THE

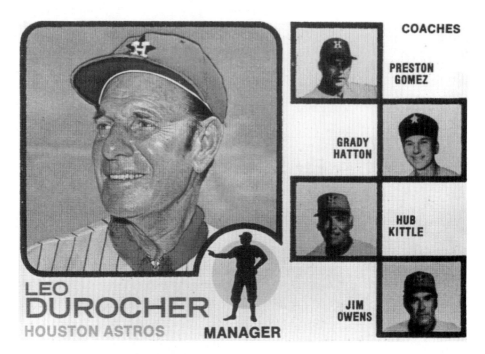

1973 Astros *Courtesy of the Topps Company*

1969 Cubs *Courtesy of the Topps Company*   1952 Giants *Courtesy of the Topps Company*

THE LIP

A BIOGRAPHY OF
LEO DUROCHER

No. 25 SPEEDY DUROCHER

1936 Cards *World Wide Gum*

GERALD
ESKENAZI

WILLIAM MORROW AND COMPANY, INC.
NEW YORK

Library of Congress Cataloging-in-Publication Data

Eskenazi, Gerald.
    The Lip : a bibliography of Leo Durocher / Gerald Eskenazi.
      p.   cm.
    Includes bibliographical references (p.) and index.
    ISBN 0-688-11895-X
    1. Durocher, Leo, 1906–   . 2. Baseball—United States—Managers—
Biography. I. Title.
    GV865.D83E85   1993
    796.357'092—dc20
    [B]   92-42006
                                                              CIP

Printed in the United States of America

First Edition

1 2 3 4 5 6 7 8 9 10

BOOK DESIGN BY ROBERT AULICINO

This page is for all those who were part of my Brooklyn roots, starting with my mom, Adella Eskenazi, Grandma Minnie, Grandpa Barney, Uncle Arthur, and the branches that encircled my wife, Rosalind, the wonderful kids Ellen, Mark, and Michael, and the newest hangers-on, Andrew Shuster, who changed Ellen's name, and Anna Grimaldi, Mark's best friend.

ACKNOWLEDGMENTS

In ways I had forgotten, Leo Durocher was part of my life in Brooklyn. Somehow, he seemed to have been a part of everyone else's I spoke to. Even people who never met him.

The man spent forty-seven years in baseball, and lived for eighty-six years, virtually all of them an adventure. Perhaps by the time you read this he will have overcome the simmering controversy, which has lasted decades after he retired, and finally made it into the Baseball Hall of Fame.

But with Leo, who knows? He was unpredictable. So were his teams. The fans, the players, the owners, the wives—they loved him and hated him.

Thus, it was an exercise of research, interviews, sifting of fact and fiction, examining and discarding, to examine his life, times, impact, and significance.

Of course, I went back to the beginning. And the man who helped me put in perspective the life that shaped Leo, the West Springfield, Massachusetts, beginnings not far from a real gashouse, was Sam Pompei. Sam retired as sports editor of the Springfield *Union-News*, but not from his love of the place and its lore.

Along the way, he was joined by these other people who helped me; the varied nature of the group says much about the life Leo led:

Red Barber, Chris Durocher, Jimmy Breslin, Ralph Branca, Laraine Day, Father Arnold Fox, Jerry Izenberg, Dick Schaap, Herman Franks, Willie Mosconi, Bobby Bragan, Monte Irvin, Buzzie Bavasi, Harvey Wineberg, Pee Wee Reese, Bob Broeg, Bob Durocher, Harry Coyle, Joe Goldstein, Dick Osgood, Joe Garagiola, Harry Shattuck, Don Williams, Ethan Allen, Harold Rosenthal, Marty Appel, the West Springfield crew of Jinx Powers, Bill Girotti, Paul McCarthy, Cy Conner, Pat Lawsure, Harold Passerini.

Dutch Garfinkel, Marvin Miller, Carlo Imelio, Chub Feeney, Jack Lang, Norm Miller (the player), Bill White, Jim Ogle, A. B. Chandler, Jr., Willie Mays, Dave Anderson, Don Gutteridge, Bo

Gill, Joe Hirsch, Sam Goldaper, Stan Fischler, George Vecsey, Bowie
Kuhn, George Freeman, Annie Perasa, Mike Shamos, Maury Allen,
Mark Koenig, Sally Williss Ort, Leonard Koppett, Red Foley, Sey-
mour Siwoff and the Elias Sports Bureau, Mike Panozzo, Jerome
Holtzman, Peter Golenbock, Bob Lipsyte, William Wrigley, Sr.,
LeRoy Neiman.

Also, the Baseball Hall of Fame's librarian, Bill Deane, and cu-
rator, Peter Clark, were helpful archivists along with the New York
Public Library, the Brooklyn Public Library, *The New York Times*,
the *Chicago Tribune*, the *St. Louis Post-Dispatch*, the *Los Angeles
Times*, the *San Francisco Chronicle*, *The Cincinnati Enquirer*, C-El
Purdy of Shelter Rock Library, and the Brooklyn Historical Society.

The creativity process was encouraged by baseball expert and
expert agent Jay Acton, and midwifed by Andy Dutter of Morrow.

To all the above, a tip of the cap.

CONTENTS

PROLOGUE

THE DUGOUT was his personal playpen, from where, unafraid and unchallenged (mostly), he could yell to his pitcher, while the batter dug in for the next pitch, "Stick it in his fucking ear!"

Yeah, that was Leo Durocher, all right. Leo the Lip, Lippy Leo, Leo the Lion. The former altar boy who used to dash across the street after church to steal a doughnut at the bakery, then go next door and hustle suckers at the poolroom.

Leo Durocher, whose baseball career spanned almost fifty years, who played with Ruth, who managed Robinson and Mays, who jetted with Sinatra to Japan for kicks, who has a better record than most of the managers in the Hall of Fame, who splashed toilet water over his face and wore suits with the pockets sewn tight so he wouldn't be tempted to put something in them to ruin the line. The guy from the West Springfield, Massachusetts, gashouse (he was part of a real gashouse gang before he helped give the name celebrity status), who could steal the dais from Hollywood celebrities, who married a movie star, a top fashion designer, a television personality—and a clerk from West Virginia. And who, at the age of seventy-two and living with a woman more than forty years younger, underwent a penile implant so he could still try to enjoy sex.

After he pushed a picketer in 1934, unions boycotted the Gashouse Gang team he played for, then he came close to being nailed in a federal action for antiunion activities forty years later. He survived player insurrections twenty-five years apart. Check his name in the FBI files under his friend Bugsy Siegel.

Leo denied to the end that he ever stole Babe Ruth's watch—but what about Lou Gehrig's ring?

Ralph Branca *and* Bobby Thomson considered Leo the best manager they ever played for, but Norm Miller considered him possibly the worst. Leo was the architect of the Giants' Miracle finish of 1951 against the Dodgers and the 1954 sweep of the Indians. He brought Brooklyn its first pennant in twenty-one years. At his playing peak, he was the fanciest fielding shortstop in the majors.

Even as an old man Leo could light up a room—that was the expression everyone who knew him seems to use. His last appearance, fittingly and with some irony, was at the annual bash of the New York Baseball Writers, America's great baseball dinner, eight months before his death. Until DiMaggio was introduced, Leo received the biggest hand, the warmest applause, more than those Hall of Famers, more than those league presidents and coaches and managers.

But before his death in 1991 at eighty-six, they still hadn't voted him into the Hall of Fame. And for this, he told his lawyer, "Screw them, I don't want you to accept it if they vote me in after I'm dead."

Yet, picture this: Leo, rheumy-eyed, eighty-one years old, going back to the Church, from which he had strayed earlier this century. It was in Palm Springs, California, and the name of the church, Our Lady of Solitude, was ironic for this man of turbulence. There, he met an even older man, an eighty-three-year-old priest. "Father," the Lip rasped, "I want you to help me learn how to stop cursing. I want to control my tongue."

CHAPTER
I

GROWING PAINS

GO BACK to West Springfield now and they remember Leo Durocher as if they had really seen him. Of course, some did, but they're not kids any longer. Leo was eighty-six when he died in 1991, increasingly embittered over the Hall snub, more reclusive as the result of a car accident that had left him unable to drive his beloved Cadillac. Leo always liked fine cars, some of which he even paid for.

Not many people in West Springfield had seen him in his last years, though. For them, it is the memory. Or is it the myth? They all have one—whether or not they actually knew Leo, or thought they knew him, or had a father or aunt or brother who knew him. As clear as yesterday, they see him with a beaming Laraine Day, wearing her sunbonnet. He is as alive today in that rail and factory town as he was during the Depression years, the favored son who would roar into town in a Pierce-Arrow, and greet old friends with a slap on the back.

They remember (or think they do) that when Leo was a young boy, he was always on the streets or in the fields. With a glove and a ball. That was Leo Durocher, always looking for someone to have a catch with.

The image that America has of Leo Durocher is occasionally at odds with his upbringing, but more often a reflection of it. Here was a man who was told to stop gambling by his bosses when he was a player and a manager, a Beau Brummel of the gray-flannel set who moved easily in mob circles, in Hollywood circles, on Broadway.

Leo Durocher was a man who remained closed up on his early life and didn't mind his life being made up of stones. After his death, Laraine Day, his third wife, was asked if he had ever mentioned his struggles as a youngster, his erratic father, his mother cooking and cleaning for boarders. "No, never," she said. "I never heard anything about that."

Tom Meany, a knowledgeable sportswriter of Leo's era, didn't know much about Leo's background. And perhaps the Lip liked it that way. Writing in *The Saturday Evening Post* in 1947 (ironically, the issue hit the stands the week Leo was kicked out of baseball for the year), Meany wrote, "Of his family or his boyhood in West Springfield, Mass., Durocher never talks. The handout biography of the Dodgers is remarkably skimpy on Durocher's childhood. It records the fact that he was born at West Springfield on July 27, 1906, and comes to a dead stop between that date and the time he reached Hartford in the Eastern League some 19 years later." That 1906 date is curious. For many years Leo used that year as his supposed birthdate. All it did was make him a year younger.

And in his fanciful autobiography of 1975, *Nice Guys Finish Last*, Leo created his background selectively. He forgot to mention his first marriage and a daughter, the only child he fathered. People from West Springfield who have read the book laugh at some of its outrageous statements—such as how he blew a college scholarship by punching a high school teacher, or how he ice-skated—ice-skated!—ninety miles to Boston. And back.

Of course, Leo never had a chance at a college scholarship (it is unlikely he even attended high school, and if he did, it wasn't for long). And he never ice-skated over the frozen Connecticut River to Boston (the river doesn't go in that direction). If these stories are absurd, how many other stories, earlier and later, in and out of his book, are pure bunk?

Perhaps making up stories was one way Leo could get them to come out right.

Dick Schaap, the television journalist and author of several best-selling books, asked to do a book with Leo, said, "I determined that Leo couldn't tell the truth, and there was no way I'd be associated with him under those circumstances."

Since there are so many contradictions in Leo Durocher's life, so many false turns, false starts, dead ends, not-quite-true stories, sensational rumors, wild speculation, I thought a visit back home would shed some light on what actually happened to him as a youngster, and what sort of place formed him. So on the day after Christmas in 1991 I drove up to West Springfield.

In Leo's day, West Springfield had a population of about eighteen thousand and it was always quite a sports-oriented town, with polo, the dog track, baseball, hockey, football, soccer, basketball (Springfield, the adjacent town, is the birthplace of that game), boxing, billiards, and bowling. One of the earliest spectator sports that drew people was the 1852 Harvard-Yale crew race on the Connecticut. And the first baseball field in West Springfield was created virtually at the time of Leo's birth.

West Springfield was Heartland, only ninety miles west of Boston. And there used to be a gashouse over there.

More precisely, it was just across the river. It was the poor section of Springfield, where the gashouse factory was located, where they stoked the coal and made the gas that they sent out to the good people of Western Massachusetts.

Leo Durocher knew all about the gashouse because he lived it.

He could see the gashouse from his house across the Connecticut River. It was three quarters of a mile away, but its smoke and noise dominated the skyline. Once you saw it, once you lived near it, looking at it every morning when you left the house, seeing its lights at night, you were dominated by the gashouse. And the gashouse symbolized a sort of sleaze, of something less than class. It symbolized something that Leo ran from, and yet always was a part of.

The rail yards in West Springfield don't dominate the town the way they did back then, when it was filled with busy locomotives and workmen bustling between tracks, headed to town for a place to spend the night or to get something to eat or find some action. West Springfield was a main switching point in the Northeast—trains between Boston and New York were routed there, along with those roaring through the busy Montreal–New England, Montreal–New York corridor. Leo wasn't born on the wrong side of the tracks. He was born practically on the tracks.

Leo wasn't even the first name on his birth certificate. He was born on July 25, 1905, the fourth son of Clara and George Durocher. When his birth was registered a week later, it was as Charles Joseph Durocher. Apparently, the midwife or doctor who delivered the baby registered it, but not as Leo Ernest Durocher, which is what his mother and father wanted and which, more than fifty-six years later, he had corrected.

Leo's mother, Clarinda, was known as Clara. She was born in Canada to French Canadians, Mr. and Mrs. Euclid Provost. George Durocher also came from a similar background. Their name originally was DuRocher, but when George's parents moved to Cohoes, New York, sometime late in the nineteenth century, they slightly anglicized it.

After the turn of the century George and Clara migrated from Cohoes to West Springfield with their first two sons, Clarence, the oldest, and Raymond. Armand was born in 1903, followed by Leo in 1905.

The original Durocher house was just near the end of School Street, number 50. It stands today like many of the wooden frame houses in West Springfield, a reminder of turn-of-the-century life.

Today, almost forty years after the death of Leo's mother, Bob Durocher, one of Leo's nephews, twenty-two years younger than Leo, remembers her as a tough bird. And Leo's father was "a small, good-natured, but very meek man," recalls Bob, a florist still in West Springfield.

George worked for the Boston & Albany Railroad, but he moved around a lot—some said because the rent somehow got misplaced before the beginning of each month at one of the town's many drinking establishments. "Leo's family wasn't a solid family. They moved a lot. His father was a drinker and come the first of the month, they'd be moving."

This is Sam Pompei speaking. Sam is more than the town's semi-official historian. He is a man proud of his city. A lifelong resident of West Springfield, until his retirement in the late 1970s he was a newspaperman. He was the sports editor of what is now the Springfield *Union-News* across the river. He wrote more and spoke more and knew more about the young Leo than anyone else in that part of the Commonwealth. "His father used to say, 'My Lay-o, he do dis...'" recalls Sam. "He used to pronounce Leo's name 'Lay-O.'"

Bob says that the other brothers were quiet, self-effacing, almost shy. All were smallish as well, not much over five feet tall. Leo, though, took after his mother: At five feet nine inches, he was the tallest man in the family.

They lived for a time in a big house at 21 Elmdale Street. After

George suffered a heart attack, Clara took in railroad workers as boarders. When George could work, it wasn't for long and his earning power was limited. So Clara washed by hand, and had to look after her frail husband, four boys, and the boarders. She also did a lot of work for Spalding. They made baseballs in Chicopee, Massachusetts, and they used to farm out the work to ladies who could stitch the baseballs at home.

Around the corner from their School Street house on Main Street was the St. Louis de France Church, known as St. Louie's, where Leo was an altar boy. Today the sons and nephews of those who knew him chuckle when they imagine little Leo in church, his hands in front of his chin, forming a demure steeple. After which he'd go out and hustle some pool in the pool hall just across the street—one of two pool halls he prowled.

George Kelly, the bighearted owner of the West Side Bakery, used to slip him pieces of pastry. Or, he liked to retell, he would look the other way when, after Leo helped serve mass at St. Louis across the street, he would help himself to a doughnut and not pay.

Tim Lynch was eighty-six years old in 1992 when he remembered life with Leo. "Leo participated in all sports except swimming. A lot of us went to the nearby Connecticut River. Then one day he decided to join us. All of us were in the nude. Leo jumped in, and as far as I know he had never done this before, but he amazed us with his natural swimming ability."

A former police officer and neighbor of the Durochers, the late Dick Blaha, recalled that even as a little kid in grammar school, Leo always had a glove with him. Blaha, walking the street, would see Leo going to school with it. He saw him coming home for lunch with it. He saw him returning from school in the afternoon with it.

Whenever little Leo saw another youngster with a ball, he'd shout, "Hey, throw it here." Soon, he'd have the kid throwing it high, throwing it low, to the left, to the right. "Try and get it past me!" Leo would shout pugnaciously. And the other kid, angry, would try to smoke it past him, usually with little success. This liking to play pepper lasted all through Leo's time in the big leagues, even as a sixty-five-year-old manager. He loved playing it right in front of the NO PEPPER ALLOWED sign near home plate—playing pepper with "Mister Leo" remains among Willie Mays's fondest memories.

Recalling Leo's earlier life, a childhood friend, eighty-eight-year-old William Pitter, says, "They should have called him the Lip or

Lippy when he was only eleven or twelve. His mouth was always going."

Leo was quite a marbles player. The sons of the owner of the variety store on School Street where he bought his marbles usually won them back in games they played, so Leo, smaller and pugnacious, would steal marbles out of the circles to keep his stock up.

One of the many disruptions to his family occurred at a pivotal point in Leo's childhood. When he was about twelve they moved to Elmdale Street, half a mile away from the Merrick section he had grown accustomed to. Leo didn't like it. And while living on Elmdale and roaming the Merrick section, he took up pool. There are some people who believe he might have become a champion player if baseball hadn't intervened.

Sam Pompei describes Leo's new friends on Elmdale as well-behaved and middle-class. Leo, says Sam, preferred the action of his old neighborhood. He enjoyed the company of children of immigrants, the Italians, Bohemians, French, Poles, blacks, Irish, and Greeks.

He was unsupervised, spending much of the day even after school in the old Merrick section of town. And Leo was popular. When he missed a meal at home, he was never hungry—his friends would have him over for dinner, a not-uncommon practice among those family-oriented people. They knew Leo was having a hard time adjusting to the new neighborhood. Other times a friend would give him a sandwich, or restaurant owner invite him in. In the days before World War I, Leo was a street urchin. And his wanderings affected Clara, made her nervous and edgy.

Leo had more time to play marbles and pepper than most youngsters because he apparently spent less time in school. He attended the Meadow and Main Street schools, but Tim Bowen of the Board of Education says there is no record of his having reached high school. Though it is possible Leo attended high school in some neighboring cities the family lived in for a while.

Tim Lynch was there when Leo began playing pool at the age of twelve at the Circle Lafayette Club. This was a place used by the French Canadians, one of West Springfield's many ethnic clubs. Usually, Lynch and Leo went in during the day, when most of the members were at work. They were always polite, and since Leo was from a French-Canadian family, he was tolerated. Before long, though, he had an audience, and the older members would wander over to the table whenever Leo started playing. However, some of the members squawked. Just what were twelve-year-old kids doing in the clubhouse all the time, shooting pool? Others said, "Forget it, let 'em stay." And they did.

After a while, Leo saw he wasn't improving. He'd play the older men once in a while, but they weren't serious about the game. Leo needed more of a challenge.

The boys tried the Railroad YMCA over on Union Street. It was only a few blocks away, but it was on the edge of the Boston & Albany yards, and it attracted a different kind of crowd. These were hard-drinking, hard-working men, most of whom didn't actually live in town. They'd stop off for the night after bringing their trains to West Springfield. There was almost a frontier quality about the place.

The boys didn't charge into the Y the way they had at the Circle Lafayette. Instead, they quietly took places around the edge of the tables and watched how the game was being played. It was on a different level.

Then armed with new techniques, and the ability to play with older fellows, Leo and Lynch would go back to the Circle Lafayette and take on the locals there—a pair of twelve-year-old pool hustlers. They became local celebrities. Eventually they moved on to Winterborn's Pool Room opposite the Main Street School, where Leo's friends were across the street studying. Leo was preparing for life in a different way.

The people at Winterborn's looked the other way when the two teenagers began showing up. Pool halls were considered breeding grounds for delinquents, and kids under eighteen weren't permitted. But the important thing was, were you good enough to compete? And could you afford to pay for a rack?

Lynch remembers they were about sixteen when they became regulars. He got money for pool by working at odd jobs, but Leo rarely worked. Yet, Leo always managed to scrape up a dollar or two. "He'd borrow it from me or his other pals," Tim recalls. "Then he could run it up to three or four bucks. Leo had the knack for making the difficult shot under pressure, especially when money was on the line."

After playing, Leo would split his winnings with the guys who backed him or lent him money. Then he would head home. But in the morning he was broke, he claimed, and, hey, could you let him have a few more bucks until the next sucker comes along. This was the beginning of a strange pattern—a pattern he continued for much of his life. He was broke repeatedly more than fifty years later when he married his fourth wife, Lynne Walker Goldblatt, a Chicago television personality. Finally, she had enough of his gambling.

Back then, though—how could Leo be broke so quickly? Tim used to wonder. Was Leo turning over the money to his folks? Or was he stashing it away? Tim never knew.

Winterborn's was the hangout for the town's big players and all-round good guys: Dom Muscolo, Boney Pradella, Leon Hamilton, and Ernie Lawsure. The good folks of West Springfield whispered about some of their associates. But just whispered. No one would dare ask these good fellas about some of their activities. Muscolo was a heck of a pool player, one of the best. But his best sport was candlepin bowling, which to this day remains the most popular form of bowling in Western Massachusetts. He became the candlepin national champ, even enshrined in the Candlepin Hall of Fame.

Leo turned out to be the best player at Winterborn's, the top money-winner there. So pretty quickly, the wise guys there realized they had a good thing, a baby-faced kid they could use to hustle strangers. The regulars soon backed him against all comers. There, in that setting of wisecracks, smoke, foul language, and macho aggression, Leo was accepted. Better—he was a star. He was to move easily, forever after, with the kind of people who had come of age in places just like this.

There was one disconcerting aspect of Leo's playing, though, that has remained with the folks who remember his pool playing, or who have heard about it from their folks: Sometimes Leo would be beaten by players he should have trounced. Perhaps if it had been someone else, the observers might not have been suspicious. But the people who backed Leo with their money often wondered: Were they being hustled themselves? Was Leo actually sharing the winnings of the other side as well?

These uncomfortably similar questions were asked fifty years later when the Cubs of 1969 collapsed under Leo as their manager. Newspaper reporters wondered whether Leo was gambling on baseball. They had even heard reports he had gambled against his own team, and that some odd managerial moves were (in retrospect) suspicious. It ended up just talk, and never got beyond that. But some people in the commissioner's office wondered.

With his expertise in pool increasing, Leo's attitude toward his opponents changed dramatically. He became cocky. Everything turned into an argument, every move by the other guy elicited a Leo remark and retort. The Lip was forming. He was also developing the ability to get to the brink of a fight and then be able to bluff his way out of it.

Eventually, he became a liability to the local pool halls. He was such a good player that no one wanted to bet against him. And then there were those suspicions. So Leo moved on. He went across the river to downtown Springfield, to Smith's Billiard Parlor on Worthington. This was where the top players from western Mass would congregate, where the stakes were high—Durocher-type people, Durocher-type money.

Leo juggled this with his growing baseball ability. In the spring, summer, and fall, he played every day, for a variety of teams. He was becoming a local celebrity, with people turning out just to see him sparkle at shortstop and doing his star turns in the field. And then after darkness pushed him off the playing field, he would head for the poolrooms. He could go day and night.

Tim Lynch remembers crossing over the Connecticut River on the Old Toll Bridge, as it was known, to play pool. As they walked to Springfield, Leo often would stop to admire the clothes in the windows of men's shops. Why the heck is he looking at those fancy clothes? Tim would wonder. He'll never be able to afford them.

Once, passing Kennedy's clothing store on Main Street, Leo stopped to admire a beautiful green suit. It was laced with a vertical thin strip of black. It was thirty-five dollars.

"Suddenly Leo started to repeat, 'I just gotta have that suit! I just gotta have that suit!' " Lynch recalls. "I thought he was just kidding."

Every day on their way to the pool hall, Leo looked in the window. One day, though, he told his friend, "Let's go in, I want to try it on." Tim would not go inside; he was embarrassed. He knew Leo couldn't afford it. Then Leo came out, very disconsolate. "They let me try on the jacket, but not the pants," he said.

The next time they passed the store, Tim noticed the suit wasn't in the window.

"I bought it the other day," Leo said. He seemed almost embarrassed.

"I never understood where he got the money," said Tim. But Tim knew that in order to be a player at Smith's, you needed a full-dress suit and tie. Leo couldn't get by there with knickers.

To make it at Smith's, which used to host Willie Hoppe and Willie Mosconi on their exhibition tours, Leo had to look and act the part. But he was only sixteen years old. If he could get in by wearing a fancy new suit, say, and rack up a game—just one game was all he needed—then he'd show them and they'd accept him. So he wore his new green suit with the black thread and they let him in. He ran fifteen balls and no one asked his age. He became known as the Green Phantom.

From then on, clothes—good-looking clothes—were part of Leo. (Tim says that he and Leo went their separate ways not long after.) "Someone told me once, says Jinx Powers, a restaurant owner in West Springfield, that one day Leo showed up at the football field on a Sunday wearing his Sunday suit and patent leather shoes and they asked him to punt, and he kicked the shit out of the ball. In his patent leather shoes!" Bob Durocher adds that "Leo was always neat and clean. When everyone else was wearing twenty-five-dollar suits, he was wearing four-hundred-dollar suits." However, Leo's obsession with clothes led the writer Barry Furlong, obviously no fan, to note, "When Leo puts on a three-hundred-dollar suit, he thinks he is putting on three hundred dollars' worth of class."

In pool, it was the soft, almost delicate, touch that mattered. On the ball field, especially in semi-pro, it was the big bat, the heavy-handed hitter, who was the big shot. Leo became the gloveman in baseball, though, the man with the soft hands just as he was in pool. Once in a while he'd loft a Chinese home run to right at the Chapin Street Field, but that was on a good day.

Leo started playing sports for the Merrick Athletic Association Club. It was run by the Fitzgerald brothers, and anyone—Italian, Greek, French, Irish, Polish, and black—could belong. The dues were fifty cents a month.

"If anyone was late with his dues, the other members would get on him," recalls one old-time member. "When Leo—who was on both the football and baseball teams—failed to pay, one of the guys pinned him against a wall and demanded he pay up. 'I play two sports for you guys,' growled Leo. 'I shouldn't have to pay anything.' He did, though."

Although Leo was a string bean as a teenager, weighing about 140 pounds, he was a standout football player. He was Merrick's best halfback, and he could throw pretty well. But best of all, Leo could kick. The old-timers still around, or their kids, still tell stories about this little guy and the distance and height he got on his punts.

Even after Leo made it to the big leagues, he would come home after the season and sit in the stands for Merrick football games. Then at halftime, he would trot on to the field in his suit, an overcoat topped with a fur collar, and spiffy shoes always highly polished. And he'd put on a kicking demonstration.

And one day after the 1928 Series, Leo suddenly showed up driving a Cadillac. He pulled the car up to the sidelines, got out, resplendent in his suit, hauled out a couple of jugs of apple cider, then started serving cider to the fans at halftime.

The home field for the Merrick baseball and football teams on Chapin Street was pockmarked with bumps and ruts. Leo later said that the unscheduled bounces the balls made there helped make him a fielder. When he joined Merrick, its regular shortstop was Harland Goldsmith. But Goldsmith suggested that Leo, who was playing second base, shift to short. He also taught Leo to be smart in the field—where to play for the various hitters, how to charge ground balls, and so on.

Soon, his best friend on the team was Boney Pradella, a hard-hitting outfielder and a football lineman. They were a Mutt and Jeff pairing. Leo was smallish, dapper, and loquacious. Boney was a big blue-collar guy and proud of it. He had a belly and dressed sloppily—a warm and friendly streetwise guy.

In later years Leo would invite Boney to sit in his private box with Laraine Day at the Polo Grounds. Boney would be chomping on a cheap Italian cigarillo, the juice running down his chin. "Leo," Laraine would say after the game, "can you talk to him about it?"

Despite Leo's celebrity status when he made it big, he never seemed embarrassed over the antics of his earthier buddies. And he never was reluctant to help them.

When Leo was with the Yankees, he was able to get a tryout for a good young pitcher, Jim Murphy, who had played with Merrick. (Murphy was perhaps the best pitcher to come out of that area until Vic Raschi fifteen years later.) Leo arranged for him to try out under Miller Huggins. Murphy was the kind of guy, though, who never really took the game seriously. And so, in Yankee Stadium, while the other pitchers were shagging balls in the outfield as they waited their turn on the mound, Murphy was stretched out on the grass, sunbathing.

Huggins turned apoplectic.

"Leo, he's your friend," said Huggins, furious. "You tell him I'm not interested. I won't even talk to him. You brought him here; you tell him."

Undaunted, Leo kept the string of old cronies coming in. Not only friends, but sons of friends.

Butsy Fiala, whose given name was Walter, was a terrific shortstop on West Springfield High's team, and then on the local semipro teams just after World War II. Butsy's dad, August, was a good customer of A. O. White's clothiers across the river in Springfield. August was fitted by the same salesman who used to take care of Leo when Leo returned home. "I'm going to write Leo and ask him to give Butsy a tryout with the Dodgers," the salesman volunteered.

And Butsy soon got a letter from the Dodgers inviting him to a tryout camp in Newport News, Virginia. The Dodgers liked the kid. A scout, Alex Kampouris, came to Butsy's house and gave him a three-hundred-dollar signing bonus. He made it up to Fort Worth of the Double A Texas League, and even up to Montreal, the Dodgers' top farm team in the Triple A International League. But the Dodgers were loaded with infielders on the big club and on the farm: Pee Wee Reese, Jackie Robinson, Billy Cox, Rocky Bridges, Don Hoak. So Butsy, a .280 hitter and outstanding fielder, spent six years at Montreal, most of that time under Tommy Lasorda. Whenever Lasorda got booted out of the game by the umps, Butsy would take over.

After his playing days, Butsy became a jail guard. He retired in the early 1980s. And up to his death, he always was grateful to Durocher and the chance he had given him by answering a clothing salesman's letter.

So there was an openhandedness, an acceptance of the other guy in the world that Leo grew up in. It was also a world of games, usually played for money, where nerves—and moxie—were required if you wanted to get along. It was where Leo developed not only his style of play, but his attitude toward the games he played—and toward life.

Leo had another passion beside hustling pool and playing baseball and football. He loved to dance. There were dance halls aplenty in the Merrick section, or in Springfield (the Butterfly Ballroom) across the river, or even in nearby Agawam and Riverside Park. Leo also could walk to the Venetian Gardens, not far from where he was born.

Helen Fitzgerald often danced with Leo. "He liked the fox-trot, the tango, and the waltz," she recalled. "He was also the best-dressed man on the floor. The perfect gentleman—and a most interesting talker. The ladies loved to dance with him. He never sat out."

Jinx Powers, the restaurant owner, remembers that Leo's best friend was Walter "Shinola" McCarthy, who "was a railroad man. But you'd never know it. Walter always dressed immaculate." Paul McCarthy, Shinola's son and a deputy fire chief, adds that "he got that nickname from their habit of being well dressed. You know, Shinola shoe polish. Leo and my father would save their money and have a suit custom-made rather than go out and buy one off the rack. He was a stationmaster but didn't dress like one.

"Both my father and Leo came from a background with no money. My father's father died when he was about eight years old and he had three brothers and two sisters.

"Leo was at our house all the time. He was sharp enough so that he hung around with guys a couple of years older. My father was three years older than Leo.

"When Leo was over at our house, he'd tell my mother, 'You ought to dump that husband of yours.' He was a character, all right.

"He was a fast mover for a young fellow. I can remember him, even though I was a kid, walking into a room and shouting out, 'What the heck you doing here?' He was loud and full of heck. I remember him always greeting my father as though they were still bosom buddies and my father said to me, 'That's pretty nice of him to do that. We don't see each other anymore.'

"My father said it wasn't that Leo was a troublemaker. He was cocky and younger than the guys he associated with, so the older fellows thought they were going to push him around. But he wouldn't back down from anybody. That was his nature as a youngster and he just retained that. It wasn't that he was out looking for trouble.

"I remember a couple of run-ins he had, a few little things. But I don't think he ever got in major trouble. Being a fireman I would have heard about it later on. Those stories die hard and I would have known about it.

"When he had a few bucks in his pocket he'd always bring gifts for my grandmother and my father's sisters. You know there are stories about how tough he was, but in our family we always remembered him with affection. You might not like what he brought home, but he always brought something home for the girls. He was generous and thoughtful.

"What I remember was how he thought of his friends. My father didn't always want to bother him and sometimes he'd buy tickets for a game and when Leo heard about it he'd scream at him. I could hear him screaming over the phone, 'You get your ass over here after the game.' You might not have seen him for years, but he'd be talking to you as if you were his best friend."

The pool playing, sports, and street life, had become his life. Then his mother kicked him out of the house.

One day he told his close friends he wasn't going home anymore. But it was known around town that his mother, working hard by keeping a boardinghouse, stitching baseballs at home, and trying to make a go of it on the erratic income brought home by her occasionally working husband, had had enough. She couldn't take Leo's refusal to work, his insistence on playing only baseball and pool.

Leo moved in with his friend Shino on New Bridge Street. Walter's folks liked Leo, who always had a few nice words to say to them. Leo was engaging, if nothing else. The McCarthy's house was only a few doors away from the Fitzgerald Brothers, Tom, Jim, and John, who, like Shino, treated Leo like a brother.

On his own, Leo was able to devote even more time to his two loves. But now there was nothing to temper his competitive style. It was almost as if he were growing up feral, lashing out at anyone who stood in his way, not bound by society's rules, and with no anchor.

Shino McCarthy recalled that living away from home put Leo under a mental strain. He acted erratically, flying off the handle. But "Leo would listen whenever an older person would try to teach him any of the fine points of baseball," recalled Goldsmith, the Merrick shortstop, who also was a surrogate big brother.

Even though Leo was living apart from his family, he often visited home. And despite this break, he always maintained close ties with his mother and father over the years. When he managed the Dodgers and the Giants, he brought his mother to live in Brooklyn and then Manhattan. When he was a player in Cincinnati and St. Louis, his mother often lived not far from him. He even got her a job in Cincinnati that was to figure in a bizarre way in his first divorce.

Following Leo's unusual stay with the McCarthy's, he moved back home and went to work for the Wico Electric Company, but he was still playing baseball. Then when his chance came at a tryout for pro baseball, his mother ordered him out of the house once again, calling him a bum.

On my last day in West Springfield I went with Bob Durocher to Jinx Powers's restaurant and we found there some of the guys who remembered Leo. And of course they swapped some more Leo stories.

I asked about Babe Ruth's watch. Bob's version was "Leo swiped Ruth's watch and Gehrig's ring and passed them out the Yankees' locker room window to Boney Pradella. Boney used to travel with Leo and got to know Babe Ruth."

But Paul McCarthy said, "Leo told my father it wasn't true. My mother said he brought Babe Ruth back here a couple of times. I don't think they were mortal enemies."

Harold Passerini is the brother-in-law of Angelo Bertelli, who in Leo's days used to own the liquor store on the corner of Main Street—and before that won a Heisman Trophy at Notre Dame. Now the owner of the liquor store Harold told of his tryout with the Giants, a four-day stay that remains etched like a game-winning home run from childhood.

"I went out there with his nephew and they gave us both tryouts," Passerini recalls, his eyes glowing. "You see, Leo always took care of his family and friends from West Springfield. All you had to do was call. You want a tryout for a major league team? Sure, Leo will take care of it.

"Leo was always testing you to see if you had balls—like Eddie Stanky. He was always referring to Stanky. At the end of batting practice, each regular would have three swings. And I was talking to him at the left side of the batting cage. The guys who were waiting to hit were on the right side. So he told me, 'Get your swings.' And I'd wait in line and there was Monte Irvin, he would jump in ahead of me and get his three swings. And then Willie Mays would get his three, and I'd say to myself, 'Wait, a minute, I'm not going in front of these guys.' But Leo would growl, 'What the heck are you waiting for? Take your swings, damnit.' He was testing. He wanted to see if you'd let these guys jump in ahead of you, if you had balls.

"Another thing I'll never forget—his dressing room. He had a closet in the locker room, with a wardrobe of suits lined up. Must have had fifteen suits. And this was just for the ballpark." (One newspaper report from 1935, when he was with the Cardinals, claimed he changed suits five times a day to keep wrinkle-free. Also, it said, he bathed a lot. But this neatness compulsion does not appear in other accounts, and former ballplayers say he might have been obsessively neat, but not the sort of guy who was constantly washing his hands.)

"I remember once at the batting cage—and you've probably heard this a hundred times—he looked out at Stanky and gave me that 'You see that guy on second base? He can't hit, field, throw, or run. All he can do is beat you.' Then he looked out to right. 'You see that guy in right field? Don Mueller? He's a good ballplayer. If he had Stanky's balls, he'd be great.'

"I remember one game, they were ahead and they made a bet with Stanky how many balls he could foul off. He just kept knocking one after the other into foul territory or behind the plate. Great bat control.

"Boy, Leo's language was something. It was amazing what he'd call those umpires. And they let him get away with it. Everything under the sun. And when the Giants were up in the first inning, he'd erase the lines in the coach's box, and he'd be halfway home arguing on a strike and the home plate ump would yell, 'Get back in the box!' But there wasn't any box because he'd erased it. Every other word out of his mouth was 'Fuck you,' or 'You son of a bitch.'

"One of his best friends from West Springfield was Boney Pradella. He played sandlot ball with Leo. Leo would say, 'That Boney, he's a good friend of mine, but he'd think nothing of coming into a meeting I'm having with Horace Stoneham, wearing those dirty boots, and ask for a couple of tickets.'

"He borrowed five thousand dollars from Boney, and wouldn't give him the money back. Finally, Boney got a judgment against him. If Leo came back to West Springfield, he'd be arrested."

Sam Pompei, the retired newspaperman, remembered 1936, hitchhiking 130 miles from West Springfield to Brooklyn. The Gashouse Gang, and Leo, were coming in to play the Dodgers. "I had about four dollars in my pocket," says Pompei. "I left really early so I could get there for game time. All I really wanted to do was see that one game. I hung around the players gate, looking for Leo. And then I saw him coming in with Pepper Martin and the Dean brothers. Leo was dressed in an all-white suit, his dark shoes shined like a mirror. He stood out fashonwise, all right. But physically, he was the smallest of the lot.

"He didn't know me but I shouted, 'Hi, Leo, I'm from West Springfield.' And I started to reel off the names of some of his old friends—Giddy, Boney, the Fitzgeralds, Shino McCarthy, just to let him know that I was from the West Side.

" 'Have you got an extra ticket?' I asked.

"He said, 'No, but you come with me.' He tried pushing me past the guy standing guard at the gate, but the guard insisted it was for players only.

" 'But he's a friend of mine, from my hometown,' " Leo said insistently. The guy finally gave in. Leo left me, but told me to meet him at the dugout. He handed me a ball and said, 'I'll see you after the game.'

"I enjoyed it so much I decided to stay overnight and come back the next day, if I could find a room. I got one for fifty cents a night at the Bedford Avenue YMCA. I came back the next afternoon, and Leo got me in the same way, for the next two games. So thanks to Leo, I was able to stay in Brooklyn for the three-game series."

Years later, when Sam had become a reporter, he was interviewing Leo and asked if he remembered the incident. Leo laughed. "Everybody from West Springfield came to Ebbets Field or the Polo Grounds to see us play, and I'm sorry to say, I don't remember them all. I wish I could."

Bob remembered Leo's glove: "It was like a rag. He ripped all the stuffing out of it. I saw it in Braves Field, where all his friends and relatives used to come when he was playing the Braves. He never forgot his friends. I went there with the chief of police and Shinola and we arrived just as he was getting on the bus. He wasn't upset or anything. He just said, 'Why didn't you tell me you were coming?'

"When he was managing the Cubs, he got us tickets to Jarry Park in Montreal. This was 1971. We had good seats, right on the field near the dugout. And we were so happy to see Leo working a game. Boy, we could see him for nine innings. And the very first inning he argues with the ump and they kick him out. He passes us sitting in the box and he says, 'Son of a bitch.' "

Paul added, "We'd always go back early in the clubhouse, whether it was New York or Brooklyn; he was always very good to the West Springfield friends. I'd be in the clubhouse and he'd come over and hand me a dozen balls and when the players came back from batting practice they'd sign the balls, and he'd say, 'Give 'em away to the people back home.'

"I can also remember sitting with him in the clubhouse before a game and he'd have his bookies in there."

"One time with the Yankees the Merrick Aid Club honored him in a ceremony and they made a big deal of giving him a check for five hundred dollars," remembers another old-timer. "The only thing was, there wasn't enough money to pay him, and the truth is, we never figured on paying him. We just wanted to show how we appreciated him. And we told him, 'Don't cash the check.' Well, you know the son of a bitch cashes the check. And the next time Leo comes to town, Bull Hardina grabs him by the collar and says, 'You come in here again and I'll drive you through the wall.' "

After Leo joined the Dodgers, he sometimes returned to West Springfield with George Raft. The actor, who had made a living as a gigolo and dancer in Manhattan before making it in the movies, would cut a rug in the era of the big bands. Raft also was quite a dresser. Leo held his own with Raft, though, and is recalled as a soft-stepping dandy with a clean-cut, all-American look.

Leo liked to return home. He'd tool around town in a big Packard or Caddy or even a Pierce-Arrow, dressed like a magazine ad. He enjoyed taking his old pals for a spin, and he'd visit the old places, the pool halls, the dance halls.

By the 1950s, though, his appearances grew less frequent, especially after his mother died. When he'd show up it would be to say hello to Shino and Boney. But on one trip back in the 1950s, he returned to the place where the old Wico Electric Company stood. That was where he had worked before he had gone into organized ball. It was now an industrial park, and he walked around quietly, asking where the field used to be, where the factory had been. One of the property owners, John Nekitopoulos, remembered seeing a well-dressed man moving around, deep in thought. Nekitopoulos thought it might have been a real estate buyer, and he asked the stranger, "Can I help you?"

"My name is Leo Durocher," Leo replied. "I used to play ball over there."

That reminded Bob of his car. "He had a Pierce-Arrow all right. I remember he came to my grandfather's funeral [Leo's father's, the day Leo was named manager of the Dodgers late in 1938], he came in that Pierce-Arrow. And a few weeks later, the finance company took it away."

Another West Springfield man remembered, "My sister used to go with Leo and she left him for this reason: One day he was in a store, and he was a big shot from New York by this time. He told the cigar store owner, 'I'm not going to pay for this stuff anymore.' "

Bob continued about Leo and money. When Leo was married to his second wife, Grace Dozier, "One thing I'll never forget is walking into that apartment," said Bob. "The first thing you saw was the bar, and I've never seen anything like it before or since. The seats on the barstools were catchers mitts. The legs were made out of bats. The front of the bar was inlaid with bats. Behind the bar he had autographed pictures of Sinatra, Danny Kaye, Tony Martin.

"One day Leo called Grace. 'Mama,' he said—he used to call her 'Mama'—'I've got to borrow ten thousand dollars.'

" 'Why?' she asked.

" 'Don't ask, but I need it.'

"He needed it because he was going to divorce her," recalled his nephew. ("The son of a bitch conned me again," Grace later recalled.)

"He spent a lot of money on Laraine's two kids." (Laraine Day was his third wife.) "My brother Bernard said he died broke.

"After his funeral Willie Mays sat with Bernard and told him how he had gone to see Leo one day. Leo was an old man. 'Then when I went to say good-bye, I took a roll out of my pocket,' said Willie. 'I had five thousand dollars there and I gave it to him.' Leo went into a rage and started screaming at him.

" 'I thought I lost my best friend,' said Willie. 'It took a while until it got back where it was.' "

One of the few who did, in later years Clara Durocher said she understood where her son's overzealous habits and excesses had come from. He had done without as a child. She knew about the life on the edge he was leading—she had to know—but to the extent he kept her placated at all, ever, it was with his attendance at church. He was always serious about that—when he was there, that is. However, whatever Leo might have done out of the house or on or off the ball fields, his Catholic upbringing remained with him for the rest of his life.

And if Clara Durocher could not accept baseball when Leo was younger, she basked in his success in later years. She sometimes even offered advice. Once at Ebbets Field, she was impatient with his continual arguing with the umpires. After one tirade, as he returned to the bench, she shouted from her box seat, "Get back in the dugout and shut up, Leo. That's where you belong." The fans applauded her.

When Leo was about fourteen, he played on the Meadow Sluggers. They were facing a team from the Immaculate Conception Church in a game behind the church. There was Leo, who was to become the baseball world's most feared umpire baiter, and the umpire that day turned out to be Father John Mullins.

He was a man in his seventies, and normally he didn't do this sort of thing. But the two teams got into an argument over who would umpire the game, and finally they asked Father Mullins. He came out in his cassock and collar and called the balls and strikes from behind the pitcher. The other players on the Sluggers griped about his calls—the man couldn't see a ball from a strike, high from low. Not Leo. When he took a third strike, he simply said, "Yes, Father." On a close play at second that Leo believed he had put the tag on, the call was safe and Leo didn't argue.

Who knows what would have happened if Leo had broken into the big leagues under the old gentleman Connie Mack, who sat on the bench in a high-collared shirt, straw boater, and business suit and managed his A's for fifty years? Or under the courtly Branch Rickey, who never allowed profanity to escape his lips? Would Leo have just been a slick fielder, subdued, and never heard from again after hitting .220 as a rookie?

Leo, though, developed under Miller Huggins, himself a small guy with a big mouth, who used his wiles. He encouraged Leo to holler from the bench, often wondering what was wrong if Leo went a couple of batters without saying anything—even if Leo wasn't in the game.

Huggins fancied himself an expert on what made players tick. Often, he'd get on Tony Lazzeri, cursing him, telling him he was going to be benched for the light-hitting Durocher.

"That busher's going to play my position?" screamed Lazzeri, who would then go out and rip the cover off the ball.

All the while, Leo kept notes of what Huggins said and did in a little black book, a book he claimed to have even thirty years later.

So from the Eastern League, where he played under the pugnacious Paddy O'Connor, to Huggins, to the Gashouse Gang with Frankie Frisch as manager, the cocky Dizzy Dean, and the combative Pepper Martin, to Brooklyn, with Burleigh Grimes, himself a madman on the field and in the dugout—Leo found himself in situations where he wasn't forced to stifle his imaginative and colorful use of words, his brawling style, or his fervor for the game.

CHAPTER II
THE LIP IS FORMED

AT SIXTEEN and out of school, Leo finally went to work for a machinery firm, and then for Wico Electric. Wico produced battery parts, but to many in West Springfield what Wico did best was field a heck of a baseball team. And Leo, with his spotty background, might have been hired as much for his fielding skills as his ability on the assembly line.

According to Harry Nunn, a railroad foreman who coached baseball, "Leo lived and thought and dreamed and acted baseball as a kid. He was playing with every team in the area he could get money from. He started playing for my church team after it had lost its first four games. When I put it up to Leo he admitted that he wanted a shot at the Eastern League. I told him to stay with us for a year and I'd see that he got his chance."

Nunn eventually got a promise from Jack O'Hara, the business manager of the Hartford Senators, to give Leo a tryout. But Leo was apprehensive. He was worried about his weak hitting—and also he was earning nearly sixty dollars a week assembling motorcycle batteries for Wico.

He worked alongside a welder named David Redd, who kept prodding him to try out for pro ball. In that melting-pot city, even in the early 1920s, it was not unusual for a white man to work side by side with a black man. Leo and Redd, a black man, got friendly enough to discuss their dreams. Leo told him he was apprehensive about leaving the security of Wico to take a chance playing Eastern League ball.

"I told him not to worry about getting a leave of absence," Redd recalled. I said to him, "You can always get a job. You're better than all the other ballplayers around here. You're different."

In later years, Leo was to gratefully remember Redd whenever the talk got around to the early years and who had inspired him. If Leo had been hesitant about Redd's advice, it might have been the last time anyone ever noticed.

Leo took two weeks' leave from Wico in the spring of 1925 to try out at Hartford. He was considered too small and sent home. They weren't offering him a contract. But the day before the season began, Hartford's shortstop got hurt. One report had it that he just disappeared. In any event, O'Hara appeared at the Wico factory gate, grabbed Leo, and brought him in his car to Bridgeport, where Hartford was playing that afternoon.

"I remember I dressed in the car behind the stands," Leo recalled. "There was skin on the field, no grass. But I handled eight chances without an error and I also got two hits. I was flying."

Nice memory, and almost accurate. Leo actually got 1 hit in 4 at-bats and handled 6 chances. The date was April 22, 1925. Leo's hit in the seventh touched off a 2-run rally, and the Senators won, 2–1. There is no record of whether Leo argued with Conroy and Stafford, the two umpires.

Paul Krichell, the legendary Yankee scout, heard about Leo in time, came over to take a look, and was impressed with his glove— but dismayed with his bat. Leo played 151 games with Hartford in 1925, batting only .220 and fielding .933 over the pebbly infields of the Eastern League. Luckily for Leo he was used to them, though that didn't help his weak hitting.

Krichell nevertheless called Ed Barrow, the Yanks' general manager, who snorted, "He's not even hitting his weight."

But Krichell persisted. "The kid's got moxie," he said.

Lucky Leo happened to be in the right place at one of the few times in the Babe Ruth era that Yankee fortunes had tumbled. In 1924 they finished second, but in 1925 they plopped to seventh, the year Ruth was ill, was fined, and was the center of a season of Yankee turmoil. In fact, it was to be the Yankees' only losing season for the next forty years. Barrow was intent on remaking the Yankees, and spent $300,000 of Colonel Jacob Ruppert's money acquiring ballplayers such as Mark Koenig and Tony Lazzeri. Barrow was less generous in trying to make Leo a Yankee.

He was the Yankees' cheapest purchase in 1925. Barrow made the deal over the phone for $7,000 with Hartford owner Jim Clark and Manager Paddy O'Connor. O'Connor liked Leo's style, and thought that Huggins, the Yankees' manager, would too. O'Connor had been a coach with Huggins on the Yankees in 1918. But Hartford gave Leo away cheaply because the year before the Yankees had lent them Gehrig for a while.

That year the Yankees paid $55,000 for Koenig and $60,000 to Salt Lake City for Tony Lazzeri, who had popped 60 home runs in the rarefied air there. The Yankees paid $2,500 down for Durocher, and Hartford, strapped for cash, took it.

The Yankees brought him up at the end of the season. On October 2 at Philadelphia, in a game that took one hour sixteen minutes, Leo pinch-hit for Garland Braxton in the eighth inning. Stan Baumgartner, later a sportswriter, pitched to the rookie. Baumgartner was a left-hander and Leo batted right. But, typically, he failed to pull the ball, even against a southpaw. He flied to Walter French in right. The A's won Leo's debut, 10–0. It was his only at-bat of the year, although he got into another game.

Leo's pinch-hitting appearance marked the first of 1,637 games in the majors. He would get 1,320 hits (24 homers, including 2 grand slams—both off Boston Braves pitchers while playing for the Cardinals). His grand slams (off Leo Mangum in 1934 and Huck Betts in 1935) accounted for nearly 20 percent of his homer total for the two seasons. He hit only 3 in 1934 and 8 the next year. In his career Leo drove in 567 runs and scored 575. His lifetime average was .247. In 11 World Series games his average was .241.

There was a two-year lull, though, before Leo made it back to the big leagues. In 1926 he was optioned to Atlanta of the Southern Association while Lazzeri and Koenig took care of second and short for the Yankees. Still, Leo, not yet twenty-one years old, made an impression there. On May 5, a Cincinnati scout, George B. Alexander, reported to August Hermann of the Reds. "This Durocher fellow," Alexander wrote, "*is big league material right now*. A ball hit into a spot where it's always a home run on these grounds today— he ran into left center, took a short throw from C.F. and with a wonderful throw to plate held it a 3 bagger. A hit too hard for third baseman to handle, a fast man batting, he backed up the play, got the ball and if the umpire had called the man out it would have been just. He whipped that ball over like Steinfeldt could. This boy covers more ground and hustles harder than any infielder you've got on the pay roll. Today he displayed even better THINKING ability at bat and in the field, he waits 'em out, bunts good, fast on his feet. The box scores are enclosed—but the sight of this young man in action would tell you more. Durocher is a rangy lad. You will do well to keep him in your mind's eye."

Leo was promoted in 1927 to St. Paul, where the records there gave him another inch or two in height. Suddenly he was five ten.

Leo had gone into professional baseball with this admonition from his father: "Keep your mouth shut. Just listen." But it was at St. Paul that, he was to explain, almost apologetically, he began yakking on the bench and in the field. His manager there, Nick Allen, used to tell him, "Talk it up. Show 'em you're alive. Make some noise. This is baseball, not a church." And his teammates on the bench supposedly told him to start gabbing. As if Leo needed encouragement.

He was the best shortstop in minor league ball in 1927. He led the American Association in putouts, assists, double plays, and even errors. The errors probably resulted from his ability to get to tough chances, which he then mishandled. He played in 171 games, and batted .253.

Something happened when Leo joined the Yankees for spring training in 1928. He arrived full-blown. He talked a lot. He dared players to slide into him. He had a collection of fancy clothes. Before long, someone called him Lippy Leo. The man did not stop chattering; the Yankees hated him. But one man loved him.

Miller Huggins was an anomaly in baseball. He was small, almost frail. Officially, he was listed as five feet six inches tall, though some thought he was only five three or five four. He weighed, supposedly, 140 pounds. Huggins "overcame" his size—he was known, affectionately, as the Mighty Mite, but derisively by the Babe as the Flea—to forge a long career with the Reds and Cardinals before managing the Yankees.

And he had a law degree. Explaining why he spent less than a year in a law office, he told *The Sporting News* in 1914, "I gave up the law for baseball because it is more than a game. For the real ballplayer employs his brains as much as the shrewdest businessman."

That may be an exaggeration, but Huggins felt he was able to use his wiles—and he appreciated others who did too.

The first time Huggins appeared in a box score, it wasn't even under his own name. He played for a team in his native Cincinnati, where his father worked for a wholesale grocery and believed baseball was for hoodlums. So Huggins played third base under the name of Proctor (which was actually a misspelling—he chose the name from Procter & Gamble, the huge Cincinnati-based soap company).

After Huggins played second base in the majors for Cincinnati and St. Louis from 1904 to 1916, he became the Cards' player-manager in 1916, then turned to managing exclusively in 1917. But that season the Cards were sold to a group led by Branch Rickey, and he fired Huggins at season's end. Ironically, Huggins was known as a man of integrity, yet was fired by the man who often quoted the Bible, who espoused morality and family values—and who twice was to have Durocher on his teams.

As of 1917 the Yankees had never finished first. One of their new owners, Colonel Jacob Ruppert, the beer baron, wanted Huggins to replace Wild Bill Donovan as manager for 1918. His co-owner, Colonel Tillinghast "Til" L'Hommedieu Huston, wanted the Dodgers' roly-poly (and his beer-drinking companion) Wilbert Robinson. Ruppert won. Huggins became the new manager of a team overshadowed by the Giants, in whose Polo Grounds they played as the tenants. The shy man who never married was to become the unlikely leader of a dynasty.

Life changed forever, though, when Babe Ruth arrived for the 1920 season. When he joined the team, the Babe put his arm around Huggins for the photographers, looked down at the little fellow, and said, "I think you and me ought to get along all right together." They didn't. Ruth was behind a minirevolt to oust Huggins and install himself as player-manager. Huggins confided to the writer Arthur Mann, "You will find that ballplayers who get too ambitious are always dumb. They are easy to outsmart. Those fellows after my job hitched their wagon to the wrong star."

The Yankees didn't win in Babe's first year of 1920 despite his outlandish total of 54 home runs (by July 16, he had broken his own record of 29 in a season). And even though they won their first pennant the next year, they lost the World Series to the despised Giants, which again led to a dump-Huggins movement. But the Mighty Mite prevailed despite the impression, in a *Sporting News* editorial, that "perhaps never in the history of the game has a manager been so flouted, reviled, and ridiculed."

Huggins became stronger than ever in 1922 when Huston sold his share to Ruppert, giving him control, and with a general manager, Ed Barrow, who also trusted Huggins's moves. Huggins in fact asked Ruppert to send the following telegram to his players: "I AM NOW THE SOLE OWNER OF THE YANKEES. MILLER HUGGINS IS MY MANAGER."

By the time Leo reached the big leagues, sluggers were revered—fancy fielding was okay only as long as you could hit. The 1927 Yankees had batted .307 *as a team.* The Babe had hit his 60th home run, Gehrig had 47, Koenig at short had hit .285, and the team had swept the World Series from the Pirates in four games, using four pitchers. Koenig had set a series record by batting .500.

Enter Leo, roaring. He took on Ruth. He dared players to try to slide into him.

Huggins began talk of moving Koenig to third. That meant the end of Joe Dugan. The Yankees had won 110 games in 1927 and had become Murderer's Row—and they were going to be upset by Leo Durocher? He criticized the veterans, and to make it worse, Huggins loved him. Huggins told writers he was the best shortstop he'd ever seen.

Huggins was concerned about Leo's batting, though. He tried to make him a switch-hitter, to bat left-handed against righties. But Leo was such a light hitter that left fielders played practically behind the shortstop when he faced a right-handed pitcher.

That was okay with Huggins. The man, Leo would say later, "loved me like a father, and I loved him like a son." Huggins told Leo he would be around for many years. "Little guys like us can win games," he told Leo. "We can beat 'em"—and he would tap his head— "up here."

Huggins also encouraged Leo's combative nature. And if Huggins felt that Leo was not as aggressive as he should be, he made sure to test him. This went back as far as Leo's rookie spring training, when he wanted Leo to get some extra swings in to practice switch hitting. All the big guys—Ruth, Gehrig, and the others—jealously guarded their batting-practice time, and their turn. No busher was going to hop in ahead of them.

"Get in there and swing," Huggins commanded.

Leo didn't. He just looked on as one after another of Murderer's Row got in his licks.

"Go on!" shouted Huggins. "Hit!"

Reluctantly, Leo tried to muscle his way in.

"Get out!" someone shouted. Leo got out.

But Huggins continued to ride him, insisting he push his way to the plate. Finally, he did.

Leo was to recall that it was Ruth who snapped at him to get lost. But Leo stood his ground. And when he became a manager, he used the same tactic as a yardstick to measure other ballplayers. Indeed, over the years, many ballplayers spoke of the delight Leo as manager would take in testing them in the batting cage. For one, his nephew's friend from West Springfield. And even a future National League president, Bill White, who recalls, "If you couldn't take it, Leo didn't want you on his team."

Huggins would encourage his aggressiveness when things were slow on the bench: "What's the matter with you, Leo? You ain't said a word since the last two batters got up."

That would stir Leo, who might take it out on Ruth, who had chronic knee problems. "What's the matter with you, Babe, always crabbing about your legs? You big stiff, go up there and hit."

When newspapermen asked this twenty-two-year-old with one big league at-bat how he dared act this way, Leo explained, "You see, I got to encourage even the manager. I get under his skin, but I know he likes to have me yipping around on the bench. Say something—make a noise, let 'em know you're around, that's my motto."

There was one thing about this constant chatter that did bother Leo, though. "I just wish," he said, "I could get in there some place where I could be nearer to the opposition so they could hear the sassy things I say."

Still, it did not appear to the writers covering the team in St. Petersburg that Leo would last.

He fooled them, becoming the first rookie to make that championship team. He did it despite the pronouncement of Dan Daniel of the New York *Telegram:* "No, Durocher will not take anybody's job as a regular, that is, unless everything goes wrong around third base and it becomes necessary to shift Tony Lazzeri. If Leo could hit an even .280 he could step right in, but he batted only .253 with St. Paul and, to speak frankly, he doesn't look as if he will be a really first-class hitter. He is light and he isn't loose enough at the plate."

But Huggins said of him, "Durocher is essentially a shortstop. He plays the position naturally. He has a fine arm and gets the ball away fast. He'll be ready to step in at short or second."

The Yankees picked up on Leo's expensive clothes, as well as his high night life. Soon, they began calling him Rudy, after the matinee idol, Rudolph Valentino. He also had a reputation for playing cards, especially hearts, bridge, and craps, and he quickly became known as a big-time pool player.

But playing on the ballfield, that was something else. For with Koenig anchoring short, Lazzeri at second, and Dugan at third, the Lip would have to wait his turn. It came up Opening Day 1928, when the Yankees were in Philadelphia. The A's, their chief rival in the late 1920s and early 1930s, had a couple of future Hall of Famers, Ty Cobb and Tris Speaker, who would finish their last season that year.

Before the opener, Huggins realized that Lazzeri, who had separated a shoulder, could not play. "You ever play second?" he asked Leo.

"Sure, Hug," Leo lied. "I've played it more than I have shortstop."

The Babe told Leo, "Listen, kid, if Cobb rides you, I want you to say to him, 'Listen, you no-good penny-pinching son of a bitch.' He can't stand being called a tightwad." It was something all baseball knew.

Early in the game, with Cobb on first, Speaker followed with a grounder between first and second. As Leo reached for the ball, he nudged Cobb, who was dashing for second. The minor collision slowed him, and Leo fielded the ball and just nipped Cobb at second with the throw. Cobb, of course, figured Leo had done it deliberately. Probably he did.

"If you ever do that again," Cobb ranted, "I'll cut your legs off." He might have been forty-one years old, but he stood six foot one and was still formidable.

Leo remembered the Babe's advice. "You old penny-pinching..."

Before Leo could finish, Cobb challenged him to a fight under the stands after the game. But Ruth trotted in from right field and said, "Look, Ty, you wouldn't hit a kid would you?" and Cobb turned and headed for the dugout.

There was, naturally, another Cobb-Durocher confrontation. It might have been Cobb's farewell year, but Leo was making up for all those years they never met.

This time, Cobb came in as a pinch hitter. Durocher was uncanny at positioning himself in the field. He knew the hitters, he knew his pitchers, and he had wonderful acumen in figuring where the ball would be hit based on the kind of pitch the batter was getting.

So Leo, playing shortstop, moved close to third, playing ten feet closer than he normally would. He thought Cobb might be able to slash the ball sharply off the hurler, rather than pull the pitch. Cobb hit a scorching grounder right to Durocher, who threw him out.

"You're a lucky busher," growled Cobb, passing Durocher as the inning ended. "Playing me way out of position and then throwing me out."

"Well, I was playing you for a better hitter than you are," retorted Durocher.

Before long, Leo became one of the most quoted players on the Yankees—not bad considering his playing only 66 games at second and 29 at short. And he could back up his talk with his fielding. He displayed excellent hands, a wonderfully accurate arm, and he covered a lot of ground. Leo constantly encouraged the pitcher with his chattering, an unusual and welcome trait for a rookie. He gave those around him confidence, even though he usually came into a game to rest the regulars.

Early in the season, he told newspapermen before a game against the A's, "Watch tomorrow's first pitch. And watch me when it comes up there."

Durocher got up, facing a rookie, Ossie Orwoll, and the first pitch sailed straight at his head. He got up out of the dirt and shouted to Orwoll, "Three more of them, pal, and I'll be on first where I belong." Orwoll walked him.

Now how could Leo have figured that would happen? To anyone who would listen, he explained that, the year before, at St. Paul, he had gotten a reputation for being yellow, and they had thrown at his head. "I became expert at dodging pitches. I got fifty-two free trips to first. Now I see this busher Orwoll. I figure if I say that he'll knock me down with the first pitch, he will. He does, but we win the game by one run, and he's not there at the finish, but I am. What does it mean? It means that he won't stay in the big leagues very long, and I will. Remember that!"

Leo was right twice. Orwoll was gone by the end of 1929, and Leo hung around until 1973.

Fatty Fothergill came to bat in Detroit one day in Leo's rookie season. Leo ran up to the plate and told umpire Moriarty, "He's batting out of turn." Moriarty took out his lineup card and said Fothergill was just where he was supposed to be.

Leo had him now. "But there are two guys at the plate," said Leo of the five-ten, 230-pound Fothergill. "Which one is batting?"

Fothergill was not amused. After the inning, he tried to cut Durocher off on his way to the dugout. The Babe, Leo's sometime protector, stepped between them.

At the plate, switch hitting proved to be only a temporary remedy for Durocher's weak hitting. He was a streaky batter (at one point at St. Paul the previous season, his average had been up at .340, but he finished at .253). In the big leagues he had a fast start, but that soon tailed off. Still, he hit .270, a highly acceptable figure for a fancy-fielding shortstop today.

If Leo had difficulty making the transition to the left side of the plate, there was nothing wrong with his other athletic skills that had been honed in West Springfield. Before long, he was ensconced in the big pool hall in New York, in a room over the Capitol Theater on Broadway. Hustlers would play each other nightly after the other rooms closed. It was the sort of place depicted in *The Hustler,* dimly lit, open all night, attracting an assortment of characters who were beyond Runyonesque. They were downright dangerous. Leo loved it.

The rookie had "caught lightning in a bottle," which was to become one of his pet expressions. The Yankees won the pennant, and they swept the World Series against the Cardinals. The money, of course, was extremely useful to Leo, who had started to spend more than he made. His salary was $5,000, his spending considerably more. He also began writing bad checks.

"You know the one about the bad check he wrote to a stationery store right near Yankee Stadium?" recalls a chuckling Harold Rosenthal, a newspaperman whose career in sports was longer than Leo's. "Leo refused to make good on a check, so the owner of the store pasted the bum check in the window. That's all Ed Barrow had to see. Everyone coming to the game would stop at the window and look at Leo's bad check. Barrow called in Leo and said, 'Twenty-four hours to make good.' "

* * *

Even though Leo spent a lot of time on the bench in 1928, he was in that year's World Series every day. All his appearances came in mop-up duty at second base for the sore-shouldered Lazzeri in the late innings. Durocher batted only twice, but the last one, he told *The Sporting News* in 1944, remained among his favorite recollections: "I missed what would have been my big thrill of that Series, losing a homer off Grover Alexander by inches." (Alexander was forty-one years old, but had posted 16 victories.)

Leo related that it was the last game of the Series at Sportsman's Park. Alexander relieved Bill Sherdel in the seventh inning. "The Cardinals didn't like me," said Leo, and Alexander threw three brushback pitches at him.

Then Leo, batting left-handed, tagged one and it went deep to right field, headed for the seats. "However, just when I thought I had a World Series homer, a gust of wind got hold of it at the last moment, and George Harper caught it with his back to the wall."

He didn't get his homer—it would have been his first in the big leagues—but there was plenty of reason to celebrate that night.

On the trip back by train, the players launched a midnight parade, marching through each car, stealing people's shirts and pajamas. Colonel Ruppert, who never married, was traveling with a friend, Fred Wattenberg. The two men locked themselves in their drawing room. But Ruth and Gehrig broke through the panels and got hold of the top of Ruppert's lavender pajamas, which they then displayed like a trophy to the rest of the World Champions.

During the off-season, disenchantment among teammates grew and stories of Leo's larceny spread. The most famous concerns Ruth's watch.

Leo used to explain that what really happened was that one night in St. Louis when the Babe was coming in after bouncing around town in speakeasies, Leo spotted him. The two were friendly that first year. The rookie gave him a helping hand, guiding him through the lobby and into his room. The next day Ruth discovered that his wristwatch was gone. Forgetting about his stops the previous night, Ruth somehow convinced himself that Leo—the last man he had seen before hitting the sack—had done it.

That is Leo's version. Others aren't so sure. The people back in

West Springfield are convinced that Leo and a friend of his had a hand in it.

In any event, Babe Ruth believed he'd done it. A few days later, the Yankees were in Scranton for an exhibition game, and the local coal miners presented the Babe with a huge mantel clock carved out of coal. Ruth took it with him, put it on top of his locker, and said, "By God, here's one the slippery-fingered son of a bitch won't steal."

The truth can never be discovered about whether or not Durocher stole Lou Gehrig's World Series ring, but there is talk that still remains in Leo's hometown. Sam Pompei says he knew of people who saw Gehrig stride into town looking for Leo. And the children of those who saw Gehrig come looking for Leo still tell about it.

Leo did have a run-in with the law back home after the season. In late November he was freed after an off-duty patrolman charged that Leo had made a turn with his car and hit him. The charge never stuck.

That same month, a newspaper item appeared: "Leo Durocher, the dugout jockey of the New York Yankees, is making speeches at athletic clubs and other places of interest in and around Springfield, Mass. He spent the Summer making speeches to rival players, but they won't be found in forensic text books for beginners."

Leo wasn't aware of the growing resentment that was building in his teammates against him. He certainly wasn't happy when that off-season the Yankees acquired shortstop Lyn Lary, considered the minor leagues' top player, for $100,000.

At the beginning of 1929, Secretary Barrow announced that henceforth each Yankee would wear "a large and easily perceived number" on his back. Each was going to be listed by his number on the scoreboard as well. The *Times* described this as "a real innovation in the major leagues." Players would be numbered according to their place in the batting order. Thus, Earle Combs was number 1, Durocher number 2, Babe Ruth number 3, Gehrig number 4, and so on.

Perhaps, it was suggested, Manager Huggins might be able to deceive the opposition? "Yeah," said Barrow. "I suppose we can give the Babe's number to Durocher and give his number to the Babe. Then the other side won't know when the Babe comes to bat."

There wasn't to be much levity surrounding Leo the rest of the year, though.

Durocher came to spring training ready to win a job. And bragging about it. He had to unseat the popular Koenig at short and do away with the challenge from Lary.

That was hardly the worst of it. For now, his teammates had, essentially, turned against him in full force. They started to talk about him, not only among themselves but to the writers. They told reporters that he hung out with gamblers, including the infamous Meyer Boston. Leo was accused of every crime in the book.

If he met friends at the clubhouse gate, they were gamblers. If he was seen signing autographs—and he loved to—it was part of some slimy underhanded transaction. Stories even spread about his family. The stories got around with no help from the writers. In those days, the understanding between press and player was that private life was kept private, unless management, or more rarely the player, chose to make it public. (Thus, Babe Ruth's so-called bellyache is today simply accepted as a bout of gonorrhea.)

Despite these distractions, Leo won the shortstop's job. But suddenly, when the season began, his fielding began to suffer. He was making errors on the sorts of plays that he had always executed. Huggins analyzed what was going on: Leo wasn't bungling grounders or liners. He was mishandling throws. His teammates were throwing him curveballs to make him look bad!

One startling play in 1929 demonstrated not only Leo's talent in the field, but his talent for talking too much and making a teammate look bad. By winning the job, Leo had shoved Koenig to third. In this particular game, Russ Scarritt, a Red Sox rookie, was batting. He was a left-hander, so Koenig, naturally, positioned himself closer to his left. Durocher, barking to Koenig to play more toward third, told him, "I'll cover for you." Koenig was not happy about his move to third, and about sharing the infield with Leo. He told the Lip to mind his own business.

Scarritt smacked a grounder toward the hole between short and third. It zipped past Koenig, and Durocher, who had been running to his right with the pitch, somehow got the ball and threw to Gehrig for the out.

Leo explained to reporters that two years earlier he had played with Scarritt in the American Association, "and every time a lefty pitched to him, he hit the ball down to third." The Yankees now had more reason to rip Leo, who had shown up one of their veterans.

And Leo loved to brag about his clothes. One of his teammates said Leo was obsessed with keeping his shoes neat—he even sat down in the center of the diamond after heading for shortstop, took off his shoes, and started to clean them. He claimed he was looking for a nail in his shoe.

Leo became a loner. He ate alone, roomed alone, went to the movies alone, "with nobody near me," he disclosed.

Why? he was asked.

"Because of all the gossip," he explained. "These guys will never get me out by bouncin' balls at me or whispering gossip."

Maybe that's how the story of Ruth's watch began. But there are so many other stories of his gambling, of his virtual criminal behavior. And those stories that began in 1929 were repeated and carried through his career.

Huggins stuck up for him. "They won't get him out. He'll stay in there when every one of them is wasting away on the bench. I'll rebuild with Combs, Ruth, Gehrig, Pipgras, Dickey, and Durocher. I'll keep Durocher because he's the greatest infielder that ever smothered a half hop. I'll take those six and I'll start over."

Huggins, who had sent Durocher to the bench and installed Lary, the former Pacific Coast League star, at short, then put Durocher back in. Leo went on to bat .246, play 93 games at second base, and, for the second consecutive year, fail to hit a homer.

He was dubbed "the All-American Out" because of his anemic hitting. Legend says Ruth gave him the nickname. More likely, it was another teammate, or a newspaperman. No matter whoever it was who tagged him with it, the nickname stuck. His more enduring nickname, Leo the Lip, probably was coined by Will Wedge, a sportswriter of the time.

On a cold, raw day in late September 1929 (*The Sporting News* reported ten years later), Leo went into the locker room between games. The Yanks were mired in second as the A's ran away with the pennant. Huggins had been suffering from a blood disorder. He stood in front of a mirror looking worried, fingering a sore spot on his chin. "I don't feel very well," Huggins said. Durocher was frightened by the way he looked.

The next day, Huggins told Coach Art Fletcher, "Take the club, Fletch, I'll be back tomorrow."

Before the end of September, Huggins was dead.

On the day of his funeral every American League game was canceled and all ballpark flags flown at half mast.

"Well," Leo conceded, "that's the finish of little Leo. Hug was the best friend I ever had."

CHAPTER III

TRAVELS WITH LEO

WITH HUGGINS'S DEATH, and the Yankees' failure to make the Series, Leo was in trouble. Not only on the job, but at the bank. He owed about $20,000.

The Yankees were trying to dump him now, but it wasn't easy. The rumors about him had taken hold all over baseball. In later years, Leo liked to say that it was his cheekiness in asking Barrow for a $1,000 raise that led to his being traded to the Cincinnati Reds—a seventh-place club, and where he had absolutely no chance of earning a postseason paycheck.

The truth is that Barrow found him an embarrassment and a player who was causing havoc in the locker room. Then, too, Huggins's successor, Bob Shawkey, didn't like the language Leo used in the clubhouse, in the dugout, and on the field. Leo had overstayed his welcome.

He remained a Yankee slightly more than four months after Huggins died. On February 5, 1930, Leo began his big-league traveling. "NEW YORK MYSTIFIED AT DUROCHER'S EXIT," a next day's headline, only partially explained what had happened. It was the subhead, "But Leo's tongue said to be cause of A.L. clubs' snub," that made it clearer.

All the other teams in the American League had passed Leo by. (Of course, that was known as "the mysterious waiver route," which was another way of saying there was collusion among the league's owners if one of them was able to make a deal in the other league.) There was all sorts of speculation why Leo had been dropped, sold for a paltry $10,000 and a player to be named later. Supposedly, the Yankees were unhappy because he had publicly announced the terms of a new contract sent to him by Barrow. And, in another story, he had argued with Barrow over salary. He had refused the offer and started out the door.

"If you go out that door," said Barrow, "you go out of the American League."

Leo himself said he had told Barrow, "Fuck yourself," when Barrow threatened him.

If so, this was quite cheeky for Leo, considering his debt load. He had moved his father and mother to a house near Yankee Stadium and was supporting them while blowing his money on clothes and dice and pool. He estimated he spent more than twice as much as he made.

Yet, Leo refused to report to Cincinnati. It would not be the only time he tried to hold up a deal by squeezing an extra thousand or so for himself. *The Cincinnati Enquirer* reported that Durocher told the Yankees he refused to report to Cincinnati unless he obtained part of his purchase price from the Yanks. But Leo backed down on his threat. Saddled with debt and marked "lousy," what were his options?

Luckily for Leo, the Reds' new owner was a compassionate fellow named Sidney Weil. Weil, who had a sense of irony (unusual in baseball, but a must in dealing with Leo), had made his money from an auto dealership and from one of Cincinnati's first multilevel parking garages. He also was a brilliant stock market investor. And although he had his problems when the market crashed, he made a big financial comeback in the insurance business. Eventually, he sold the team to Powel Crosley of the Crosley radio family.

Weil's version of Leo's joining the Reds is probably the most accurate one. It comes from his witty reminiscences, published by his family after his death in 1966. He spoke of how he acquired Leo, how he gave him up, and why.

"My manager told me that the Yankees wanted to get rid of Durocher, who had been a pet of Miller Huggins. . . . He also reported that while he was a great fielding shortstop, he might as well have a toothpick . . . in his hand. . . . I went to see Mr. Barrow who ran the club for Mr. Ruppert. Yes, Durocher was for sale for $25,000 plus one minor league player. I was willing to part with the player, but not the money.

"After further talk, he gave me an opening to make an offer. I mentioned $7,500 and the player he wanted. He just swiveled around and looked out the window. I looked at his back so long I began to feel uncomfortable and then I said, 'Well, I've been thrown out of better offices than this.' And I started to get up and get out. With that he turned around to face me . . . in a few minutes I had bought Durocher for $10,000 and the player.

"No sooner did I arrive home than I began to get letters from hotels enclosing bills that Durocher had run up and not paid. . . . When we went south in the spring, I called Durocher to my room and showed him the bills. He admitted that he owed them and said that eventually he would pay them. They amounted to nearly a year's salary. We made an agreement that I would withhold all of his salary except just what he had to live. . . . "

With that, Weil was able to convince Leo not to file for bankruptcy. He began a systematic payment schedule to pare his debts. So much for good intentions.

"Leo . . . was a very natty dresser," Weil continued, "and . . . it wasn't a week later that I received a haberdasher's bill for $350. I called [Leo] at once and asked him which of the purchases he had already worn. I gave him enough to pay for it and told him to return all the other stuff, which he did. With all his faults, one couldn't help liking him.

"The morning of Opening Day I received a telephone call from Judge Landis. He said, 'Well, Durocher owes a lot of money in New York. Do not permit him to play until he pays.'

"'Judge,' I said, 'I know he owes the bills, but . . . if he can't play, he'll never have any [money].' I told him of the agreement that Durocher had made with me and that eventually the bills would be paid. So the judge reversed himself.

"Durocher played great ball for us, although he did not do much hitting. . . . One winter a social club asked me to talk to them one evening and to bring a player along. I invited Leo. He was a wow. He just talked about his experiences. One anecdote he told [happened in] the period when he was playing with the Yankees, with Babe Ruth. One season, only two or three weeks after opening, Leo was .300 and the Babe only .250, so Leo commenced to ride him about it, and the Babe said to him, 'Kid (he called everyone 'Kid'), when October comes and I look for your average, I'll run my finger down the percentage column to .220 and I'll go to my left, and there I'll find Durocher.' 'And I was there,' said Leo. He brought down the house. On the way home I told him that in the future he was to be the speaking representative of the club . . .

"He kept his word and gradually I paid off the New York hotels. It took about two and a half years. He would ask me for $100 and we'd finally settle for $25. He soon got the name of C-note Leo."

Leo might have been put on an allowance by Weil, but he once reminisced about Cincinnati, "It's possible to spend money anywhere in the world if you put your mind to it—something I proved conclusively by running up huge debts in Cincinnati."

Leo, naturally, did not become a Cincinnatian without creating just a little stir in the press. First, there was his refusal to report. Then, before he had even donned a uniform, Leo bragged, "The boys in the National League will be glad to see me—and beat me. There'll be Hack Wilson to ride. Won't that be fun?" Wilson just happened to be the league's leading slugger and star of the pennant-winning Cubs.

During spring training, though, Leo did not get treated with the respect he expected. He rode the bench while Hod Ford appeared to retain his job as shortstop. Leo did not endear himself to his new manager either with some late-night exploits.

His new manager and the Reds' new manager, Dan Howley, was trying to turn around a franchise (he would have spectacularly poor success, as did his successors). He was not enamored of Lippy Leo the way Huggins had been and the way Weil apparently was. In fact, spring training hadn't even ended when Howley, miffed at Durocher, threatened to send him packing.

Durocher missed a train in Atlanta that would take the Reds to an exhibition in Birmingham. He had been out late, as usual. So he got to an airport, hopped on a plane, and still arrived later than the train. He showed up on the field during batting practice. "Say," bragged Leo, when he stepped to the batting cage. "Did you fellows notice that plane that swooped down low a little while ago? I was on it."

Howley, not happy, said, "Next time you have to take a plane to join the team, you just keep going all the way to the Coast."

Ford started every game at short during spring training. This was not what Leo had in mind.

Weil recalled, "One spring he missed the train on the way home and as punishment, Dan Howley took him out of the Opening Game. Leo was heartsick."

Leo finally got into a game on April 18, the fourth of the season, as a late defensive replacement at second. He didn't get to bat, though, until April 28. After 27 games his batting line read 0 for 1.

There was no stopping Leo, though, or his ability to produce startling defensive plays. Within a few weeks the Reds traded their second baseman, Hughie Critz, to the Giants and moved Ford to second—and Leo stepped in as the shortstop. Weil, who used to involve himself in the on-field activities, explained, "While Leo may not be such a good hitter, we feel he will fill the vacancy in admirable fashion."

Leo soon became a darling of the Cincinnati fans, who had virtually nothing to cheer about. They had been seventh the year before he joined them. They were going to be seventh again and then mired in last place for a few years. They had the aging Harry Heilmann and Bob Meusel. The only pennant the team had won since the turn of the century had come in 1919, but the World Series victory that followed was tainted. The Reds had faced the Chicago White Sox, whom history would remember more dramatically as the Black Sox.

Still, the accounts of the day were almost in awe of Leo's wonderful fielding ability:

Leo had "caught the fancy of the crowd by his rapid maneuvering around second," the *Enquirer* reported before long. "Durocher has been fielding brilliantly, but hitting very lightly, mainly because he insists on batting from the left side of the plate when facing right-handed pitching."

Finally, on May 31, "On advice of Manager Howley, Durocher gave up his idea of batting left-handed, at which he has never been successful . . . "

"Undeniably a memorable defensive player although a light hitter," the *Enquirer*'s Jack Ryder noted.

Whatever problems he had at the plate, and off the field, did not affect his fielding. With Durocher at short and Ford at second, the Reds led the league in double plays.

In Cincinnati, Leo found himself virtually in the center of the gambling capital of America. He was a short gallop from northern

Kentucky, where crap games, bookie joints, casino gambling, and nightclubs flourished. And he loved the action across the river in Covington. There he befriended a legendary Covington gambler named Sleepout Louie, along with Cigar Charley and the Dancer. In later years he regularly visited them even after he had joined the Cardinals and then the Dodgers.

He also got involved with Ruby Marie Hartley. Ruby's name disappeared from Leo's background data after a while, but she was a fascinating part of his life—one might say unbelievable.

He got to know her soon after coming to town. She quickly became pregnant and before long they were married. It took place on November 5, 1930, at St. Andrew Church in the Avondale section—exactly nine months after Leo had been traded. She was a clerk, living in Walnut Hills, although she listed "none" when asked for "occupation" for the marriage license.

Although Ruby said she had no job, Ruby made some money. Weil knew quite a bit about this West Virginia–born woman. He recounted in his memoirs that before meeting Leo, Ruby had sued Daniel L. Bauer III, the son of Weil's partner in the auto business. She claimed breach of promise—that he had walked out on her after promising to marry her—and asked for $53,080 in damages. She contended that Bauer had proposed in 1927, that she had accepted, and the engagement had been announced. She also disclosed that Bauer had given her an $11,000 diamond ring but later had told her he couldn't marry her because he was a drug addict. She claimed he said he injected drugs through his mouth. Coincidentally, she filed this suit only four days before Leo was traded to the Reds.

The newspapers described her suit as being settled "amicably" on September 12, 1931—after her marriage to Leo. Weil said she received a $50,000 settlement, a sum that would not make her unattractive to Leo.

The night of Leo's marriage, Weil's wife said to her husband, "Guess who Leo married?"

"I can't begin to guess," said Weil. "Who?"

"Ruby Hartley," she replied.

"Can't that woman stay out of my family tree?" said Weil, still able to see the humor in the situation.

A little more than four months after their marriage, on March 27, 1931, Ruby gave birth to a girl named Barbara Lee Durocher.

THE LIP ◊ 59

She is the only child Leo is known to have fathered; each of his other three wives had children when he married them.

The controversy, the mean-spirited nature of the Leo-Ruby relationship would consume Durocher for many years and the marriage was rocky from the start. (It certainly wasn't helped when Leo brought his mother to Cincinnati and got her a job there as a hotel maid.) "I had one black eye a month after I was married to that man," Ruby testified in 1934 at their divorce trial. She filed for divorce in December 1933, by which time, they had been living apart for quite some while.

Leo did all right in his first season with Cincinnati. On one afternoon late in July, he handled 22 chances in a doubleheader, thought to be a record, and committed 1 error. And batting right-handed, he wound up at .243, struck 3 homers, 3 triples, and 15 doubles. Not bad playing for a team the *Enquirer* described as having "only a minor league punch at the bat, the pitching was erratic and the defense . . . only mediocre."

He was then looking forward to 1931. He explained in spring training, "I've got to do some real batting this year. With a family to support, a man has got to extend himself to the limit."

The family man, though, apparently had a weakness or two. For just after the 1931 season began, Howley lifted a ban on poker playing for the team—excluding Durocher. Everyone else could play cards to his heart's content. Howley never explained why Durocher was banned.

Durocher was at his fielding peak that season. He did not commit an error between May 15 and August 5. At the height of the streak, *The Sporting News* noted, "His irresponsible habits gradually are leaving him, now that he's a husband and a father."

He handled 251 chances perfectly, the streak ending on a little roller tapped by the Cubs' Kiki Cuyler. The Reds went on to tie their own 1928 record of 194 double plays. The *Enquirer* described his style as covering "a wide territory, [he] has a keen eye and a quick pair of hands, and his throwing is always right to the mark. He gets the ball away very rapidly. He is, also, quite clever at going back for short fly balls.

"But the best thing about Leo's work is . . . that he was never known to shirk a play. In many years of observation, [this] writer has seen a good many players who, under such conditions, would be careful not to take a chance on a very difficult play for fear of breaking the [streak]. Not so with the Reds' shortstop. Leo goes after everything regardless of his record . . . he lets his fielding average take care of itself, which is the sign of a good, game ball player."

Leo had another goal in this dismal season. He wanted to help the Reds set the team double-play record. It went down to the final game of the season, the second of a doubleheader. But he and Tony Cuccinello managed to pull off three.

Working in Cincinnati quieted Leo's voice. It wasn't that he talked any less, was any less outrageous or argumentative, but he was like a tree falling in the forest at night. If no one heard it, did it make a noise? And few people were listening to what was going on in Cincinnati and its hapless Reds. Leo's reputation as a fielder grew, but he produced the second lowest batting average of any regular in the league: .227.

His penchant for suspensions and brawling were just around the corner, though. In spring training of 1932, when the talk was that Joe Morrissey was going to come up from St. Paul to battle him for the job, Leo was hit in the shin. He had to sit down for a while. Morrissey, meanwhile, was holding out. "Maybe Joe Morrissey will sign up and come down when he hears about this. Let him come," said a defiant Leo. "He will have quite a battle on his hands to take the shortstop job away from yours truly."

Yet, when the season began it was Morrissey at short. Leo, losing a job for the first time in his career, began to press. He was 0 for 15 when he broke the slide with a scratch single. Finally, he got a solid hit by batting left-handed, a line double, and he decided to switch to being a full-time lefty hitter. Huggins had always wanted him to, claiming that with his speed Leo could leg out some grounders. And because he didn't have any power, Leo needed all the edge he could get.

That included nailing anyone who stood in his way. Early in the 1932 season, Leo, who had already stolen 2 bases against the Phillies, tried to steal another late in the game. Harry McCurdy's throw was in time to Dick Bartell. And as Bartell tried to tag Leo, Leo slashed at his wrist with his spikes. Bartell held the ball though, and growled to Leo, "If you ever try that again, I'll smack you right in the nose."

"I don't think you're man enough!" Leo retaliated. Bartell took a step forward, but Leo sucker-punched him right on the chin.

The umps ruled that Leo was the aggressor. He was kicked out of the game, suspended for three more, and fined fifty dollars.

"Leo says he swung because Bartell called him a fighting name, and also because Dick led him to believe he was going to throw a punch," wrote one newspaperman. He was always claiming the other guy started it, and that he would always have to defend himself.

Bartell, though, claimed he made no motion toward Leo. In fact, he said, he was trying to head for his own bench.

It was another crummy season for the Reds, who finished last for the second straight year. Leo played in 143 games, got 400 at-bats for the first time—but batted only .217.

"If Leo could add 50 points to his batting average," wrote John Drebinger of *The New York Times*, "he would easily stand as one of the stars of the game."

Another reporter said that Leo was the guy Mike Gonzalez was speaking about when the Cuban-born catcher coined the expression "Good field—no hit."

One of his best hits, though, was another shot with his foot—this time to a fan. On the club's final trip to Boston, Leo had been getting the needle. After the game, the fan made the mistake of going down on the field to continue jawing at the Lip. Leo stepped on his foot. After the season, Leo had to travel to Boston to answer a charge of assault and battery. Weil, his godfather, accompanied him. The judge ruled the fan had no business going on the field and threw out the case.

This sort of behavior—the incident with Bartell, followed by ejection, and stepping on a fan's foot—was to become more frequent. Indeed, it symbolized Leo's career almost as much as his managerial skills and way with a glove.

CHAPTER IV

THE GASHOUSE KID

C HARLEY GELBERT, the Cards classy shortstop, had shot himself in the foot while hunting before the 1933 season. Gelbert had anchored the position for the Cards since 1929, had hit .300 when they won the pennant in 1930, and worked the double play well with Frankie Frisch, the Fordham Flash, at second.

Leo, his battles with Ruby in full flower, started the 1933 campaign miserably. He was batting down near .200 after the first three weeks. The Reds were en route to their third straight finish in the cellar.

They had a new manager in Owen "Donie" Bush, who was moved to say of Leo in spring training, "There's the greatest ballplayer in the big leagues—that is, he would be if he could hit. He needs fifty points added to his average."

Then, Weil got a phone call. The Reds owner recalled: "One morning in New York, I received a call from Branch Rickey . . . That evening I went up to his room where he told me that he needed a good shortstop desperately in order to win the pennant. Finally he got around to Leo. I told him not to think of it—he was untouchable. But he persisted and said, 'You will listen?' He led out with Pitcher Derringer, whom I had been trying to get for a long time. Well, Derringer was worth $125,000 to $150,000 even in those days. . . . In return Branch wanted Durocher—who was worth only $35,000 to $50,000 if that much.

"The next morning I sent the club secretary to Durocher. About fifteen minutes later, Durocher came storming into the room, shouting, 'I won't go. I won't play for that Rickey. I won't join the chain gang,' and plenty more. I said to him, 'Leo, you must be filthy rich. You can't make the money out of baseball that you do in it. In it, you can only play for the Cardinals.' He acquiesced. We went over to Rickey's hotel and up to his room, where he was still in bed, reading the Bible. Leo didn't wait for introductions, just opened up with the same barrage he had given me."

Rickey was patient. He had to be. He needed a shortstop and he needed someone to cover for Frisch at second, where his range was limited. "Now it's my turn to talk. I have heard many tales about you, young man," Rickey finally said.

Leo was never one to allow others to explore his thinking and emotions, but he let Rickey. "I don't make friends easy," said Leo in an uncharacteristic admission of weakness. "I made only one real friend and he died on me."

Rickey reminded Leo that he would make more money from baseball than anything else he could do. The clever Mahatma then worked on Leo's ego: He told Leo, what if you don't join us, and at the end of the season we finish one game from the pennant and our shortstop had let a few go past him? How, said Rickey, would you feel then? Leo agreed to report that day. He was part of a deal in which the Reds also received, besides Derringer, another pitcher, Allyn Stout, and thirty-eight-year-old infielder Sparky Adams. In return, Durocher came to the Cards along with a pair of minor leaguers.

Leo also defended his financial situation, saying he was still paying off debts but was on schedule. Rickey knew otherwise.

Just as he had done after the Yankees had traded him to the Reds, Leo attempted a holdup. This one worked better. He told Rickey he would need more money than his $6,000 salary to come to New York and Rickey was noncommittal. Then, after Leo left, Rickey spoke to Weil about Durocher's demand, and Weil, solicitous of Leo to the end, threw in the $1,000 and the deal was done.

A few months later, Weil declared bankruptcy and sold the team to Crosley. The deal was brokered by the Reds' new president, Larry MacPhail, who just missed connecting with Leo in Cincinnati. The pair would get another chance in Brooklyn. But that was some years away.

The Sporting News trumpeted Leo's arrival as "Deal for Durocher Makes Cardinal Infield."

Rickey certainly believed he had a necessary key to the team's future success. After winning consecutive pennants in 1930 and 1931, the Cards had slumped to seventh in 1932. Still, Rickey knew his second-year right-handed pitcher, Dizzy Dean, was on the verge of greatness. With Pepper Martin at third, Frisch at second, Ripper Collins at first, twenty-one-year-old Joe Medwick in the outfield, and another pitcher, Tex Carleton, Rickey felt he had a potential winner.

After Gelbert's accident, the club had tried to move Frisch to short and use Rogers Hornsby at second base. But that clogged up the bag because Hornsby tended to play the position tight. And Frisch had trouble going to his left, so he stayed close to second as well. That left big holes between first and second and second and third.

Although Derringer did become a Reds star, helping them to consecutive league championships in 1939 and 1940 as part of a three-season string of 20 victories, there were those in Cincinnati who thought that losing Leo was a bad deal. "In addition to being a smart and aggressive fielder, Leo has fire and pepper on the field and is one of the most colorful athletes in the business. He will be missed by both fans and players, with all of whom he is a popular member." That was Ryder's farewell in the *Enquirer*.

Thus, the eternal search for a winner led Rickey to begin his association with Leo. It would last through the St. Louis years, be interrupted by Leo's trade to Brooklyn, then be rekindled in their final, improbable Dodger reunion during which Rickey alternately was appalled by, and reveled in, Leo's style.

In baseball's tobacco-chewing, cussing milieu, Rickey was the odd man out. He never attended Sunday games. He never uttered epithets stronger than "Judas Priest!" He preached. He moralized. The people who worked for him could not reconcile this part of him with the fact that he was a tightwad, and never missed an opportunity to make a deal that would screw the other guy.

Rickey knew all about his image. And it bothered him. He once admitted he was upset with the image of a Bible-spouting do-gooder. It painted him virtually a hypocrite since he didn't attend Sunday baseball but certainly reaped in its profits. "A deeply personal thing," he once explained about Sundays. "A man's promise, a promise to his mother."

By not attending games he was not condemning baseball, or those who played it on the Lord's day. It was simply a promise that could easily have been a promise "not to attend the theater," he told Gerald Holland in a 1955 *Sports Illustrated* article. " 'Hell's fire!' " he shouted, conceding what people thought of him. " 'The Sunday school mollycoddle, the bluenose . . . ' " He was upset. Instead, he declared, he was " . . . a *liberal!*"

Here was a man born in Ohio in 1881, a former big-league catcher, who often claimed he was torn between the pure idea of the game and how it actually was run behind the scenes and on the field.

He acquired a law degree and even tried to practice. He moved to Boise, Idaho, to recover from tuberculosis, but was so frightened by his first client—who turned out to be a pimp—that he left the state and wound up in St. Louis. There, he got a job with the St. Louis Browns, intending to stay only a year. But after the year, his wife gave birth, he was offered a raise, and he stayed. He was, he explained, "a moral coward."

It often bothered him that he had devoted his life to something he derided as "a game played with a bat and a ball." Yet, he also saw the beauty in baseball, and how it was somehow American, how its verbiage was part of the broader language. Baseball, he once said with typical Rickey verbosity, "points the way to our salvation."

Rickey's legacy was the mass production of ballplayers. It is why Leo derided Rickey's operation as a "chain gang." But the Cards were three years ahead of all the other clubs in establishing tryout camps. They looked at four thousand boys a year and once signed, they needed places to play. The Cards created the farm system.

Rickey had brought innovation with him from the Browns, where he had started Ladies' Day. With the Cards, he developed the Knothole Gang. It got youngsters to become fans. In effect, he created a farm system for crowds. But the first inductees into the Cardinals Knothole Gang were required to sign a pledge that they neither smoked nor used profanity. Leo would not have qualified.

In 1955, twenty-two years after he first hooked up with Leo, Rickey reflected, "He has come a long way, off the field as well as on. A quick mind, a brilliant mind, an indomitable spirit. But when he came to St. Louis, Leo was in trouble. No fewer than thirty-two creditors were breathing down his neck, suing or threatening to sue. An impossible situation. I proposed that I go to his creditors and arrange for weekly payments on his debts. This meant a modest allowance of spending money for Leo himself. But he agreed."

So Leo had never rid himself of debt with Cincinnati, despite Weil's extraordinary efforts. Indeed, it is likely Leo still was paying off money he owed to people in New York.

Leo immediately was placed at shortstop alongside Frisch. The Fordham Flash had joined the Giants in 1919, never playing minor league ball after starring at Fordham University in the Bronx. His father was a lace manufacturer, who didn't like the idea that his son, who had a degree, was a ballplayer. But Frisch played with the Giants eight seasons and would have succeeded John McGraw as manager, except the volatile Frisch had a fight with McGraw, jumped the team in St. Louis in 1926, and eventually was traded to the Cards for Rogers Hornsby.

Frisch was a volatile, almost violent man in a gray flannel suit. He was a study in contrasts: a devotee of classical music and gardening at his suburban home in New Rochelle, New York, but a tiger in uniform. To the public he was an accomplished, hard-nosed infielder with a strong arm and strong features, quick though bowlegged, and a strong batter with a .316 career average as a switch-hitter.

Even in his twilight as a manager, when he was fifty-three years old and managing the terrible Cubs, he led the National League in being thrown out of 6 games. And he was fired after only 80 games were played.

Columnist Red Smith once walked into Frisch's room in a hotel in Philadelphia and asked if he had sent his fine to Frick. Smith was astonished when Frisch whipped out a check, signed it, and wrote in a note: "Dear Ford: Here is my check for $25 to pay for the fine. Please use it for a good cause—like buying your umpires new caps. They now look like Civil War veterans."

Frisch didn't like modern ballplayers, at least the 1950s version. He complained, "Rampaging, dictatorial managers have vanished with the bunny hug and the hip flask. Gone are the feuds, fines, profanity, and fun. This is an era of love and kisses, of sciences and psychology." Leo would echo these thoughts himself when he said in the 1970s: "Whatever happened to 'Sit down, shut up, and listen?' "

Leo described an angry Frisch as "letting go with a full display of fireworks. It's like the Fourth of July. I love to get the Dutchman riled." The Frisch-Durocher relationship was of a very different nature from the Huggins-Durocher, father-son love-in. Somehow, Leo couldn't escape relationships that were at once clinging and repellent.

Frisch had been one of the few athletes in the early years of the century to graduate from college and go on to the big leagues. He was a daredevil baserunner and a true son of McGraw, whose Giants won four straight National League pennants starting in 1921. After his run-in with McGraw and departure from the Giants, he helped the Cards capture pennants in 1928, 1930, and 1931.

Before Leo was on the team very long, Frisch became his manager. Just after the midway point of 1933, Rickey dismissed Manager Gabby Street, whose team was barely over .500, and inserted Frisch in the dual role of player-manager. The move angered the players, who enjoyed the easy-going Gabby. They found a harsh, loudmouthed disciplinarian in Frisch.

Frisch realized he had created a difficult situation on the club. His sarcasm alienated most of the players. When the season ended he visited his key players at their homes around the United States to mend fences. "It isn't easy managing men," he conceded after the season. "But if anybody should get tough, I can get tough too."

In December 1933 Ruby sued Leo for divorce. Soon after that, one May E. McDonald also filed for divorce from one Charles McDonald, who was a well-known concessionaire at ballparks and racetracks. In the suit, Mrs. McDonald claimed that her husband "had been too friendly with Mrs. Durocher."

The round-robin continued. The Durocher suit dragged on. Early in 1934 Leo charged Ruby in a cross petition with "gross neglect of duty." "On numerous occasions," he said that she "associated with other men; that she neglected to care for her home; that at various times she attended parties in hotel rooms, apartments and nightclubs unescorted by her husband."

Leo asked for custody of the child.

A month later, Ruby roared back. Leo, she said, "was wholly unfit to have the care, custody and control of [the] child [because of] his association with women of immoral character." Ruby claimed she had proof of Leo's philandering—letters and messages written to him by other women. Why, she said, the Ohio Humane Society even had filed charges against him because of his "neglect to provide for his aged mother."

Further, Ruby showed the love letters to the court. One was

signed "Virginia." Another came from "Sis." Still another was from "Marie." Virginia, Sis, and Marie wrote or wired often. Marie was a New York chorus girl and also had been with the Atlantic City beauty pageant. In one of the letters read to the court, Marie said she was lonely because as a chorine she dated only "old fossils" who were "not like my loving Leo." She closed with "All my love."

All these letters, claimed Ruby, were found in Leo's hotel room in St. Louis when she had visited him in June 1933—barely a month after he had been traded from Cincinnati.

Still, they managed to see each other. In fact, just a month after she filed for divorce, she said, Leo tied her up with a bed sheet and punched her in the jaw. She displayed a photograph showing her jaw swollen and face disfigured.

"Isn't it a fact that you were highly intoxicated and that was the only way your husband could subdue you?" Durocher's lawyer demanded. "You drink quite a bit, don't you, Mrs. Durocher?"

"I do," she replied, "on occasions."

Then Leo took the stand. Why, yes, he admitted, he had struck her. And here's why.

"I got home about eleven o'clock and went to bed. About two o'clock my wife came in. She . . . snatched the covers off the bed. I . . . smelled liquor on her breath. I took the covers back and she snatched them a second time, cursing me.

"I tried to quiet her by telling her she would wake the baby, and out of a clear sky she said, 'The baby needn't concern you. It doesn't belong to you.' I said, 'What did you say?' She said, 'You heard me; the baby doesn't belong to you.' Then I struck her."

And as for the letters from Virginia and the rest?

"Fan mail," replied Leo.

Leo's side was just getting warmed up.

That maid's job that Leo had gotten for his sixty-year-old mother came in handy. Leo claimed that Ruby had been seen with a man in the Netherland Plaza—the same hotel that Leo's mother happened to work in. Ruby denied she was ever there.

Not according to Mrs. Clara Durocher, though. In a remarkably fortuitous (for Leo) circumstance, Clara claimed that while working at the hotel one night, she happened to be passing room 1706, when she heard the voice of her son's wife.

Clara and another maid knocked on the door. "A man came to the door and asked for some towels," Clara Durocher testified. "He was in his shorts. I saw Mrs. Durocher in a dressing gown. When the room was cleaned up there were whiskey bottles and face powder there, and lipstick on the pillow slips."

And could Clara identify the man with her son's wife?

"Mr. McDonald," she replied.

Ruby did admit, however, that McDonald had called on her at her apartment. She said he never gave her money. She lived on the hundred dollars a month that Durocher, who was still earning six thousand a year, had sent her. Well, McDonald did buy her a fur coat, she conceded.

In an unusual action for that time, a domestic relations court judge ruled in April that Ruby, and not Leo, was guilty of gross neglect, and granted Leo the divorce. But the court gave custody of Barbara to Ruby and ordered Leo to pay child support of twenty-five dollars a week until October, and ten dollars weekly thereafter. Leo was given visiting rights to the child. There was no alimony.

The final legal wrangling in the Durocher divorce case apparently took place in July 1936. One Murray Kane, a hairdresser identifying himself as Ruby's new husband (he had married her the previous year), asked the court for permission to adopt Barbara. In the application, Kane said Durocher had consented to the adoption. The judge granted the adoption request soon afterward.

The record is scanty on Leo's relationship with Barbara, though he kept her picture in his apartment.

During spring training of 1934, Frisch seemed ready for a challenge. Little did he know that Rickey was about to undermine him by insisting that Leo become the field captain. "I'm the boss," said Frisch. "I'll call all the shots. The boys will come to me for all instructions. No one will nod me off on a signal. I'm the yes-guy on this ballclub."

He and Leo were to battle so often that the Gashouse Gang came to symbolize their infighting as well as the Cards' brawling and style of play against enemy players.

It is likely that Leo gave the club the nickname, or at least helped make it a household name. But there are references to the name Gashouse before he used it.

The funny thing is, the 1934 Cardinals—the team synonymous with the term "Gashouse Gang"—was not called that when they won the pennant. It has been awarded retrospectively.

The first time the Cardinals were associated with "gashouse" is believed to be 1932. But it was not a name that stuck or gained popularity. Warren Brown of the Chicago *Herald-Examiner,* in describing Pepper Martin, noted that his scruffy play and appearance made him look like "a refugee from a gasworks." And during the 1934 Series, Joe Williams of the New York *World-Telegram* claimed, "I picked the Tigers but the Cardinals have got me worried. They looked like a bunch of boys from the gas house district who had crossed the railroad tracks for a game of ball with the nice kids." Six days later, a writer for the *World-Telegram* used the term "Gas House Gang" in describing the Cards.

But it wasn't until the following spring that the name was widely quoted—after Durocher used the term, or something very close to it. Someone asked him if he thought the Cardinals could make it in the American League as well. Frank Graham of the New York *Sun,* one of the country's most widely read sportswriters, quoted Durocher as saying, "They wouldn't let us play in the American League. They'd say we were a lot of gashouse ballplayers."

If the greatest player on that team was Dean and if Medwick was its enforcer, Pepper Martin was its soul. Even his nickname connotes the quality that lifted that club to baseball legend. However, unlike Murderer's Row, or the A's under Connie Mack, the Gashouse Gang never accomplished a string of pennants.

But in Martin, it had the gashouse image. Here was a player who did the unheard of—he slid headfirst! His uniform not only got dirty, it got shredded. The center fielder was always running, and dangerously. First basemen never kept their feet on the bag when he was hurtling toward it on a grounder, even if he was out by five feet.

When his former teammate, Rip Collins, was playing first for the Cubs, Martin smacked a ground ball. The field was wet from that morning's rain, and so the runners used the inside of the baseline rather than run in the mud. "Out of the corner of my eye I saw Martin coming up the inside like an express train," Collins recalled. "I gave him the whole bag, stepped off, and took the throw."

The Cards ran out of the dugout yelling that Collins's foot had never been on the base. After the argument ended, the umpire whispered to Collins, "How far off the bag was your foot?" The umps knew.

But it was the headfirst slide that seemed to symbolize the Cards' combativeness and that gave even more meaning to Martin's nickname, the Wild Horse of the Osage. It was, of course, a more efficient way of stealing a base or legging it into second or third—you can maneuver your arm much more easily than your leg. The trouble is, it takes some nerve to go diving into the ground.

When the Cardinals invited Martin to spring training as a rookie in 1930, he "rode the rods" underneath a freight car. He was arrested and jailed overnight. By 1931 he had taken over as the Cards center fielder, and had a creditable season, batting .300. The Cards were going to face the A's, who had captured two straight World Series. In fact, the American League had handed the National League consecutive World Series losses for four straight seasons.

This was embarrassing, and so before the Series, John McGraw, the most famous manager of his time, addressed the Cardinals. He was joined by Branch Rickey in an emotional appeal to the team. "McGraw with his cussing and fire and brimstone and Mr. Rickey with his shrewd understanding of psychology and his wonderful command of the language—when I left that dressing room I was floating on air. No team could beat us. In my mind we were champions already!" Martin recalled.

The Cards captured that series in seven memorable games. Martin belted .500—12 hits in 24 at-bats. No one else on his team even reached .300 against a staff that included 31-game winner Lefty Grove, George Earnshaw, Rube Walberg, and Waite Hoyt. These pitchers were so good and played for such a powerful team (the A's had won the pennant by 13½ games) that they rarely saw base runners take chances against them.

Before the series, though, Martin had told his roommate, George Watkins, "I'm going to run the bases against these guys." His 12 hits not only set a Series record, but he had stolen 5 bases—and made a running catch of the final out. His popularity had become so widespread that in the final games of the Series he needed a police escort. He became a national figure.

By the time Leo arrived during the 1933 season, the Cards were stumbling. Twenty-two-year-old Dizzy Dean, who had won 18 games as a rookie the year before, would win 20 in 1933. But the league was closely matched when Leo joined them, and the Cards finished fifth, even though they were 11 games over .500. They wound up 9½ games behind the Giants.

The 1934 campaign made Leo a Gashouser forever and enhanced his reputation as baseball's best-fielding shortstop. It also produced his second marriage. The Giants had jumped out to such a huge lead, and the Cardinals under Frisch had turned into such a feuding family, that the pennant chase seemed to take a backseat to the Cardinals' squabbling that year.

There were several points of controversy on the club, and Dean and his arrogant, off-the-wall ways were at the core of them. Here was a man who would win 30 games—despite a 7-game suspension. He boasted before the season, when pressed for a number, that he and his brother Paul, a rookie, would win 40 to 45 games between them. They won 49. He argued loudly and often with teammates, half of whom seemed to be angry at him at any given time because he criticized them if they blew a fielding play while he was pitching, or if they failed to deliver a clutch hit to give him a win.

In one dugout scrape with Medwick, who failed to run down a fly, Dizzy and Paul made a threatening move toward the outfielder. Medwick picked up a bat and challenged, "Come on, I'll break up this brother act right now."

Later in the game, Medwick hit a home run with the bases loaded, got a swig of water in the dugout, spat it over Dean's shoes, and snarled, "Okay, let's see if you can hold that lead, gutless."

The young Medwick had been the brunt of his teammates' jokes since coming up two years earlier. He bragged and was hotheaded, and he usually responded to his teammates' razzing by shouting back or shoving. He was, however, a terrific player with a career average of .324 and the National League record holder of doubles in a season with 64.

Medwick actually pummeled teammate Tex Carleton in 1934 over a batting-practice lick. Before one of the games, Medwick broke protocol—as he often did—by trying to get into the batting cage during the fifteen minutes allotted for pitchers. This time, Medwick had a reason beyond sharpening his batting eye. He was being paid by a magazine to pose. Carleton didn't know, or care, about that. All he knew was that Medwick was being his usual contentious self by usurping someone else's time. When Carleton tried to stop Medwick from getting into the cage, Medwick bopped him across the top of the head. "They never stopped me again," Medwick later recalled with some misplaced pride.

Meanwhile Durocher at shortstop—right next to the playing-manager—would stick his two cents in all the time, questioning Frisch's decisions. Yet, Frisch also came to rely on Durocher's baseball smarts, at least the way some players remembered it. Others weren't so sure, contending that Leo's contributions to Frisch's decisions were exaggerated by none other than Leo.

Leo almost got into a dugout slugfest with Rip Collins, who was to tie for the league's home run title, in a game against the Reds. It was the twelfth inning, with Leo on deck. Collins was on second with a double. Chick Fullis lined a hit to right, and Durocher ran down the third base line shouting to Collins, "Slide! It's going to be close." Collins crossed home plate standing up. In full view of the crowd, Durocher yelled at Collins after he scored. Later, in the dugout, Durocher screamed, "You ought to be fined for not sliding."

Collins shot back, "You're trying to show me up."

When Collins questioned Leo's authority to tell him anything, Frisch said, "I give Leo my approval to criticize, Ripper, and he's right."

Dean, meanwhile, disliked Leo because he publicly belittled him for claiming he had a sore arm. Dean also believed Durocher had betrayed him when he said, of the Dean brothers' holdout, "It isn't right for two players to think they are bigger than a ball club, and you watch our smoke from now on. We'll show those two guys a thing or two." Leo dared to suggest the Cards could win without the Dean boys. In fact, Leo was to "testify" against Dean in a hearing to determine if Dizzy should be suspended because he refused to pitch.

Through it all, Rickey believed in serenity at home. That is why he liked his ballplayers married, and that is why he encouraged Leo to date, and then marry, Grace Dozier, a woman of fashion and style who epitomized Leo's search for class.

They had met at the end of Leo's first St. Louis season. She was a well-known figure in the fashion industry. Three years older than the twenty-nine-year-old Leo, with a daughter, she was said to be the first person since Huggins to believe in him. And like Ruby Hartley some years earlier, she had more money than he did; she probably earned twice as much.

Bob Broeg (pronounced Bregg), the longtime columnist and sports editor of the *St. Louis Post-Dispatch,* who had a forty-year, often combative relationship with Leo, remembers Dozier: "Grace was a little older than Leo, what you'd call a handsome woman rather than beautiful. She had money. Leo didn't have much. She saved him. His famous line at shortstop, when they were horsing around before a game in 1934—and I'm sure it's true—was, 'Damn it, Diz, I'm $10,000 in the hole now. I need that World Series money.'

"I had seen his contract for 1934. The Cardinals were throwing away stuff after they moved into their new stadium. They stupidly threw away history. There was a cabinet filled with salary information." Broeg might have been the first reporter ever to have seen a team's entire salary structure. In the 1930s baseball was in a serfdom situation. "In the Depression, ballplayers' salaries were cut," said Broeg. "Frisch told me at one time he got $28,000 as a player, but he was making $18,500 as a player-manager. That's how much these guys were cut. The next highest on the club were Bill Hallahan, the pitcher, and Pepper Martin, getting $9,000. Leo was getting $6,500.

"But stapled to Leo's contract were codicils, conditions: If this man does this—paying off his debt... If he does this, paying off his first wife, and providing child support... If he does this, he gets an extra thousand." So Rickey had put in good-behavior clauses for Leo.

Sally Williss, now a tough-talking librarian on the North Shore of Long Island, worked for Grace Dozier years after she and Leo were divorced. "I'm from St. Louis and I worked for her in 1951. Grace ran the Carole King division of a St. Louis clothing manufacturer named Forest City. But she was a nationally recognized designer because she helped popularize junior sizes.

"Grace still carried the torch for Leo. We all knew that and that was the story. She was a very pretty woman, but very tough. She also was unforgiving.

"I was nineteen years old when I went to work for her. I had brought in my designs and she hired me. Finally, I decided to go to New York and she was furious, as if I was betraying her. 'You don't have any talent. You have no right to go to New York,' she said.

"But I came to New York and I went to a designer and I lied about my age. After all I was just a kid. I got a job designing in Manhattan. One day she came to New York and when she found out where I was working, she went to my boss and said, 'Sally lied to you about her age.' The bitch tried to get me fired."

Sally Williss was a successful New York designer for many years until she tired of the rough-and-tumble life in New York's garment industry. But anyone who has spent any time in that business knows that foul language, rough handling, and few diplomatic niceties are part of the business. Leo could have been a cloak-and-suiter. He liked shiny suits and he enjoyed four-letter words.

Leo married Grace on September 26—at the height of the 1934 pennant race, with five games remaining. Only Leo could get away with marrying with a week to go in a nail-biting season. Grace had even gone to Rickey and told him she didn't think it would be right to get married while the season was under way. But Rickey knew that marriage would help Leo, who had continued his wild spending. He told her to forget that, that it would be better for Leo to be able to concentrate on fielding and hitting once he was married.

Frisch was not happy. "What a time for a wedding," he fumed.

The ceremony was at the Municipal Courts Building. Records show that she originally was married to Vernon Dozier in 1918 (when Leo was thirteen) and separated ten years later. She obtained a divorce from Dozier two days before she married Leo. Ernie Orsatti, the center fielder and the team's other clotheshorse, was Leo's best man. He made a show of juggling the ring, amusing the few people in the judge's chambers.

That afternoon Leo went 0 for 3 against the Pirates.

And the day after their marriage, Grace sat down and wrote out a dozen checks to clear up all his debts.

Leo was loyal to Grace, and in fact got into trouble the next spring over her refusal to honor a picket line. It was the type of incident that many times led Rickey to say of his wayward boy, "Leo has the ability to make a bad situation infinitely worse."

It began when Leo accompanied Grace to work during a strike at the Forest City Manufacturing plant. She crossed the picket line. People vilified her. A garment worker named Doris Smith razzed Leo for being with Grace. Leo claimed Smith tried to get in his car and he called the cops. She was arrested and fined $240 on the basis of Durocher's testimony. She was charged with "disturbing Durocher's peace." It seemed an ironic charge: Durocher's peace?

Soon, Leo was an outcast as far as labor was concerned. He may have been the first ballplayer ever boycotted.

The Central Trades and Labor Union voted unanimously on April 28 to boycott the Cardinals until Durocher was removed from the lineup. Delegates charged that Durocher had made antiunion statements and appeared in court as a witness against Smith. The union said it would ask its seventy-five thousand members to stay away.

Rickey knew Leo was wrong and tried to avoid a confrontation.

He finally was forced to acknowledge what was going on and issued a statement that said, in part, "It was a matter that concerned Leo off the field and in his personal life, where the club cannot exercise control. I hold no brief for conduct of any player, on or off the field, which may be offensive, and I am not making a defense of such conduct."

Sam Breadon, the Cards' owner, who was still trying to turn a profit, was furious with Leo and with the boycotters. Leo, though, claimed he did not deride the efforts of striking workers. "I have nothing against the union and don't understand why I should be singled out," he said, surprised as always that his behavior should be misinterpreted.

Union leaders said it could be settled if Durocher apologized. He declined.

This was happening at the height of the Depression, during a time in this country when unions still were fighting to be accepted, which generated heat and emotion on all sides. Union busters and scabs were just about the most vile characters organized labor could imagine. And now they were imagining Leo was one.

The ILGWU complained in a letter to Commissioner Landis that Durocher had told them, "You are walking the streets for nothing, and while you are starving my wife is getting as much in one day as you would in a week."

The pickets included the ILGWU, the Bartenders Benevolent and Protective League, and the Ticket-takers and Ushers Union. In the first game played while the picketers marched, the Braves came in. For many fans it was their first—and only—chance to see Babe Ruth, then playing in the National League. Yet, only four thousand fans showed up.

"It's an average weekday crowd," said Breadon, bravely.

Eventually, Rickey met with the unions, issued an apology that satisfied them, and life went back to being as normal as it could be in Gashouse Land.

Leo's marriage in the final week of the 1934 season was one of the minor distractions for the Cardinals.

There had been early signs in the season that this would not be just another baseball year. The Yankees handed Ruth a $17,000 pay cut. Now he was down to $35,000 from his $80,000 high of 1930. All Ruth had done in 1933 was belt 34 homers, drive in 103 runs, score

97 more. That didn't earn him a raise by the standards he had established, or the standards of the times. And there was a Depression to boot.

The Cards were bathing in austerity now. They were dropped by the radio station that covered them. They didn't even have a public-address system. A fellow named Jim Kelley, who sat on a stool, would pick up his megaphone, march to home plate, and trumpet whatever announcements had to be made.

Leo protested before spring training that he was asked to take a pay cut himself, and he claimed it just wasn't fair. But he reported to camp. Not so with Diz's brother Paul, a minor leaguer who held out for an additional $1,500. Instead, he played for $3,000.

Although the Cardinals were in or close to first place for most of the spring, the Dean brothers moaned and complained. Actually, it was Diz who did the screaming. Paul never said much. But Dizzy contended his little brother was still underpaid. They threatened a strike. Then they pitched and usually won. But on June 1, Dizzy told Frisch he had a "sore arm." Frisch told Dizzy to go home, whereupon Paul announced that he, too, had a sore arm.

Now Dizzy was getting worked up, and every day he began complaining about his own salary, not just Paul's (who had captured his first eight decisions in the big leagues). Dizzy was earning $7,500 a year—the same he had made in 1933 before becoming a 20-game winner.

Before they refused to pitch, the club had still managed to get along despite the infighting and was 25–14, in first place on June 1. But they went 11–11 over their next 22 games, and the other pitchers were sulking. So was the team. In desperation Rickey acquired forty-three-year-old Dazzy Vance, who had been in baseball since 1912, to try to bolster the staff. Dizzy was 10–1, Paul was 10–3, but everyone else was under .500. Hallahan had fussed and fumed all season, since Dizzy had gone to the press complaining that he and his brother were earning less than Hallahan.

Finally, in mid-August, with the club in third place, 7½ games back of the Giants, the brothers refused to accompany the team to Detroit for an exhibition. The wrangling was in earnest now, and Dizzy was fined a hundred dollars while Paul was hit with fifty.

In full view of all the players in the clubhouse, Dean demanded that Frisch rescind the fine. Frisch, backed to the wall in front of his players, refused. "Then me 'n' Paul are through with the Cardinals," said the volatile Dean. He then went over to the trainer and said, "Take a look at my arm. It's sore."

The other players continued to stare. Finally, Frisch, thinking the bluff was over, said, "Okay, boys, it's time to play. Let's go, Paul, c'mon, Dizzy."

When they refused, Frisch shouted, "Take off those uniforms!"

Dizzy did more than take his off. He tore it off, ripping it apart. Then he ran around the room kicking over stools and benches. At his locker he snatched his road uniform and shouted, "Nobody's gonna wear this either," and he proceeded to shred it too. Carleton and Collins tried to calm him down, but the rampage continued. On Diz's way out the door, a photographer, who had missed the scene, said, "Can you do that for me again?"

"Sure," replied Dizzy, who always accommodated photographers. He held up a piece of torn jersey and, while the camera clicked, tore it asunder.

The next day Dizzy led his brother into the front office and said he was trying to get things worked out. But first, he said, the fines would have to go. He had also been assessed for the uniforms he destroyed. Frisch declined, and Dean was mystified. Why, said Dizzy, those uniforms could have been patched up.

Neither side would budge. Frisch told Diz he could go to Florida, as he was threatening. But Dizzy said no, he was going to stick around for the series against the Phillies. "The Cards don't need us none now," he explained. "Anybody can beat them Phillies, but the Giants are comin' in here next week and we figure Rickey will be beggin' us to let him give us our money back. It takes ol' Diz 'n' Paul to stop them Giants and he knows it."

The next day Frisch welcomed Paul back. But not Dizzy. He would have to sit for ten more days. So Diz demanded an audience with Commissioner Landis. Leo showed up—to testify against Dean. The meeting was supposedly closed, but it being summertime in St. Louis, and air-conditioning still a luxury enjoyed by the few, the transom to Landis's hotel room was open. Reporters heard the exchanges.

Leo actually didn't say anything derogatory about Dizzy, but suggested that Dean never had a sore arm and simply was so angry he refused to play. "He came in storming," said Leo. "I told him he put himself in a fine mess." Then, Leo testified, he offered to bet the distraught Dean twenty dollars that he'd be fined.

Dean never much liked Leo after that. His testimony made worse Durocher's earlier statement about the Deans' acting bigger than the team.

Landis upheld the suspension but suggested that perhaps the Cardinals would like to make it only seven days instead of ten. That was acceptable all around, and Dizzy rejoined the club. The Cards were 6½ back, still in third place, with a 68–47 record. During the two months of the Deans' wrangling, the team had fallen into a rut, playing 43–42 ball. They had sunk to the level of a .500 team.

But then they roared through the rest of the season, winning 27 of their last 38 games. Leo produced some key extra-base hits earning him the nickname (temporarily) Captain Slug.

But the Cards lost a Labor Day doubleheader to the Pirates while the Giants won a pair. With only 24 games remaining, the Giants had a 7-game lead.

The next day, Frisch gave the speech of his life as the Cards opened a series in Brooklyn.

Casey Stengel, the Dodgers' new manager, had angered the Cards when he got the job. He declared, "They're not all that good."

Frisch had the players come in an hour early. "Are you fellows going to quit now?" he shouted. "This race is just getting hot. It's not over yet. We're going to fight to the finish."

Reflecting a few days later on his speech, he recalled, "The change in their expressions was remarkable. They started kicking the benches around. They grabbed their uniforms and I saw them dressing with fire in their eyes."

"We ain't givin' up, Frankie," Dean told him in front of the players. "I'm pitchin' today and I'll show you we ain't beat. Are we boys?"

He pitched a 3-hitter for his twenty-fourth victory. Then with two weeks remaining, the Cards took three of four from the Giants in the Polo Grounds and now that lead was down to 3½ games. But would there be enough time left? Fourteen games remained.

On the next-to-the-last Saturday of the season the Cards visited Brooklyn. The Dean boys produced their famous double shutout— Diz's 3-hitter in the opener, and Paul's no-hitter in the second. "What makes me mad," said Dizzy later, "is I didn't know in that first game that nobody had got a hit off me until the eighth inning. I shoulda knowed, then I coulda really breezed 'em in there and we'd both had us a no-hitter."

Two days after Leo and Grace got married, the Cards began their final weekend, half a game behind the Giants. The Cardinals were home against Cincinnati, while the Giants were host to the Dodgers. On Saturday, St. Louis shut down Cincinnati, 6–1, while Brooklyn beat New York, 5–1. For the first time since early June, the Cardinals were in first place.

The Cards then captured the pennant the next day behind Dean's thirtieth. Even if they had lost, they would have taken the pennant anyway—the Dodgers again defeated the Giants, in the tenth inning to boot. Durocher charged into the clubhouse shouting "Give us some beer!" Leo should have remembered that Breadon, the Cards' owner, didn't believe in overspending. There was no victory brew for this pennant celebration.

The 1934 World Series against the Detroit Tigers would be the first national showcase for Leo's glove, and he established himself as the game's fanciest fielding shortstop. His fielding style included an uncanny ability to know where on the diamond he should be, and how the hitter would react to the pitcher. His arm wasn't especially strong, but it was wonderfully accurate. He could go to his right and, off balance, quickly get off the throw. On double plays, he was consistent in getting the ball to Frisch at second chest-high so that Frisch could release the throw to first with a minimum of effort. And when Leo was the middleman on the double play, his acrobatic ability allowed him to jump over a sliding base runner and release the ball accurately to first.

As soon as the Cards settled into their Detroit hotel, Leo and Grace went for a stroll in the lobby. He promised everyone he met that he'd buy them a hat if the Cards didn't win the Series. His more practical bride suggested, "Listen, honey, don't you think you'd better go slow on those hats? Hats cost money and it's a long winter, and you know, darling, you might lose."

Dizzy pitched the opening game, even though he had started in 6 of the club's final 25 games and had relieved in 3 others.

The Tigers' top power-hitter was young Hank Greenberg, who had belted 26 homers. He also was a rarity: a Jewish slugger.

Leo knew exactly how Dean should pitch to him. It was now the third inning, and Dean was struggling. He had lost some hop to his pitches because of all his late-season work. He was nursing a 3–1 lead, with runners on second and third, two out, and Greenberg up.

"Don't waste your fastball," Durocher yelled to Dean from short, loud enough for the bleachers to hear. "Throw the son of a bitch a ham sandwich. He won't touch it."

Diz struck him out. He held the Tigers to 8 hits, including an inconsequential Greenberg homer in the eighth.

The Cards, counted out a few weeks earlier, now had taken the opening game of the World Series. But Leo had a history—and a future—of screwing himself when things were looking brightest.

As the Series ground along to the maximum of 7 games, the thirty-five-year-old Frisch was wearing down. The season had taken its toll, from the Dean wars to the remarkable pennant race, to the pressure of being player-manager for every pitch.

It happened almost unnoticed, but it was a foreshadowing of Leo's inevitable exit from St. Louis: As the Cards took the field one inning, Frisch said to him, "How about playing a little closer to second and giving me a hand? I'm getting pooped."

Durocher didn't hesitate. "Go get yourself a wheelchair if you can't cover your territory. I'm not going to make myself look bad just to make you look good."

If he reacted this way to friend, how about foe? One thing you never wanted to do with Leo the Lip was give him ammunition. He could find it anywhere. So when Edna, the fiancée of Schoolboy Rowe—the Tigers' top pitcher—was writing a column about the Series, Leo filed away the information. What made Edna's appearance even juicier to Leo was the fact that Schoolboy's mom objected to the marriage. She boycotted the Series.

Rowe, the Tigers' 24-game winner, pitched the second game. The Cards touched him for runs in the second and third, with Leo chortling from the bench, "How'm I doing, Edna?" "Oh, Edna, honey, watch this!"

The Cards also knocked the Tigers' player-manager, Mickey Cochrane, off his feet in the third. Medwick crashed into the catcher attempting to score. Cochrane held the ball but limped to the dugout with two spike gashes in his right leg. But Rowe recovered and went on to pitch a 12-inning victory.

The Tigers then captured two of the next three games. Frisch called on Paul Dean to keep them from elimination in Game 6. Rowe pitched for the Cards.

Before Game 6, Leo was determined to get the team moving somehow. They were down 3 games to 2, and he had been 2 for 18.

He began jawing to his teammates, "C'mon, guys, we can do it. C'mon." From the opening pitch he began taunting Rowe, bringing the pitcher's mother and his fiancée into his diatribe.

Leo finally spoke loudly at bat, too. He was robbed in his first appearance when third baseman Marv Owen made an outstanding fielding play. Then in the fifth, with the score tied at 1–1, Leo began a 2-run rally by topping a grounder toward second. Charlie Gehringer fielded it and tossed to first, but Leo beat it out.

Detroit tied it in the bottom of the inning. With a timely hit, the Tigers could bust open the game and take the Series. With two out and runners on second and third, Owen hit sharply toward the hole.

"That," Leo recalled, "was the play that kept me in the big leagues." He grabbed it behind Martin and made the long throw to first to end the inning.

Leo then scored the winning run in the seventh after hitting a two-out double off Rowe.

Leo produced his third hit in the ninth, putting two men on. On a subsequent hit, Orsatti tried to score. He was out by ten feet, but still hurtled into Cochrane, knocking the already injured catcher into the dirt.

As Goose Goslin came in from the outfield with the inning ended, he passed Durocher and said, "You fellows think you're pretty tough, don't you?"

"No, we just play that way," replied Leo.

"Well, by God, you'd better not cover if I come down to second. I'll knock you on your ass."

"You come down, Goosie," Leo answered, "and I'll make you eat that goddamned ball."

On page one of the *Detroit Free Press* the next day was a photograph of Cochrane in his hospital bed. The caption read: "OUR STRICKEN LEADER." That was all Leo needed for Game 7.

Frisch was uncertain about pitching Dizzy in the game. In the opener he had gotten by without his usual speed and had survived early-inning troubles. But Leo talked Frisch into using his tired star again. As usual, Leo had a sense of history. He also knew players and tempo and how to grab the moment. The Cards generated 7 runs in the third inning. But 1 was all they really needed this day as the magnificent Dean produced a shutout.

The Lip was never better. "How's our stricken leader?" he would ask whenever Cochrane appeared. And he kept after Dean to remain focused. But, of course, Leo couldn't keep out of trouble.

In the bottom of the sixth, Medwick tripled and slid hard into Owen. The third baseman fell on Medwick, who began kicking him. The dugouts emptied, the umpires rushed over, fans stood. Medwick put his hand out, offering to shake, but Owen refused.

The next inning, Medwick was greeted by more than boos when he trotted out to left field. Fans pelted him with apples. Some of the players, including Medwick, threw them back and forth, as if they were having a catch. That really infuriated the fans, who now were being made fun of, so they started to throw at him in earnest. Medwick came in from left field toward the infield.

"It's nothing, Joe," Leo told him. "Don't let it bother you."

"If you think so," said an angry Medwick, "then you play left and I'll play short."

It was getting serious now.

Judge Landis, sitting in his box, began to get worried that if this didn't stop, there could be a riot and a World Series game would end in a forfeit, an intolerable situation. Landis waited seventeen minutes. The public-address announcer could not be heard when he asked for order. Suddenly, Landis decided to hold a hearing right there. He ordered Frisch, Cochrane, Umpire Bill Klem, Owen, and Medwick to his box. He demanded to know if Medwick was justified in kicking Owen.

"No, sir," replied Owen.

Medwick conceded, "I ain't mad at him."

"Mr. Medwick," said the judicial Landis, his white mane of hair dramatically falling over his ears, "you're out of the game to prevent bodily harm from fans."

That got Medwick even angrier, since he had already produced 11 hits and lost a chance at tying Martin's Series record. He slammed his glove to the ground. Four policemen escorted him off the field.

The only thing that remained was to preserve Dizzy's shutout, which the Cards did. They won, 11–0. But at one point late in the game, Frisch got furious at Dean. Dizzy was fooling around with the big lead, and daring Greenberg to hit the ball. "If he hits, you're out of the game!" Frisch yelled at his pitcher.

The victory gave the Cards the world championship—the only one the newly named Gashousers would capture.

Leo had come on with his hitting, finishing with 7 hits in 27 at-bats. And in the field he handled 30 chances without an error. With his newly acquired affluent wife and his Series check for more than $5,000, Leo was at long last debt-free.

At a twenty-fifth reunion in 1959, Branch Rickey said of the Gashouse Gang, "They loved the game so much, they would have played for nothing."

"Mr. Rickey, we almost did," quipped Martin.

Jim Mooney, a Cards reliever of 1934, was asked about Leo many years later by Robert E. Hood, who was writing a book on the Gashouse Gang. Mooney, a man of some substance who had both a bachelor's and master's degree, changed his expression. "Nobody liked him. When he put on his street clothes, nobody associated with him. He was a prima donna. Carried a couple of trunks of clothes on road trips. Everytime you saw him he was dressed differently."

But was this a reason to dislike a man? Perhaps in the rough-and-tumble of 1930s baseball—especially Gashouse Gang baseball—it was.

Another member of that team, right fielder Jack Rothrock, once was asked if Leo really was the brains of the team, as a teammate had said. "No way. I think Leo must have been the one who said that," he suggested.

And Jesse Haines reflecting on Leo, said, with a laugh, "It'd take an automobile to keep up with him." Yes, said Haines, Leo was quick, and had good release—"If he wanted to. He loafed."

Indeed, Leo and Frisch often went to war over Leo's attitude. Many times Frisch claimed Leo was taking it easy, certainly an impression that the public never had of him. Frisch once got angry at Leo for not hustling, getting off a lackadaisical throw, and in front of the players fined him. They went back and forth: Frisch told him the poor throw would cost fifty dollars.

"Make it a hundred," shouted Leo.

They continued jawing until it was up to two thousand and both realized how absurd the situation was. Frisch backed down.

Even though Frisch wanted to be the dominant man on the club, he often consulted Leo on pinch hitters and pitching changes—at least, the way some teammates remember it.

Despite Rothrock's downplaying of Leo's role, most of the Cardinals thought more highly of him than they did of Frisch, according to Robert Gregory in his book *Diz*. "Two-thirds of the players didn't grade [Frisch] high as manager," wrote Gregory. "They said he couldn't think ahead, called for too many curve balls to opposing hitters, and that Durocher, as much as they disliked to admit it, was a better tactician."

From afar, Bill Terry, no fan and no teammate, said of Leo, "You can have him."

With his championship ring (presumably his own), Leo would now take on anyone. In a 1936 game against the Dodgers, Leo got into a shouting war with Casey Stengel in Ebbets Field early in the season. "He called me vile names," Leo would recall, with an insulted tone.

They met under the stands after the game. Leo claimed Stengel came at him with a bat but that Leo got in the first punch, an uppercut, before the Dodgers stepped in.

But Stengel, who at forty-five was fifteen years older than Durocher, contended, "I didn't use a bat on him. I didn't have to."

Even without a championship, the Cardinals still retained their aura of brawling and winning. They didn't care who was watching. Indeed, they once fought in their own dugout in full view of enemy fans at the Polo Grounds.

One time it involved Ed Heusser, a pitcher with the nickname the Wild Elk of the Wasatch, who played for the Cards in 1935 and 1936. He got angry at Ducky Medwick.

What happened is related by Don Gutteridge, who was with Leo in 1936 and 1937, the Lip's final two seasons in St. Louis. Gutteridge was eighty years old, still active as a Midwest scout for the Dodgers in 1992, and one of the few surviving ballplayers of the Gashouse era. The Cardinals were celebrating their hundredth anniversary in 1992, and he was one of the few from that wacky era left to invite.

"It was a tight ball game. Medwick got fouled up on a fly ball and a run scored, and Heusser thought Medwick should have caught it.

"When Medwick got into the dugout, Heusser said, 'You Hungarian bastard, why didn't you catch that ball?'

"Medwick said, 'You can't say that to me,' and they started swinging right in the dugout.

"We finally separated them, but that was nothing new for the Cardinals. They fought among themselves, somebody else, whoever."

Martin and Dean were the ringleaders, Gutteridge recalled, "and the players just followed them. Frisch didn't start things, and he'd just turn away when they fought."

Gutteridge remembers Leo was nice to him, even though many of his teammates didn't share that vision. "Leo and Frisch got at it pretty good," said Gutteridge. "They both had that sort of personality. They liked confrontations. They didn't agree all the time and they told each other about it.

"In 1936 Frisch hit a grounder and thought he'd be thrown out and he just sort of trotted to first. But the infielder missed the ball, then he recovered it and just barely threw Frisch out.

"Martin and Durocher met him on the top step and started to yell at him, 'Hey, you so-and-so. If you don't want to win, get the heck out of there. You tell us to hustle, you do the same thing yourself.'"

As for Leo and his teammates: "They liked him as a player. He was a fine shortstop and they wanted to win. But they didn't see eye to eye with Durocher because he was a spiffy dresser. He was an uptown dude, you know, and the rest of them were farmboys and they kind of resented his looking so good and trim all the time.

"Durocher didn't associate with them. There was a bit of a clique there—Durocher and Medwick were buddies and they stayed away from Martin and Haines and those kind of guys. Medwick was his best friend, by far. He kind of took Medwick under his wing and got Medwick dressing up and buying all those fancy clothes."

The rookie Gutteridge learned quite a bit about the game playing alongside Leo, and also appreciated his skills. "He did everything well. He had a good arm, a very accurate arm. He had good range. I don't think there were many better shortstops than Leo Durocher, as far as fielding is concerned. Of course, he couldn't hit. He drove in runs once in a while. But he was good in the field, he was good on the double play, he could go to his right.

"He'd tell me where to play. He knew as much about the hitters as anybody. The fact of the matter is, he took care of the infield. He'd call Jimmy Brown, the second baseman, and tell him where to play."

Gutteridge also remembered Durocher as a "guy who would give you a fight—he might not win, but he'd sure give you a fight. On the bench, he was rabid yelling at the other guys. Leo could also look at talent and grade it as good as anybody I knew."

Gutteridge eventually was traded to the Browns and because he and Leo were in different leagues, their paths didn't cross. But in the 1944 World Series, Gutteridge was sitting in the dugout before Game 1.

"Leo came over to the American League dugout and said, 'I wish you luck, son.' I thought that was very nice of him to say that. He was the only National Leaguer to come over and wish me luck. I saw him again in 1970 when I was managing the White Sox and he was managing the Cubs and we played in the annual charity game in Chicago. I have a picture of him and me together that I value very much."

There are many snapshots of the Gashouse Gang in Gutteridge's memory. Such as the 1937 free-for-all involving Dean and the entire Giants team. "They promoted it as the Game of the Century," recalled Gutteridge.

The great Carl Hubbell, who had 21 straight victories going back to 1936, was pitching against Diz. Baseball's top righty against baseball's top lefty. Early in the game, they called a balk on Dizzy. He got so angry he left the mound, only to return when the crowd chanted, "We want Dean!"

"He got mad and he started throwing at the Giants—everyone except Hubbell and Burgess Whitehead, who was his friend." As each Giant came up, he knew he'd be dusted at least once.

Baseball etiquette, 1930s-style, called for retaliation by the Giants. It came in the form of Jimmy Ripple, an outfielder. He waited until the ninth inning, and until he had been knocked down on consecutive pitches. Ripple then turned toward the Giants dugout as if to say, "Now's the time. Be ready to storm the field." He would try to bunt the ball toward the first baseman, Johnny Mize, so that Dean would have to cover first—and then Ripple would barrel into him.

"The first bunt he tried was a foul ball, and Durocher said to me, 'Hey, kid—he always called me "kid"—there's going to be trouble at first, let's get going.' "

Ripple bunted the next pitch. But the ball went toward second base, where it was fielded by Jimmy Brown. He tossed it to Mize at first. Dean, however, decided to cover first as well, perhaps just to see what Ripple had in mind. Dean reached the bag just as Ripple did and the pair bumped, not too hard, but meaningfully.

"Both teams ran out and Durocher and I got in front of Dizzy. We locked arms in front of Diz so no one could get to him," Gutteridge remembered. With his arms locked, he was an easy target.

"Somebody hit me in the eye and knocked me down. After that

a big fight was on. My injury wasn't serious but it was a big black eye. You could almost have hung your hat on it. Pepper Martin jumped in there and tossed guys around. I don't know what happened to Durocher during the fight. I was on the ground and couldn't tell where anyone was.

"After the fight was over, we all got back in the dugout and Pepper came up to me and said, 'Who hit you?' I didn't know, and Pepper got mad and ran over to the other dugout and challenged the whole Giant team: 'Whoever hit that kid, come out here. You're nothing but a whole bunch of cowards.' "

Dean was a baseball anomaly—a flaky great. From his 18–15 rookie season of 1932, he posted 20–18, 30–7, 28–12, and 24–13 records by the age of twenty-six. In his first five seasons, he had amassed a 120–65 record.

Then came the All-Star Game of 1937, and Earl Averill's line drive right back at Diz. It caromed off his foot to Billy Herman, who threw Averill out. The effect on Dean was longer-lasting.

He was supposed to be out three weeks. Instead, two weeks later Frisch—whose team was slumping—asked him, "Can you pitch?" And Dean said, "Sure." He pitched against the Braves, remarkably, but lost, 2–1.

"He wasn't the same that afternoon," Mickey Owen recalled. "His fastball had nothing on it, nothing at all."

And Dizzy described the troubles in more ominous terms: "I was unable to pivot my left foot because my toe hurt too much, with the result I was pitchin' entirely with my arm and puttin' all the pressure on it and I felt a soreness in the ol' flipper right away."

Yet, he started again four days later, limping out to the mound between innings. This time, though, "Somethin' snapped up there in my shoulder."

He continued to pitch. Frisch was concerned, but he also knew that Diz had this habit of complaining about a sore arm all the time anyway.

But he was hurting for real. With all sorts of bad medical advice, he continued pitching. He'd take time off, then go back to the mound. Finally, Rickey told him that he needed a good long rest—in fact, he told Diz to take all of 1938. Dean asked to be traded. He was sent to the Cubs. Baseball's greatest pitcher was washed up at twenty-seven.

But the Cards also played sweet (sort of) music together with their band known as Pepper Martin's Musical Mudcats. He strummed the guiter or played a cheap harmonica while Frenchy Bordagaray, a former music student in college, played mandolin or washboard. Then there were the pitchers—Bill McGee (fiddle), Bob Weiland (jug), and Lon Warneke (guitar). Turn on a radio, pick up a newspaper, and there was often a story involving the Cardinals.

They couldn't help it sometimes. Often, it was thrust upon them. When they played their first night game in Cincinnati, the Reds set up special trains and buses. This was the Gashouse Gang, the world champions, after all. The crowd arrived late, and people from the upper-deck seats rushed down to take the empty seats. Others ran onto the field, encircling it. Fans even sat in the Cincy dugout, forcing players out, and taking places sitting against the backstop. The crowd was so close to the players that Durocher noticed Medwick standing near third, arguing with a blonde. She was razzing him, telling Ducky she could hit better than he could.

In the eighth, the Cards were leading, 2–1, with Medwick batting. The blonde woman walked out of the crowd and took the bat from him and, wearing high heels, took her stance in the batter's box.

With incidents such as this, many Cardinals became celebrities. And Leo's fame spread because he was with a team that everyone noticed. He had been appreciated for his many baseball skills, and now he was becoming a celebrity. He also had generated a career high in homers in 1935 with 8. The next season he produced his best batting average, .286 and was the starting shortstop in the All-Star Game.

Six members of that 1934 Gashouse Gang, five of them players, were to make the Hall of Fame: Frankie Frisch, Dizzy Dean, Joe Medwick, Dazzy Vance, Jesse "Pop" Haines, and Branch Rickey.

But the deterioration of the Gashouse Gang did not take long. It just missed a pennant in 1935, beaten by the Cubs. In 1936, the Cards tied the Cubs for second. At season's end, Dizzy announced the club was a "bunch of bushers except for four guys." He included himself, of course, and Durocher, Martin, and Medwick.

Within three years of the anointing of the Gashouse Gang, Dizzy suffered his broken toe. Within two years, Paul Dean came down with a sore arm. Having won 19 games in each of his first two seasons, he developed arm trouble in 1936 and was traded to the Giants after the 1939 campaign. He wound up back in St. Louis at the end, when he pitched 3 games for the Browns in 1943. With a career record of

50–34, he was sixty-seven years old when he died in 1981, surviving Diz by seven years.

Perhaps the breakup of the gang began with Leo's trade to the Dodgers after the 1937 season. The crumbling was on: Dizzy, sore-armed, went to the Cubs; Medwick joined Durocher in Brooklyn in 1940; Frisch was fired after the 1938 season; and Martin remained a Cardinal until 1941.

Rickey lasted until 1942, when owner Sam Breadon, unhappy with Rickey's power over his team, dismissed him. Breadon, however, was not unhappy with the crop that Rickey produced, including Stan Musial, Walker and Mort Cooper, Harry Walker, and Howie Pollet. They would, ironically, prove the stumbling block to the Dodgers' hoped-for dominance of the 1940s under Durocher. Indeed, it was the Cards that won pennants from 1942 to 1944, and in 1946, chased by Durocher and Rickey.

CHAPTER
V

BORN TO
THE COLORS

RICKEY CALLED IN LEO one day during spring training in 1937 and asked him, in that peculiar Rickey phrasing, "You and Frisch have been fighting lately?"

Leo said, "No more than usual."

"Well, he's asked me to trade you," said Rickey, stunning Durocher.

Durocher called Frisch an "ungrateful rat." But Rickey calmed Leo and said there was nothing in the works yet.

Frisch and Durocher quarreled constantly. Even on the bench.

In early May, angry because Leo had missed batting practice, Frisch ripped into him. He didn't keep it private either. *The New York Times* reported it the next day.

"If you think you're too big for the club you can take a train back to St. Louis tonight," Frisch said before a game in the Polo Grounds against the Giants. Frisch did not believe Leo's excuse that he had sore kidneys. "You're not showing the proper spirit, and you're acting as though you're a little too big for this ball club. You'd better get that idea out of your head." After the game, Frisch told the press, "It's all over now and everybody's good friends."

Despite their differences, the captain and manager still were able to make things happen on a ball field. "Leo and Frisch together, when they surrounded an umpire, that was something," recalls Broeg. "But I think Frisch feared Leo was getting too close to Rickey. Leo was one of Rickey's pet reclamation projects. Frisch wanted to get rid of him.

"I'll say this for Leo. There were pluses and minuses, but one of the pluses is that when he was managing the Giants, Frisch wound up coaching under Leo, briefly. Leo might have done that just to placate Horace Stoneham. But most managers don't have anyone as an assistant they don't want. So I give Leo credit for that."

That reunion was fifteen years away. In 1937, the pair barely talked during the season, even though Leo was the captain and Frisch even played a handful of games at second base.

Leo batted .203, his puniest average yet. Then Frisch demanded Rickey trade him. Rickey had to go through his most earnest speechifying to convince Leo it really was for the best. Leo was furious. Even though the Dodgers were sending four players for him—Joe Stripp, Johnny Cooney, Roy Henshaw, and Jim Bucher, that didn't mollify the Lip, who still roared at Rickey.

Branch soon calmed him down. Why, son, he told him, they're going to need a manager over there (Burleigh Grimes had replaced Stengel). The front office is in turmoil (for years warring banks acted as executors of two different estates). And you, my boy, are just the fellow to do it.

Rickey knew that Grace was a key to Leo's accepting the deal. He called her in too. "Brooklyn," Rickey told her, "isn't as bad as it is painted. Just don't let Leo paint it too often. Don't be surprised if he becomes a manager."

Brooklyn, a poet—or someone poetic—said, is a state of mind. It had an off-center quality. It evoked laughs on radio comedy shows with the mere mention of its name. There were movies about the place: *It Happened in Brooklyn,* and *The Kid from Brooklyn.* It had its own poet, Marianne Moore. During World War II every politically correct film included a soldier from Brooklyn. The Brooklyn Bridge was sold, in legend, to hayseeds who wandered into Manhattan. Tarzan even dived off the Brooklyn Bridge in his cinematic visit to New York.

Brooklyn's baseball team had earned the nickname of the Daffiness Boys with these strange incidents: A bird flew out of his cap when Manager Stengel doffed it to an umpire; three players wound up on the same base after a hit; Babe Herman tried to catch a fly ball, but stopped it with his head instead; Uncle Wilbert Robinson got splattered when he tried to catch a baseball dropped from an airplane (Casey Stengel had switched the ball to a grapefruit); and they had hit into the only unassisted triple play in World Series history in 1920.

The talent had names like Frenchy Bordagaray and Van Lingle Mungo. Small wonder that since that 1920 pennant, the Beloved Bums had finished in the top half of the league only five times in 17 seasons.

Brooklyn was the Dodgers and the Dodgers were Brooklyn.

Life in Flatbush then probably was similar to what I experienced in my corner of the borough known as East New York. (I was, I suppose, a typical Brooklyn fan, although my time was the late 1940s and early 1950s, when the Dodgers were also good.) You needed to know how the Dodgers were doing, and you needed to know right then. So at 6:30 in the evening, with the day's heat still hanging over the streets, you would go to the local candy store and wait for the papers. The truck delivering the New York *Daily Mirror* would soon be followed by the one with the *Daily News*, "New York's Picture Newspaper." The papers were only two cents apiece. Every day every paper brought you nearer the team.

Many of the players even lived in Brooklyn, at the St. George Hotel, or in Bensonhurst and Bay Ridge. They car-pooled to work and some of them even took the subway. If you got on it early enough, you could take the train to Ebbets Field and sit next to a ballplayer.

Leo was traded just days after the 1937 season ended. Before long, Larry MacPhail—recommended by Rickey—would join him to run the club from the front office as president. The Roaring Redhead was a tame nickname for MacPhail. Teamed with Leo, the innovative hothead was to transform the Dodgers into a team that has remained a contender for more than half a century, laughed at no longer.

There are almost as many legends about MacPhail as there are about Durocher. And most of them approach the truth, if not completely.

One story involved MacPhail's attempt to kidnap the kaiser after World War I. A few days after the Armistice, Captain MacPhail, who had been wounded and gassed, went to Paris on leave. He visited an old friend, Colonel Luke Lea—a former United States senator from

Tennessee—and they got to drinking wine. Lea spread some maps out on the table and proposed his plan of motoring to Holland to kidnap the kaiser.

MacPhail, who made many of his most interesting decisions when drunk, asked for some more wine and decided that the venture was perfectly sound. "I figured I'd like a little trip," he would explain, "and if it involved picking up the kaiser, that was okay too."

On New Year's Day, they climbed into two touring cars and headed toward Holland. They took along six soldiers from Lea's Tennessee regiment, who were told only that they were on a secret mission. Lea, armed with an entry permit thanks to his influence, was able to cross into Holland with his party.

Along the way to the castle where the kaiser was staying with a friendly count, they stopped several times at local inns. They cut all the telephone lines in sight so that word of the kidnapping couldn't be broadcast. When their caravan finally sputtered into view, a sentry at the castle rang an alarm.

The count came down to greet MacPhail and Lea. The kaiser, explained the count, was at dinner. Suddenly, one of the American soldiers ran in saying that Dutch troops were headed toward the castle. The would-be kidnappers beat it, but not before MacPhail, mindful of the historic importance of this moment, swiped an ashtray. He claimed he survived a board of inquiry ordered by General Pershing. The ornate ashtray was destined for MacPhail's home, the subject of endless retelling of his adventure.

After the war MacPhail grew rich in real estate, helping liquidate some factories, and he ran an automobile agency. He also fronted for the Cardinals in buying the American Association team in Columbus, owned by Leo's old friend Weil, that was having financial problems. MacPhail enjoyed running a ball club considerably more than practicing law. He began to dress in vivid colors. One Columbus associate described him as a municipal eyesore.

Then there was MacPhail's gaudy spending. When the new stadium for Columbus was built, MacPhail wound up with an office more ornate than Rickey's or Breadon's at St. Louis. "Do you see any wood paneling on the walls of this office or Oriental rugs on the floor?" asked an irate Breadon. And Rickey did not buy MacPhail's story that the designer office was a gift of the contractor.

There were also reports that MacPhail was paying some of his players more than $400 a month, which was a violation of minor league rules.

Rickey eventually fired MacPhail for several sins over and above his best-known failings—drinking, profanity, and erratic behavior—that were never made public. Yet, Rickey eventually later was persuaded by Leo and several influential friends, to get MacPhail back into baseball. Weil was still in financial trouble. And after Leo left, the banks had taken over the Cincinnati club. The man they wanted to run it was Rickey. Rickey declined, but recommended MacPhail, whom the banks hired as vice president.

He lined up Powel Crosley, Jr., as majority owner. Crosley was making millions selling radios, and most of those radios were tuned in to his powerful radio station WLW.

Red Barber, then a college boy radio announcer at the University of Florida, auditioned for WLW—three times. Finally, early in 1934 he got a wire to come work for WLW and to join the Reds in spring training. He was told to see a fellow by the name of Scotty Rustum, whose real name was James "Scotty" Reston. He was the Reds' PR man, hired by MacPhail from the University of Cincinnati. Before long, though, Reston left writing publicity releases to go write for the Associated Press, and then went on to win a Pulitzer as a political reporter and columnist for *The New York Times*.

Barber was one of the early announcers. Baseball believed that it would kill attendance if it broadcast the games for free. In fact, in New York the three clubs—the Yankees, Dodgers, and Giants—had signed a five-year pact in 1933 that none would broadcast any games.

But Leland Stanford "Larry" MacPhail wasn't bound by baseball tradition. In his first year with Cincinnati, he flew the team to Chicago, making the Reds the first major league club to fly during a season.

He started a profit-sharing system based on attendance. He set a goal of 275,000 paid admissions in 1934. At that number each player would receive a 5 percent pay increase, 10 percent at 325,000, and 15 percent at 350,000.

But he was having a problem with attendance, especially after an early-season heat wave. So he proposed night baseball. Landis gave him permission to install lights and in 1935, the Reds played the first night game.

Besides creating a broader farm system, MacPhail painted the

old park and spiffed up the ushers' uniforms. And since Crosley man-
ufactured refrigerators as well as radios, MacPhail placed a Crosley
icebox in deep center field and announced before each game that any
batter who hit it could keep it. The fans loved it.

Late in 1935, though, MacPhail got into an argument at a hotel
party and wound up fighting with a couple of house detectives, one
of whom bashed him on the head. It made front-page headlines.

MacPhail, who had helped create a good team (the Reds went
on to win pennants in 1939 and 1940), was let go for good after 1937.
He went back to his father's banking business in Michigan.

Thirteen of the twenty-five players on the 1939 pennant-winning
Reds were obtained by MacPhail, including Johnny Vander Meer,
who pitched consecutive no-hitters, and Frank McCormick, who led
the league in RBIs.

Leo's first spring training with the Dodgers set the tempo for
his life with the Bums.

He was leaving his hotel in Jacksonville for the park.

"What's that I smell?" someone in the lobby asked. "Oh, it's the
Brooklyn Dodgers." Durocher pushed him, knocking him into Manager Burleigh Grimes.

A month into the season, Leo almost got into a fight with teammate Bill Posedel. He was pitching batting practice to Leo before a
game against the Cards in St. Louis. Leo was on edge, returning to
the park for the first time since the trade. He refused to take his full
turn, claiming Posedel almost hit him in the kneecap. Durocher returned to the bench.

"If you threw that hard in a regular game, you'd win twenty,"
Durocher shouted. Posedel left the mound and started for the dugout
but Babe Phelps, the catcher, intercepted him.

Leo wasn't the only interesting character who arrived in Brooklyn
in 1938. So did Babe Ruth.

He was forty-three years old, disillusioned with the game he
loved. He had quit the Braves three years earlier after serving as a
sideshow following his retirement. He thought he had been promised
a job as the Braves' coach, but all the Braves, a lousy club, really
wanted him to do was show up at batting practice so they could sell
extra tickets.

Ruth became a Dodger on June 18. MacPhail signed him for
$15,000 a year, but also warned him that he should have no illusions:

He would not become the manager. To underscore that fact, MacPhail was joined by Manager Grimes and Durocher, who had been named the team captain.

Yet, to many people, it seemed that Ruth and Leo were heirs apparent to Grimes's job. That never could have happened. In fact, Ruth could barely get the signals straight as the first base coach.

And that led to the clubhouse fight between Leo and the Babe.

It was an extra-inning game, and Leo was up. Leo relayed the hit-and-run sign to the base runner. But the pitch was outside. In desperation, Leo threw his bat at it, was lucky to connect, and it fell for a hit. The Dodgers went on to win.

A young reporter for the *World-Telegram* wrote that Ruth, coaching first, had cleverly signaled for the daring maneuver. The next day in the clubhouse, Durocher was furious and yelled that Babe didn't have the brains to give such a sign. Babe heard it. "Durocher, I've been wanting to smack you down for a long time," roared the Babe. They scuffled and Ruth wound up with a mouse under his eye. And Leo had a story he could tell to his grandchildren.

Leo also figured prominently that year in one of baseball history's greatest feats. One of MacPhail's first construction projects was to put lights in Ebbets Field, making it only the second park (after the Reds') to have night ball. Little did it matter to MacPhail that he didn't have the cash. He went to General Electric, ordered $72,000 worth of equipment and told them to charge it.

That first night game in Brooklyn, June 15, 1938, brought in the Reds, ironically enough, and Johnny Vander Meer, a young southpaw who had pitched a no-hitter in his last start.

MacPhail made the most of the evening, offering extra attractions: He started with a fireworks display. Then Jesse Owens, the Olympic star of the Berlin Games, sprinted against several ballplayers.

People didn't come to see no-hit pitchers merely because they expected to see another one. No one had ever pitched back-to-back no-hitters. But then again, there had never before been a night game played in Ebbets Field. Into the ninth inning, Vander Meer soared with his second straight no-hit bid. But he loaded the bases on walks with two out. Leo stepped up.

In a way, he did do something dramatic. He lined out to Harry Craft in center, thus allowing Vander Meer to do something no pitcher has ever done since.

This historic moment was never heard by anyone outside Ebbets

Field. For to MacPhail's chagrin, his Dodgers were bound by the final year of the five-year blackout agreement they had signed with the Yankees and Giants—no broadcasts, either for the New York market or to the visiting teams, could emanate from any of the three local clubs. Not even play-by-play Western Union ticker reports. Thus, the first that the people of Cincinnati heard about that second straight no-hitter was when the Associated Press wires sent a bulletin to newsrooms and radio stations.

This defeat could have been construed as just another part of that unbroken line of Dodger craziness. But MacPhail wasn't going to allow that to happen. He was serious about building a winner and losing put him in bad temper. It would make his red face even blotchier with anger. It would send him into deep bouts of despair with the bottle.

When MacPhail talked, he could ramble on while those around him looked skyward for help or at their shoes in dismay. A reporter quoting him noted, "MacPhail delivered himself of a few thousand words, out of which the following brief facts were winnowed." Another ended a story about him by writing, "On he rattled."

One thing he knew he must do: fire Grimes. MacPhail needed to revive a moribund team that accepted losing and stupidity as its legacy.

The Brooklyn club had been around since 1890, when it was built with the remnants of the old Baltimore Orioles. It was owned by Charles H. Ebbets, a Flatbush architect. He had a charming, you could even call it enlightened, view of the team. He saw it as a public trust, with himself as its guardian, for the people of Brooklyn.

A genial, easygoing, bespectacled man, he roamed the streets of his beloved borough discussing his baseball worries with anybody with the time to listen. He would even step into bars and ask advice on who should pitch the next day. When times were bad, his wife washed the players' uniforms by hand. And he sold the tickets.

Although the Dodgers, under different names, had actually finished first three times between 1890 and 1900, they had soon become perennial losers—very bad losers. They finished in the second division for twelve straight years starting in 1903. Ebbets decided the advice he had been receiving in bars and on the streets was not that good. He hired Wilbert Robinson, a former Oriole catcher and lately a saloonkeeper, to manage the club in 1914. Ebbets also sold a half interest in the team to a Brooklyn contractor, Stephen McKeever, for $100,000. Ebbets Field was built.

The Dodgers won pennants in 1916 and 1920, having the bad fortune in the first to run into a Red Sox left-hander named Babe Ruth, who pitched a 14-inning, 1-run game and beat them, 2–1. Four years later the Dodgers again entered the record books (negatively) by hitting into the unassisted triple play.

After that the Dodgers slumped into mediocrity, and then transcended that status by becoming, simply, screwball under Robinson's distracted leadership. By the end of the 1920s, the Dodgers were floundering under front office strife, with Robinson handling the dual role of president-manager. He had wanted to give up managing but realized that he would have had to give up the salary as well. The embattled owners didn't want to pay a president as well as a manager a salary.

Every washed-up or troubled star seemed eventually to pass through Brooklyn: thirty-five-year-old Lefty O'Doul, thirty-two-year-old Hack Wilson, forty-eight-year-old Jack Quinn.

Robinson remained with the team through 1931, unable to get them any higher than fourth his final two campaigns. After that, Max Carey, for two years, and then Casey Stengel for three, tried to do something with this team.

In 1937, Burleigh Grimes—one of the last spitball pitchers in the majors—was hired. His credentials for managing? The year before, umpires had tossed him out of 21 games when he was managing Louisville. This was the guy to bring spirit, thought Dodger management. In spring training, he told his boys he wanted fight and spirit. Instead, Grimes arrived to find, and add to, chaos.

The heirs of Ebbets and McKeever disagreed violently over everything from the spending of money to the deployment of players. Each side owned 50 percent. At last they agreed to a sort of steering committee, but that had difficulty making decisions. Grimes couldn't get anything done. He was angry and moody, and it showed on the field.

He was bringing up players, sending them down. John Gorman was the club's harried president, making deals that seemed merely to keep the Dodgers on a treadmill to nowhere. His last year he shipped four players out and got one back—the trade for Durocher.

By the time MacPhail arrived, after months without a general manager, the club owed $1.2 million, arising in large part from a

$500,000 loss from 1935 to 1937. The team also owed $500,000 to the Brooklyn Trust Company, a mortgage of the same amount on the ballpark, and $200,000 to other teams for ballplayers and to equipment companies. More creditors than fans were knocking on the gates.

Brooklyn Trust finally said no more money unless the management was improved. Enter MacPhail, but only after having turned the job down several times. "The situation smelled to heaven," he later explained. He agreed to come only under the following conditions: He would be vice president and general manager, with absolute authority, and the bank would furnish him with a reasonable amount of capital to rehabilitate the sagging Ebbets Field.

After getting $200,000 to touch up the park, he then told the heirs he was going to ask the bank for the outlandish sum of $50,000 so he could buy a first baseman. He had in mind Dolph Camilli of the Phillies, who had struck 27 homers.

The heirs didn't quite understand. "You mean $50,000 for a whole new team, don't you?" one of them asked.

Camilli's arrival signaled the Brooklyn fans that a new era was upon them. There would be responsibility now, players who could produce. Camilli had a wonderfully productive year, not only driving in and scoring 100 runs, but in also amassing what today would bring fame—a triple double. He stroked 24 homers, 25 doubles, and 11 triples.

The team also was competitive for much of the season before inevitably collapsing without a pitching staff. Still, attendance grew by 250,000 as fans sensed that, finally, someone was there who cared about this public trust, these Dodgers.

Grimes, however, knew his tenure was over. With three weeks remaining in the season, he told Leo he wasn't coming back. "Leo, why don't you apply for the job?" Grimes asked.

When Durocher went in to see MacPhail, the redhead said, "You can't even handle yourself. What makes you think you can handle twenty-four other players?"

"That's the funniest thing I ever heard," MacPhail added.

"I don't know if I can handle the guys," Leo replied. "But I want a chance."

MacPhail was noncommittal.

The season ended. Unlike many ballplayers whose teams are out of it, Durocher liked to go to the World Series. He also enjoyed hanging around baseball meetings. During the 1938 Series, in which the Cubs played, he went to the Congress Hotel in Chicago. He saw MacPhail, who unexpectedly introduced him to a friend, "I want you to shake hands with the new manager of the Brooklyn Dodgers."

The official announcement came on October 12. But almost as quickly, the next question was: What about the Babe? Everyone knew Babe wanted—expected—the Dodger job. Instead, Ruth was canned as coach.

This wasn't his doing, Leo explained. Instead, he said, "I was told Ruth was not available for a coaching job." Leo was to claim in his autobiography that Ruth had expected to succeed Grimes, and in fact had told Leo he was attempting to undermine his manager. Leo said he wanted no part of this nefarious scheme. Leo played by the rules, he told the Babe.

When Durocher was named, Ruth was asked for his reaction. "Say this—no matter what the future holds in store—my heart will always be in and with the great game of baseball."

Leo had no chance to savor the moment. The day before the announcement, his father had died. As soon as Leo was named, he caught a train for West Springfield, where his father was being buried later that day. The obituary said he died at his home at 114 Maynard Street. In addition to his sons, he left three brothers and six grandchildren.

He probably also left, in Leo, unresolved conflicts about their relationship. Leo downplayed any adversarial incidents he had had with his father. But the turbulent growing-up years, the street life, the weeks he lived with a friend when he was kicked out of his own house—this background helps explain the battling, tempestuous sort of manager he would become.

MacPhail explained some time later why he hired Durocher. Under Grimes, there was little hustling or togetherness on the club. MacPhail wanted a do-or-die attitude. And in Durocher he had someone who had, to say the least, a background of ferment and action, the hustler from West Springfield, who had been the captain of the Gashouse Gang, the brawlers of their day.

Also, unlike the previous Dodgers management, who thought a Max Carey or Casey Stengel or Burleigh Grimes could mold the team because of his stature, MacPhail was smart enough to know that he needed to give Leo the players. "He will be as good a manager as we can make him," said MacPhail.

In setting about rebuilding, Durocher said what the Dodgers needed most was a left-handed–hitting outfielder who had extra-base power. He also brought in his own coaches, including the experienced and savvy Chuck Dressen.

Durocher not only became the sixteenth Dodger pilot, but he remained as shortstop as well. He enjoyed being player-manager, and anyway, he could still cut it in the field. For the second time he appeared in the All-Star Game, and in 1938 he also led the National League shortstops in fielding average.

He didn't find it unusual to try to take on both roles. This was, in fact, the era of the player-manager. In the National League, a player-manager had won the pennant seven straight years. In the American, two teams with player-managers, the Washington Senators (Joe Cronin) and Detroit Tigers (Mickey Cochrane), had broken dominance of Joe McCarthy's Yankees.

And the timing was right. Gabby Hartnett had taken over the Cubs from Charlie Grimm with ten weeks left in 1938 and won the pennant—just as Grimm had done in 1932 when he took over for Rogers Hornsby.

Leo loved being player-manager. He was in the game, with everything revolving around him. The two main things a manager can do when his team is on the field is to position the players and make a pitching change. He used to believe that he could move players around more readily since he was in the middle of it. He had been doing this anyway with the Cards as their captain. And as far as making pitching changes, he was the closest one to the pitcher. The shortstop could see what the pitches were doing, could see if the pitcher was tired.

Also, from short he could directly signal the pitcher what to throw, rather than waiting for the catcher to look in the dugout, get the signal, and then in turn relay it to the pitcher. All Leo had to do was a simple move. If he left his glove open, it would signal, say, a fastball. A fist could signal a curve.

Leo almost never had the chance to try them. For one of MacPhail's first acts after Durocher became manager was to fire him.

The Lip had brought the pitchers and catchers down to Hot Springs, Arkansas, for early conditioning. After a banquet, Leo played bingo with the rest of the crowd. He happened to win. The next morning MacPhail telephoned him to say he was fired for gambling.

Leo talked MacPhail out of it, or perhaps MacPhail simply never remembered firing him. MacPhail tended to do that—fire Durocher, then forget about it, or if he remembered why, simply chose to ignore the reason.

But Leo had a little bit of the erratic in him too, Red Barber recalled before he died in 1992. The broadcaster was imported to Brooklyn by MacPhail in 1939. This was, on its face, another odd selection, a geographical misplacing. Barber talked funny with his Southern accent. How could the good folks of Brooklyn hope to understand him—or he them?

And if you could get past the drawl, there were those unfathomable expressions—a club was "tearin' up the pea patch," it was engaged in a "rhubarb," it was "sittin' in the catbird seat." Was this a baseball announcer or the Grand Ole Opry?

After he retired, Barber did quite a bit of reflecting and writing. And he retained a sense of history about his time in Brooklyn: "Earlier that spring of 1939, the first televised baseball game of any sort—Princeton-Columbia—had been shown. Doc Morton—he was in charge of TV programming at NBC—asked me if I would do a major league game.

"I went to MacPhail. Now, you've got to remember that Larry wasn't crazy about radio—neither were the Giants or Yankees—and I said to him, 'Do you want another first?' MacPhail was interested but he said, 'I'll do it on one condition—that we get a monitor to put in the clubhouse so the players can see the game.'

"Well, that was a big deal back then. There were probably only a hundred, a hundred and fifty monitors in all of New York. So that was the Dodgers' payment back then in the first television game. A TV set. Quite a difference from what they're getting today, don't you think?"

During his five years with the Dodgers, MacPhail made America Brooklyn Dodger–conscious. He also installed a $100,000 lighting system, spent $1 million on players, wiped out the mortgage of $1.25 million, and called in notes of $520,000. He put on track meets, beauty contests, fashion shows—and riots.

One of the keys to the Dodgers' future was MacPhail ending the pact with the Yankees and Giants not to do radio broadcasts. Indeed, with Barber, the fans had to—needed to—listen to the games. It didn't keep them away from Ebbets Field either. If anything, it brought new fans to the games.

Barber was forthright about Leo's style. "Leo didn't make any mistakes on the field. All the mistakes that Leo made were off the field."

Barber remembered, though, that on or off the field, "He was impulsive. But that was Leo. He was also square with me. After the war, you couldn't get cars and you couldn't get gas. But [there he was] in Florida driving a big Lincoln and he had a girl in the front seat with him. He saw Connie Desmond [Barber's broadcasting sidekick for thirteen years] in an old beat-up car and he asked, 'Where you going?' and Connie said he was going to pick up my wife and daughter in Daytona. Leo said, 'Not in that, you're not.' And he said to his date, 'Get out,' and he gave the car to Connie. My wife and daughter came back in a shiny new Lincoln."

Leo never spoke to Barber about his love of fine cars and clothes, nor did he ever mention his background which was so different from the way he lived. "And I never asked him about it," said Barber. Leo's wife, Laraine Day, also said that Leo had never spoken of a childhood in which there was almost a desperate need for money and material things.

Red didn't see much of Leo in later years, especially once he left the Cubs in 1972. "I was sorry no one did much about Leo when he died," said Barber with some sadness. *The Sporting News* doesn't even run obituaries anymore."

Except for Cronin of the Red Sox, who was thirty-two years old, Leo was the youngest player-manager in the big leagues at thirty-three as he tried to mold his first team in spring training.

MacPhail insisted that Leo get the pitchers in great shape early. He wanted the Dodgers looking good on their return to Brooklyn, for there was a 2-game exhibition set with the Yankees at Ebbets Field, and MacPhail figured if he could pack the place he could pay for all of spring training. And if he could beat the Yankees, the world champs the previous three years, it would be a heck of a start to this hoped-for new Dodger era.

Leo took instantly to managing. All the years he had second-guessed Frisch, had spent learning under Huggins, had bellowed orders from the dugout, had aligned his infield, paid off—now he was officially in charge, and he had learned well. But it was not going to make him change his style, lose one F word, or say nice things about the opposition.

Hartnett, the Cubs' player-manager, had picked the Dodgers

for last. Durocher, the rookie manager, was furious. Interviewed in a nationwide radio broadcast during spring training, Leo made his own prediction in a slap at Hartnett, whose team had lost four straight to the Yankees in the 1938 Series. "If we should happen to get into the World Series, I'll promise that we won't fold up against the Yankees and also that I won't bench myself after losing three games." Hartnett had gone 1–11 against Yankees, and had taken himself out of Game 4.

When the season began and Hartnett came into Ebbets Field, he refused to pose with Leo for the photographers.

That spring, during Leo's quest for a left-handed–hitting power-hitter, a nineteen-year-old from Class D ball appeared. His name was Pete Reiser, and he was one of those golden boys of sport, a natural, who could do everything so well—but who had a flaw that kept him from reaching greatness. Pete's flaw was running into walls that would not get out of the way.

The Dodgers had acquired Reiser for a hundred dollars in a dispersal sale of Cardinals farm players ordered by Commissioner Landis. Rickey's farm system had been determined to be too large and built not in accordance with baseball's rules. The Cards had money in more than one team in the same minor league. Rickey couldn't compete with rich, big-city markets such as New York and Chicago by buying ballplayers. Thus, he had painstakingly constructed a network of farm teams, tying up many talented youngsters with Cardinal organization contracts. The best he ever signed was Reiser, who also happened to have been a St. Louis boy. But Branch had overstepped himself, and the Cardinals had to lose a goodly number of players for a hundred dollars, which even in the Depression was not much for a player who would be tied for life to the club that signed him.

Reiser had just joined the Dodgers before an exhibition against the Cards in St. Petersburg. It was hot and Leo wanted a day off. "Can you play short?" Durocher asked. The rookie said no, but Durocher inserted him anyway. Leo wouldn't take no for an answer, and anyway, what kind of answer was that? Your manager asks if you've played shortstop, you're supposed to say, "Hey, I was born at short."

Reiser played and began a stretch in which he got on base eleven straight times, including 4 homers. Here was the answer to Durocher's prayers. And certainly this teenage phenomenon could be just the gate attraction MacPhail wanted in the opening exhibition games against the Yankees.

Instead, MacPhail sent a wire: "DO NOT PLAY REISER AGAIN." Perhaps MacPhail felt that at nineteen, Reiser could not make the big club and would be better off playing exhibitions with the minor leaguers in camp. More instruction was given to those ballplayers.

But Durocher played Reiser again. The team had moved north, to Macon, Georgia, for an exhibition against Detroit. MacPhail had just flown in and sent for Leo.

"Take off your uniform," MacPhail bellowed. MacPhail began to curse Leo and fired him on the spot. The cursing didn't stop. Durocher shoved him. MacPhail bear-hugged Leo and started to cry. Leo was still the manager.

Durocher, who couldn't stand being second-guessed, was to find MacPhail constantly meddling in his decisions.

Early that first season, MacPhail fumed over Mungo's pitching in a loss to the Reds. Just as Leo often reacted uncontrollably and irrationally when facing his former Cardinals team, MacPhail went nuts when the Dodgers lost to the Reds, *his* old team. Durocher threw him out of the locker room.

Much of the information about such prewar conflicts was written down, or admitted, much later. There was a conspiracy of silence in the locker rooms for the most part. Yet, a remarkable amount of information actually surfaced during those days regarding Durocher. For if Leo was unhappy, he didn't keep it secret. And if a friendly newspaperman could help him make a point with a player or management, why, Leo would certainly not be averse to speaking.

Leo's remarkable access to the press helped give him a broad base—especially since he was in the hotbed of America's newspapers, with more than half a dozen daily papers reporting on the Dodgers. More important, he was delivering as a manager and his players were delivering as a team. Thus, before too long, judgments and pronouncements on Leo's managerial style appeared. Following is a typical pro-Leo review from Herb Goren, for many years the writer of a column called "The Old Scout" in the Brooklyn *Eagle:* "Leo has a tactful way of pointing out mistakes to pitchers. Durocher takes pains to point out errors in his judgment by his men, doing so almost immediately after they have appeared, but never upbraids any of his players for a mistake that is purely mechanical.

"Leo developed a wonderful team spirit within the ranks. He inspired much respect for his own judgment."

Many of the players contend, said Goren, "Durocher is the best manager I ever worked for." And this was after three months on the job.

Leo took over so swiftly, it seemed the man was born to manage. He was never unsure about where he was headed, and never tentative. The locker room belonged to him, the bench belonged to him, and the field belonged to him. If he wanted his friends around, they showed up. In fact the locker room—his locker room—was for friends, and kids, as much as for players. He would actually take sons of friends on baseball swings through the West (not, of course, the far West—St. Louis was as far as the majors went in those days).

There was a protocol on trains: The regulars slept in the lower berths, the rookies in the upper berths. The manager had the lower in the stateroom, with the traveling secretary sharing the room but stationed in the upper.

When Durocher took over, Ed Staples was the traveling secretary. One night Durocher stayed up late and Staples went to bed before him. When Durocher went to the room about 2:30 in the morning, he found Staples fast asleep in the lower. Durocher started screaming at the porter, demanding another room. The conductor quickly found him one. Leo was conscious of his status. Manager equaled lower berth.

A few years later, when Harold Parrott, a former newspaperman, became the traveling secretary, he took his oldest son, Toddy, on a western trip. Durocher immediately took a liking to the boy. "You'll have to find somewhere else to live," Leo told Parrott. "Tod and I are rooming together."

In the morning, Parrott went to the stateroom to take the boy to breakfast. He found Leo in the upper berth and Tod in the lower.

"What are you doing up there, Leo?" said Parrott.

"What do you think?" he replied. "When the kid woke up he wanted to look out the window, didn't he?"

This was the generous, affable Leo that so many people also remember, the one who didn't care for stuffed shirts or stifling conventions. It was the Leo who gave a young boy something to remember.

* * *

Leo seemed none the worse after his first dismissal in Arkansas. He ran spring training—or, rather, made sure that many of MacPhail's solid ideas were followed. Leo was happy with his pitching staff by the time spring training ended in Florida. He liked the new guy, Boots Poffenberger, as well as Luke Hamlin, Freddie Fitzsimmons, Whitlow Wyatt, and Hugh Casey.

There even was a set outfield in Ernie Koy in left, Gene Moore in right, and Goody Rosen challenging Tuck Stainback in center. With Camilli at first, Pete Coscarart at second, Cookie Lavagetto at third, and Leo at short, it appeared to be a Dodger team that was ready to break with its past.

But not until Poffenberger's pitching career came to a premature end. Poffenberger had been too hot for Del Baker, Detroit's manager, to handle. But MacPhail figured Leo would keep the playboy straight.

Boots didn't like curfews. He skipped a game in Cincinnati, explaining to Camilli, "Tell Durocher I am tired of the way he is keeping me, like a bird in a cage."

Boots also broke curfew in Philadelphia. The lobby of the Bellevue-Stratford had several clocks displaying times of major cities around the world. MacPhail, no early-to-bedder himself, caught Poffenberger coming in late. "You are two hours late!" MacPhail cried.

Poffenberger pointed to the clock for Honolulu. "Not by the time I go by, I ain't."

In his short spell with the Dodgers—he wound up pitching a total of five innings—he also rigged a dummy in a train berth so he could be in a more accommodating part of the train during bed check.

Boots aside, Leo spent a considerable part of that rookie managerial campaign getting across his point: You're responsible for your actions. The Dodgers are not a joke to me.

Leo was managing and playing. Although he was thirty-three years old, his batting average would wind up at a respectable .277. But he happened to be sick one day for a game in June at Cincinnati and stayed in the dugout. Lee Grissom, who was pitching for the Reds, taunted Leo before the game the next day. "You came down sick yesterday when I was working. I guess you didn't want to bat against me."

Durocher popped out of the dugout and ran over to the Reds bench. Then he started yelling at Grissom with such colorful language and volume that fans streamed over to hear what was going on.

"You'll be batting against me one of these days," said Grissom.

Leo snorted back, "I could hit you if I was using a fungo bat. If I didn't want to hurt my hands I'd slug you right now, you son of a bitch."

A few weeks later, on the Dodgers' first western trip, Leo tried to snap the players out of a 6-game losing streak. He closed the door after a game in St. Louis, not even allowing the players to shower. If there was one thing these guys weren't going to do, it was play stupid baseball. Leo lashed into them: "Listen, you bums, don't you like playing in the major leagues? Do you want to go back to the sticks? Me, I like living in good hotels and eating good and getting a good check twice a month and I'm going to fight like hell to stay up here. I'm not going to have a bunch of clumsy nitwits like you drive me out.

"If you lose another game because of your dumbness you've got a surprise coming. I'll ship you off this team and out of the major league so quick you won't know what hit you."

Then he went around to each player in turn, telling him what he was doing wrong. The Dodgers went on a winning streak. It was further evidence that the era of the Daffiness Boys was over.

Then came Leo's first major scrape and it was the kind of incident that defined his career. From then on, when fans saw him, *their* adrenaline shot up, for they knew Leo was capable of the unexpected. Indeed, they demanded nothing less of him.

It was midseason, a Sunday doubleheader at the Polo Grounds. Durocher stepped to the plate in the fourth inning of the second game. The Dodgers had rallied for 3 runs and had a man on. Hal Schumacher, a wild righty, promptly low-bridged Leo with a beanball. That was in retaliation for what the Dodgers' Wyatt had been doing earlier—throwing at the Giants' heads, presumably under orders from Durocher.

Leo poked at the next pitch and grounded into a double play. He reached first just after Zeke Bonura took the throw on the bag. That didn't stop Leo. He stepped right on Bonura's heel.

Raging, the six-foot, 210-pound Bonura wheeled and threw the ball at Leo, whose momentum was carrying him down the line. Leo continued to run as Bonura suddenly took after him. Bonura chased him into right field and dragged him down. Leo got in a punch to the nose. Words, pop bottles, and punches started to fly. Forty-five players milled about. Coach Pancho Snyder of the Giants yelled at Leo.

Later, Leo was irate at his treatment. "I didn't know I had stepped on Bonura's foot until he threw the ball at me and then ran after me and started to hug me," claimed Leo. "Anyway, his foot was in the middle of the bag in my right of way, not at the side where it should have been. Pancho Snyder ran at me and said I had intended to step all over Bonura right from the start because Hal Schumacher had thrown at me. Looks like Terry's team can't take it when Wyatt threw a few inside pitches at them. They will get more of them when we see them next weekend, and it looks like a nice party."

"Durocher's a liar!" charged Terry. "He went out of his way to spike Zeke. Only a beaten team starts throwing beanballs."

Bonura had his say, too, "Durocher admitted in his own clubhouse he spiked me intentionally. I think what he did is the lowest trick in baseball."

For his pains suffered in punching Bonura, Leo was fined twenty-five dollars by National League President Ford Frick, a former newspaperman he knew well. There had been other fines before, but this began the rock-solid, hard-core roster of fines, and later suspensions, that pockmarked Leo's career. And with almost every one, Leo screamed his innocence. MacPhail backed him up.

MacPhail wrote to Frick complaining not only about the fine, but that Terry and the Giants were "trying to intimidate National League umpires." Frick fined Bonura fifty dollars, agreeing that the Giants first baseman had started it, but that Leo was wrong in throwing a punch of his own.

"What," asked MacPhail in the letter, "did he want Durocher to do—stand there with his hands down and take it?"

"Terry has been getting away with murder in this league," claimed MacPhail. "If Durocher had pulled this stuff, he would have been out of there."

MacPhail even asked for a hearing. A week later a meeting of the league's board of directors upheld Frick.

In August, two of America's most widely read magazines, *Collier's* and *The Saturday Evening Post,* profiled Leo after barely the first half of his first managerial campaign. "Only Cobb was more hated by fellow players," claimed Arthur Mann in the *Post* story. It was entitled "Baseball's Ugly Duckling."

In 1939 there was a naïveté about athletes, and the people who wrote about them. Consider that Mann, who knew a lot about Leo and the Dodgers' inner workings, wrote that Leo had "become a property owner, and big-league manager at thirty-three, with enough money in the bank to leave baseball right now."

If Leo voiced any regrets in this upbeat article, it was about Huggins. For it was ten years after Huggins's death—and Leo's trade from the Yankees—that he took over as Dodger manager. "It's a shame that Hug isn't alive to know about it. That guy sure went through a lot for me."

There was also the defiant Leo as well as the wistful one. Asked about the Yankees who disliked him ten years earlier, he said, "It's too bad none of them is in baseball. I'd like to thank each of them personally. I don't think I could have made the grade if they hadn't tried to get me out of that lineup."

And in a less sentimental *Collier's* profile by Quentin Reynolds, perhaps the country's most famous journalist, Leo was called the Pop-Off Kid. It described his carousing, of how he would go to a nightclub and wind up playing gin rummy in a back room, winning or losing a thousand dollars in a night.

It also gave Leo a chance to describe his managerial philosophy. "Secrets of managing? There's no such thing. Get a lot of good ball-players together, make them hustle all the time, and the percentage is bound to be with you."

By season's end, Leo had escalated his fines to two hundred dollars, after he was hit for a fifty-dollar tab. This time it was for profanity in a shouting match with Umpire George Magerkurth in a game against the Boston Braves. One can only imagine how creative Durocher's language was. Magerkurth was hardly prissy, and foul language was the verbiage of the day.

Still, Durocher had become quite a package: playing, managing, feuding, fighting—and winning. His Dodgers posted an 84–69 record and finished third, an improvement of 15 games, and their best showing since 1932.

There were some quality players on the club, but not enough to take it all the way. Hamlin had won 20, Casey added 15 more, but no other pitcher was in double figures. Camilli had a fine season with more than 20 homers and 100 runs batted in and runs scored. Lavagetto at third batted .300. But not one outfielder hit even 10 homers. In fact, there was no outfield. Only Koy played in as many as 100 games. MacPhail had picked up Dixie Walker from the Tigers, but Walker suffered a knee injury.

If Leo's first year as manager showed that winning mattered, 1940 was to be the year that the club became a contender. And Leo, going on thirty-four, wanted it to be with him in the dugout and not on the field.

In spring training, Camilli tried to get extra expenses for his wife and four children. Leo, as usual, got in the middle since he liked to protect his players and often stuck up for them when they argued for more money. MacPhail, however, screamed at Camilli, "I won't pay for your wife and your eight kids." Camilli grabbed MacPhail by the throat. When he released him, he went to his room and refused to play unless they paid for spring training expenses for the entire family.

MacPhail relented but refused to let Camilli think the money was coming from the Dodgers. MacPhail insisted that Durocher tell Camilli it was Leo's money.

During that training camp, MacPhail also argued about whether Durocher should play. Leo said he liked the new shortstop they had gotten from the Red Sox farm, Pee Wee Reese. MacPhail insisted, however, "I'm paying you an extra $5,000 to play short, and if you don't..." Leo was, of course, again fired.

With MacPhail barking orders, and Leo refusing to follow them, it seemed a formula for disaster. But somehow these two volatile, warring personalities kept it together, perhaps because each wanted to win so badly and each had a common enemy: everybody else.

The Dodgers zoomed at the start in 1940, with Reese hitting and fielding. Brooklyn was leading the league, until Pee Wee got beaned. Then he also suffered a knee injury. Pee Wee, and the Dodgers, would have to wait till next year.

But it was a terrific start. The Dodgers reeled off 8 victories to begin the season. Then they were in Cincinnati, hoping to tie the Giants' major league mark of 9 straight victories from the start of the season. Carleton, Medwick's old nemesis, was going to pitch for Leo. Tex was a thirty-three-year-old who had been chased to the minors the year before. MacPhail, in his wisdom and juggling, thought Carleton deserved another shot.

Carleton took his place in history. In all of the 1930s only two National League pitchers had thrown no-hitters—Paul Dean in 1934, and Vander Meer's back-to-back gems of 1938. Here was Carleton, though, taking the National League champs to the bottom of the ninth inning, without a hit, the Dodgers leading, 3–0.

As usual, Barber was broadcasting the game—or, more precisely, reading a ticker tape report from Cincinnati back in a New York studio, since it was too costly to set up a radio booth on the road in those days. (Some announcers became especially adept at faking live broadcasts. A broadcaster might say, "Medwick knocks the dirt out of his cleats." Or, "He fouled that one off to the fans behind first base." That was all made up. The broadcaster had no idea what was going on except for the ball and strike count and the score. If there was a delay in the game, or in the ticker report, an announcer might have a batter fouling off three or four pitches, or stepping out of the batter's box, or the umpire examining the ball for scuff marks.)

There were now two out and Barber and all of Brooklyn waited for the next pitch to Lonnie Frey. Barber usually wouldn't anticipate what happened until the ticker stopped. But as soon as he saw the words "Frey out . . ." Barber shouted into the microphone, "It's a no-hitter! I don't know what happened yet, but it's a no-hitter."

It was, and the Dodgers had punctuated their record start.

It was more than fifty years ago, but Reese remembers that season, his first, as easily as he scooped up grounders over the Ebbets infield. And Leo was the dominant image. "He was the only manager I've ever known that I think people came to see. He had that certain charisma that can't be learned.

"I knew that he wanted me to succeed—but he could be a little tough on you. Especially on a young ballplayer. I'd get a little bit leery about making a boot, making a bad play, not getting a base hit. Something like that. Leo could come in the clubhouse, and if you made a mistake, he'd kind of eat you out a little bit in front of everyone, and it kind of embarrassed you at the time. I always said that for young ballplayers, it was a little tough playing for Leo. But the older fellows, they could take it. He liked to manage the older guys. But when I look back at it, the best thing that happened to me was playing for Leo.

"He fined me fifty dollars one time for not being in the right spot. Fifty dollars then, this was 1941, was a hell of a lot of money. The ball was hit between right and center field, and I'm supposed to be backing up the second baseman for the throw back in. I didn't do it because I knew it was going to be a double. So I didn't get there but the ball rolled away from the second baseman and it rolled in the infield and a guy scored who shouldn't have scored.

"I always thought he and Charlie Dressen were an inning or two ahead of everyone else. Playing for him, you were always in the ball game, I'll tell you that. Leo was not exactly against going to Dressen for information." Is this a suggestion that Dressen might have been—at times—the brains behind some of Leo's decisions? Pee Wee isn't saying.

Leo, who was so tough on Pee Wee, also treated him with kindness. "He kind of took me in. He gave me sweaters and pants. In fact, in 1940, after I broke the bone in my ankle, I went to spring training and lived with Leo and Grace Dozier in Sarasota, and Nellie, Grace's daughter. I really enjoyed being around Leo. He was very good to me. Got on me a few times when I first went up, but we became very close friends.

"I remember when I first went to Brooklyn, every time the name 'Brooklyn' was mentioned, everybody would laugh. It was a little derogatory, but it was a beautiful town. I'm glad that I got to play there. I was unhappy when I didn't go to the Red Sox because I was supposed to go to them, and I was sold to Brooklyn and I was disappointed. But if I had it to do over again, I wouldn't have done a thing differently."

In late spring, with the Dodgers the talk of the league, Leo got MacPhail to make a move for a slugger he wanted. It just wasn't any old outfielder, though. It was his old Gashouse pal, Ducky Medwick, acquired in a deal with Rickey.

Although Medwick had won the Triple Crown in 1937 and had led the league in runs batted in from 1936 to 1938, his mean temper had overshadowed his play, especially when he continued to jaw with fans. He had overstayed his welcome. It was time to send him home, or close to it, anyway. And the fact that Rickey's farm system had produced a slew of talented youngsters made unloading Medwick easier for Rickey.

His career batting average was close to .340. He might still have been considered the best hitter in the National League, but Rickey made a name for himself not only for his astuteness in developing young players, but knowing when to unload older ones—better to find a market for a star a year too soon than a year too late. Along with an aging pitcher, Curt Davis, Medwick went to the Dodgers, who sent $125,000 and four players to St. Louis.

His arrival put the exclamation point on what MacPhail and Durocher had been doing for two years. Now, a full-fledged slugger was wearing a Dodgers uniform.

Medwick was a rascally sort, unloved even by his Cardinals team-mates. But when he started to lobby for the Hall of Fame many years later, he became suddenly personable, going out of his way to grant interviews with the press he had stiffed so often.

When he came to Brooklyn, Medwick moved into the Hotel New Yorker, where Leo stayed, and where visiting teams stayed. Soon after he was traded, the Dodgers faced the Cardinals in a series in Brooklyn. In the first game, Ducky went hitless.

The morning of the second game, Medwick got into the elevator—only to find his ex-teammate, Bob Bowman, who was going to pitch against him in just a few hours. Bowman had been feuding with Medwick ever since he believed Ducky had loafed on a fly ball that cost him a run. By the time the elevator had reached the lobby, Bowman and Medwick were shouting at each other, with Bowman getting off and saying with a sneer, "We'll get you."

They did, too. In Medwick's first at-bat, a Bowman fastball, thrown *behind* him, thudded into his head, knocking him out. He looked dead. He was spread out across home plate, his arms wide. Even Bowman ran to look at him.

Barber, who broadcast the game, recalled that MacPhail might have been the most enraged guy in the ballpark. As was his habit, he ran to field level whenever anything displeased him. He stormed out of the stands, charged the Cards dugout, and jumped on top of the roof, challenging players to come out and fight. He had a folded newspaper in his hand and tried to swat Bowman. He was restrained by the police.

Barber believed that from that moment, MacPhail became disenchanted with Rickey, his former mentor. In his Brooklyn paranoia, MacPhail convinced himself forever that Branch had somehow put Bowman up to this. The next day, MacPhail went to the D.A. He brought along an affidavit showing that Bowman had threatened Medwick in the elevator before the game. MacPhail even got District Attorney Bill O'Dwyer, of Murder, Incorporated, fame, to look into it.

MacPhail came up with a new expression for the Cards. "Beanball, Incorporated." He got someone to make protective inserts for the caps and told his players to wear them whenever they faced the Cardinals.

Later, Bowman explained what was behind the beaning, virtually admitting throwing at Medwick's head. "That wasn't my fault," he said. "Dressen was stealing the signs and tipping off the batters. He'd whistle when he thought a curve was coming."

So Bowman and catcher Don Padgett decided to cross up Dressen—and whoever happened to be batting. Padgett would signal for a curve but Bowman would come in with a high, hard one. "Poor Medwick was looking for a curve and he couldn't get out of the way," said Bowman.

Medwick was never great again. Although hitters naturally tail off as they get older, Medwick's decline as a slugger was quite steep. He had averaged a home run every 30 at-bats until he was hit in the head, then for the rest of his career, he hit one every 53 at-bats.

Some baseball people thought the beaning had taken his resolve. He returned in a few days but never hit with the same authority (he was famous for his humming line drives). His career had one more highlight though. After he failed to make the Yankees in 1947, he retired to the golf course and waited for the phone to ring. Suddenly he got a call from Breadon, his old Cardinals owner.

Would Ducky like to come back as a part-timer? He was only thirty-five years old, and said sure. He went to Sportsman's Park, put on a uniform wearing the strange "21" instead of his familiar "7," he sat on the bench and waited. Soon, they needed a pinch hitter. Manager Eddie Dyer called on Medwick, who walked up swinging a couple of bats. The fans had no idea who he was. And then, at the announcement, they rose and cheered. Medwick faced the Pirates' Fritz Ostermueller and swatted an outside pitch to right. It went for a double and scored the game's only run. When he left the field for a pinch runner, the fans stood and bellowed. The old curmudgeon cried.

MacPhail was as busy off the field as on it during 1940. He had always been intrigued with the possibility of moving baseball teams by air rather than rail. In 1934, MacPhail, with the Reds, took several players by plane to Chicago. Two years later, he put the team aboard a Puerto Rico–bound flight from Miami during spring training. And in 1939, some Red Sox players made the St. Louis–Chicago flight, but most took the train. MacPhail decided it was time to break new territory: For the first time, an entire team would fly during the season. It became one of the major events of Brooklyn's season, the kind of offbeat happening that endeared the borough to all who lived there, charged it with energy, made it different.

On May 7, the Dodgers ended a series at St. Louis. There, they boarded what was described as two "giant" airliners for the trip to their next destination, Chicago. The Dodgers' six-feet-two-inch catcher, Babe Phelps, announced he didn't want to go. He was scared. Durocher sat next to him on the flight. Today that hop takes fifty minutes; Phelps was aloft three hours and ten minutes. When Phelps deplaned, he swore he would never fly again.

Three days later the Dodgers were flying again, this time coming home—without Phelps, who took the train. Thousands of people started arriving late at night at Floyd Bennett Field in Brooklyn. According to one estimate, there were ten thousand waiting for the flight, scheduled to arrive at midnight. Brooklyn Borough President John Cashmore had a speech ready.

At 11:00 P.M. the crowd was told the team was delayed and wouldn't be in for another two hours. Still, thousands remained, although the departing crowd caused a jam from Flatbush Avenue to Avenue U. The early arrivals had included Mrs. Ebbets, but the doings were too much for the eighty-year-old and she left before the plane arrived.

And then, suddenly, at 12:48 A.M. out of the Brooklyn night— there it was! The first of the two planes. A brass band began playing. After the plane landed, as the door opened, Durocher stepped out. It was as if Lindbergh had landed at Orly. The cast-iron fence surrounding the administration building, where Cashmore and players' wives waited, broke in three places. It took 175 policemen, holding a two-inch-thick rope they stretched and used as a barricade, to prevent the fans from charging the airliner.

Durocher and the players were ushered to a stage. Dignitaries couldn't speak because of the roar of the crowd, although they plugged on. The president of the Flatbush Boys Club, the treasurer of the Knothole Gang, the chairman of the Flatbush Chamber of Commerce, Councilman Sharkey—all were on hand. They were joined by two American Legion bands—the Bugle Corps of Kings County American Legion and a delegation of helmeted Legionnaires.

To the Dodgers equipment man, Dan Comerford, who had been with the team since 1905, this was "the greatest thing that's happened to me since I've been with the Dodgers."

And Durocher said this is the only way he wanted to travel "from now on, if I can get the players' support." Even three players who had backed Phelps in not flying, Tot Presnell, Koy, and Coscarart, agreed they would start flying.

The next thing to do was to get the Dodgers to soar in the pennant race. The Dodgers might have finished second in 1940, but they were quite a distance from the first-place Reds—12 games.

WAIT TILL
NEXT YEAR

MACPHAIL WAS SCHEMING for a way to get something out of Rickey. After the 1940 season, MacPhail and Durocher agreed that they needed young pitchers and a right-handed–hitting catcher. Fitzsimmons, who was thirty-eight and had posted a remarkable 16–2 record, and Wyatt, who was thirty-two, were the club's top pitchers of 1940. Phelps, the catcher who refused to fly, also was thirty-two.

Leo was going to be thirty-five years old, but he was still eligible for the military draft. He knew he'd be around for this season. Early in 1941, he was placed in Group 3 by a Brooklyn draft board, a deferred classification guaranteeing at least a year with the team.

MacPhail went after Kirby Higbe, the last-place Phillies' best pitcher, who had led the league both in walks and strikeouts, and Mickey Owen—the Cardinal catcher who had fought with Durocher during the Medwick beanball incident—who was an outstanding defensive player.

In getting Higbe, MacPhail told Phils' owner Gerry Nugent to keep the deal secret until the Dodgers could get Owen. The reason? MacPhail also was negotiating with Rickey at St. Louis, and if Rickey heard that the Dodgers would be getting Higbe as well as Owen, Rickey might kill the deal. Rickey had no problem in selling Owen to the Dodgers—how much can a catcher hurt you if there's no pitching? Besides, Rickey's farm system had produced Walker Cooper, who would certainly nudge Owen out of the way.

All it took was money to acquire these important players—$100,000 for Higbe, another $60,000 for Owen. Perhaps because Brooklynites have problems with what speech experts call a "glottal click"—"Lwan-Guyland" for "Long Island"—Higbe quickly became known as Higglebe.

Higbe, a free spirit who described himself as "strong as a bull and twice as smart," would have to bone up on his Spanish first—the Dodgers were going to spring training in Havana.

That clinched Owen's job. Phelps, known as "the blimp" for his size and not his flying proclivities, refused to cross the ninety Atlantic miles to get to spring training from Miami.

The Dodgers had a sweet deal in Havana, guests of the Batista regime, which was looking for publicity to attract tourists. It was the first time in ten years the Dodgers had trained there. During their earlier trip, a brewery had underwritten them.

The Dodgers continued to try the innovative under MacPhail. Leo had been around when the Yankees started putting numbers on their uniforms. And in this camp the Dodgers unveiled something called a "batting cage." Babe Hamberger, the club's factotum, with the aid of a young Cornell engineer, put the contraption together early in the morning. It rested on six pneumatic tires so it could be readily wheeled about.

"The idea," said MacPhail, who bought the blueprints from a Fort Worth man, "is that any ball hit foul will strike the cage. Only fair balls will go out. It will save a lot of baseballs."

"It looks a little dangerous to me," said Dixie Walker.

Danger was mother's milk to Leo and Larry. And now they had inherited another wild man in Van Lingle Mungo.

Leo and his key aide, Dressen, were having drinks one night in Havana's glitzy Hotel Nacional. Mungo came in around midnight, beaming, and offering to buy drinks for everyone. The pair hustled him up to his room. He was pitching the next day.

Unbeknownst to Durocher and Dressen, Mungo didn't stay in his room. He had gotten tangled up with the latter half of a husband-and-wife dance team that was entertaining in the hotel nightclub. When he found his way to the park the next day, he was in no shape to pitch.

Leo told Mungo to go back to the hotel. Mungo respectfully declined and they started to rant and rave. Finally, he went back by himself. But when the team returned to the hotel after the game, the police were there with a warrant for Mungo's arrest—sworn out by the husband half of the dance team.

Hamberger, described by the sportswriter Tommy Holmes as the "superintendent of Dodger loose ends," spirited Mungo out of the hotel through the entrance to the swimming pool, hid him behind a closed door at the airport, and at the last moment dragged him onto the plane. "It was," reported Hamberger, "as exciting as stealing home."

There still were things to do, niches to fill, when the club left Havana and began its swing northward. MacPhail never had been entranced by Dixie Walker, the People's Cherce. The popular outfielder was a .300 hitter, but MacPhail wanted more stature in center. So he obtained Paul Waner, a thirty-eight-year-old future Hall of Famer who had played forever with the Pirates. But Big Poison wasn't the answer, which quickly became apparent. Finally, MacPhail decreed that Reiser, now twenty-two years old and a rookie, would be the center fielder and Waner, who had hit well in Havana, would anchor right.

When the Dodgers worked their way up north to start the season, Durocher received a telegram signed by five thousand Brooklyn fans who threatened to boycott Ebbets Field unless Dixie was returned to his right place—that is, center. "If you pay attention to that," stormed MacPhail at Durocher, "I'll fire you."

So the 1941 season opened with old man Waner in right, Walker on the bench, the rookie Reiser in center, Mungo in Leo's doghouse, MacPhail threatening to fire Leo, and Leo, irate at Mungo being allowed to return by MacPhail, threatening to quit. "Who's running this team?" Durocher asked his newspaper pals. "And I'll promise you this. If I ever catch Mungo drinking anything stronger than a Coca-Cola, either he'll go or I will." Of course, there was also the boycott threat.

The Dodgers lost their opening series to the Giants, then settled down. Leo was after MacPhail, though, to get him a second baseman. He felt good about the way the club was progressing and believed he could make a run for the pennant with a solid double-play combination. Leo was merely asking MacPhail to get him the Cubs' Billy Herman, the best second baseman in the league for most of the 1930s. He was a good number two hitter, adept at hitting behind the runner, the kind of smart player Leo liked.

They got him two weeks into the season, thanks to some lucky timing. Herman had wanted, and expected, to be named the Cubs' player-manager to replace Gabby Hartnett, for the Cubs had a tradition of going to their own stars to fill the manager's post. Instead, they chose Jimmy Wilson. This did not sit well with the fans and the press. The front office was getting a razzing. The Cubs were looking to avoid embarrassment by unloading Herman.

So one night at the Hotel Commodore, where the Cubs stayed in New York, MacPhail went drinking with Wilson and Jim Gallagher, who was Cubs' owner Phil Wrigley's man in charge of hiring. The Chicago brain trust, knowing that MacPhail enjoyed drinking late and long, ordered Napoleon brandy to keep him happy and perhaps vulnerable. "I fooled them, though," MacPhail later said. "I poured myself a lot of drinks—but most of 'em went down the bathroom drain."

About 5:00 in the morning, they agreed on a deal. Herman was his. MacPhail promptly went up to Herman's room, woke him up, and told him what had happened. Then MacPhail picked up the phone and dialed Durocher. "I want to introduce you to your new second baseman," he said proudly, and promptly put Herman on the phone.

Now the young Reese had a solid player alongside him, and Leo could do the kinds of things on offense that were to mark his style—hit-and-run, hit behind the runner, and squeeze plays.

But before Reese could establish himself, he got off to a shaky start. And for a while Durocher even decided to take Reese's place. "I opened the season with a brace on my ankle because I had hurt it again in Baltimore," recalled Reese. "So Leo, being a shortstop, and watching every move that I made—I was having a tough year, losing a couple of balls—so he decided to go in. I guess MacPhail really wanted him to. But one day Leo went back for a ball over his head, a pop fly, I think he fell down. After that, he decided he'd let me go [in] whether we won or lost."

There was another story of why Leo decided to quit playing. Going in at short in a game against the Reds, he failed to throw out the notoriously slow catcher, Ernie Lombardi, who had hit a grounder. "Cut the uniform off me," moaned Leo. Certainly, that incident showed him, and MacPhail, that at thirty-five he might not be the alternative to the inexperienced Reese.

The 1941 season turned into the most grueling two-team race in league history. Since early May the Dodgers and the Cardinals never were more than four games apart. And that margin, enjoyed by the Dodgers, was only for a day. The Cards never had more than a 3-game edge. Each team had been in first ten times, each tied eight times. They faced each other twenty-three times—each won 11, and there was one tie.

Durocher's failed benching of the light-hitting Reese was only one of the Dodger controversies that season. Babe Phelps, the catcher, refused to join the team for a big series against the Cardinals in St. Louis. Owen was the only other catcher, and he would have to be behind the plate for all four games, including a double-header. Leo explained to the writers why Phelps hadn't come: "He told me he was worried about his heart, but he said he'd give it a try."

Instead, Phelps stayed home. "I've had the misery in my chest all spring," he explained to a writer in New York while the team traveled west. "And I've had pains in my head, too. I packed my bags and was ready to go when I got to feeling worse." The Dodgers dispatched two doctors to Phelps's Brooklyn hotel room. Their conclusion: He was a neurasthenic—"a person who imagines things," a newspaper reported.

To Leo and MacPhail, though, Phelps was a quitter, a guy who dogged it. "First, he doesn't go to spring training," Leo groused. "Then he has a sore arm. Then he gets his finger in the way of a pitch and he's out for four weeks. Now this thing. Imagine going off and leaving us with only one catcher when we're on one of the most important road trips in years. I'm through with Phelps."

Phelps was gone the next year—the last ballplayer from the Casey Stengel era of the Daffiness Boys.

In late August, Branch Rickey brought up a young left-hander from the Houston farm named Howie Pollett. Rickey of course wanted Pollett for the stretch run (in September he would bring up a young outfielder named Stan Musial). "How dare Rickey raid his farm team," cried MacPhail. He was going to ruin the minors in an attempt to win a major league pennant. Rickey countered with the fact that MacPhail had brought up Reiser from Elmira the year before.

On Labor Day in Boston, playing Casey Stengel's worthless Braves, the Dodgers lost the second game of a doubleheader when it was called on account of darkness. Leo charged that Stengel stalled long enough for the sun to go down, and asked for a league investigation.

The season's pivotal series was a 3-game stand in St. Louis in mid-September. The Dodgers led by a game. Fitzsimmons, who had suffered an injury to his thirty-nine-year-old arm and could be used only part-time, somehow lasted eleven innings to win the opener. Fitzsimmons had blown up at Umpire Al Barlick over a called ball, and then Cardinal shortstop Marty Marion argued with the home plate ump over a called strike. Durocher and Cards' manager Billy Southworth both left the dugout to argue with Barlick.

This was not going to continue, said league president Frick.

Before the next game, Frick called the umpires and two managers into a conference. He told them that the baiting of the umps had to stop immediately. Frick explained that Barlick could have tossed the managers out but because of the importance of the series he was swallowing hard.

Durocher tried to interrupt Frick.

"This is not an argument," said Frick sharply. "We are telling you that we are going to run the ball game. We are going to treat you as though you were eighth-place teams, and if a man's actions call for his dismissal from the game he will be dismissed."

Then the recently arrived Pollett came back to even the series.

In the rubber game, Wyatt went against Morton Cooper. It was scoreless going into the eight. Dixie Walker smacked one against the right-field screen for a double. On second base, he could see Walker Cooper calling for a curveball against Billy Herman at the plate. The sign was relayed to Herman. He also hit a double to right. It was the only run of the game.

The next day against the Reds in Cincinnati, Walker got into an argument with Umpire Larry Goetz before the first pitch even was thrown. It was over an incident that had happened in St. Louis. Goetz, short-fused, ordered the Reds' pitcher, Derringer, to throw. While Walker argued out of the batter's box, Derringer threw a strike. After that one pitch in the game, Leo, out of the dugout, was arguing and gesturing and shouting. Leo stood fast on home plate so Derringer couldn't throw another pitch. The Dodgers won in seventeen innings.

On September 19, still holding a slim lead over the Cards, the Dodgers finished a western trip in a blowup. They lost in Pittsburgh, 6–5, after trailing by 4–0 going into the eighth. But they rallied after two out, scored 5 runs to gain the lead, and then lost the lead in the bottom of the inning. But not just in any old way. The tying run crossed the plate on what Umpire George Magerkurth called a balk.

The scene unfolded: Luke Hamlin pitching against the Pirates' Vince DiMaggio, who led off with a single to left, where Medwick fumbled the ball. Leo immediately called on his top reliever, probably the best in the business, Hugh Casey. DiMaggio reached third on a long fly and stayed there on a groundout.

Then, Al Lopez was batting. Casey, who was among the early relief specialists, knew what to do with a runner on third. He stood on the rubber, set his hands in position, and looked over to third at DiMaggio and then at the plate. Just then, Lopez backed out. Casey relaxed—and let his hands fall. But the game was still in play. Before Magerkurth could bellow, "Time!" Lopez shouted, "Balk!" In the confusion, attempting to confound Magerkurth further, Coach Jake Flowers charged in from the first base box and Manager Frankie Frisch charged in from the dugout.

Magerkurth, momentarily confused, hesitated a bit and then motioned DiMaggio home.

"How in hell can a pitcher balk when the batter is out of the batter's box?" Leo kept asking. "Lopez pulled a job on us and nobody but a chowderhead umpire would have fallen for it." MacPhail, back in Brooklyn listening to Barber's re-creation, began to bellow at the radio. "A balk? In a game like this?"

That tied the game, and then Casey got two strikes on Lopez. Then, apparently in violation of the old rule that you don't purposely put the winning run on—and apparently with the blessing of Durocher—Casey threw at Lopez's head, not once but twice. Of course, it could be argued that with two strikes, you waste a pitch or two.

But Casey really was throwing at Magerkurth as well, and Magerkurth, who had been around, knew it. The umpire charged the mound and pointed a finger at Casey, threatening to throw him out if he threw another one close to Lopez. That was too much for Leo. He immediately dashed out of the dugout and began roaring at Magerkurth. Leo was kicked out, but not before challenging the entire Pirates bench, then smashing every light bulb in the entryway to the clubhouse. For good measure, he threw a chair through the window of the umps' dressing room.

Lopez walked and then Alf Anderson tripled him in with the winning run.

Durocher shouted afterward, "I never want to see Magerkurth again."

When the game was over, a few Dodgers chased after Magerkurth under the stands on his way to the umps' room, cursing and yelling.

DiMaggio conceded later the Pirates had pulled a standard Pittsburgh trick—and that the coaches running toward home, with everyone yelling, was designed to confuse the home plate umpire.

This road trip had exacted quite a toll on Leo. He dropped twelve pounds. And it wasn't over yet. The season was winding down with the Dodgers playing 17 of their final 19 games on the road.

The next day the Dodgers played their final series in Philadelphia. Leo found out he had been fined $150 by Frick for his behavior on the field after the balk call, and that the ballplayers who had harassed Magerkurth were assessed $25 apiece, despite Owen's testimony that before the game had even begun, Magerkurth had cursed him. Frick didn't buy it.

The Dodgers stayed at the Warwick Hotel in Philadelphia, where Leo was stopped by Ted Meier of the Associated Press. "You're not talking to Magerkurth now," Meier quipped.

"You'd better get out of here now before there's trouble," Durocher replied.

In Leo's version, Meier then asked him to make up a quote about being able to sweep the Phillies. "Don't quote me on things I haven't said," Leo yelled back.

"Watch your mouth. You're not talking to Magerkurth," Meier shouted back. They agreed to settle it elsewhere.

Both walked to a nearby alley to continue talking, when suddenly Durocher threw a punch, the writer said later. Meier got up and was knocked down twice. After those three shots to the jaw, with Meier on the ground, the Dodgers' club secretary, John McDonald, arrived to break it up.

There was no complaint from Meier to his office, no lawsuit charging Leo had abridged the reporter's First Amendment rights. Instead, McDonald got both to return to the hotel and shake hands. That was the end of it. Baseball the way it used to be.

Meier, of course, said later it was "silly" to suggest he'd attempted to put words in Durocher's mouth. And McDonald suggested that Meier even deserved it "for asking three less than tactful questions."

So Leo was fined again. A Leo Durocher fine was becoming commonplace. But what wasn't ordinary was a pennant for Brooklyn. And that happened some days later in Boston. At a few minutes after

5:00 P.M., with two out in the bottom of the ninth inning, Lavagetto fielded Max West's sharp grounder. Cookie juggled the ball, but just for a moment, then fired it to Dolph Camilli at first base. It sealed a 5-hit, 6–0 shutout for Wyatt.

That, coupled with the Cardinals' loss in Pittsburgh, clinched it. After twenty-one years, the Dodgers won the pennant. It was only Leo's third season as manager. Little did he know he was about to be fired in just a few hours.

Stengel, himself a symbol of Dodgers' nuttiness both as player and manager, congratulated Durocher. "A great ball club, Leo," Stengel told him, "and your boys won it by themselves, which is the hard way."

Durocher invited Stengel to come by in Brooklyn at the World Series and Stengel grinned and said, "The way you fellows played, you don't need me." But they would meet in World Series play ten years later, Leo as manager of the Giants, Casey with the Yankees. Who'd have thought it?

Manager Billy Southworth of the Cards congratulated the Dodgers "who have just won the greatest pennant race in history."

The victorious return train trip—the one that roared through Harlem without stopping, which it was supposed to—fills yet another improbable part of the Leo and the Dodgers' saga. The players took over the dining car for the five-and-a-half-hour ride home. Champagne flowed, clothing suffered. Reese and Lavagetto took a knife and cut off all neckties below the knot. Tony Martin, the singer and one of Leo's closest friends, lost his tie and shirt. Mrs. Dixie Walker's hat was filled with champagne. Pee Wee ordered Martin to stop singing the aria from *Pagliacci*, Leo escaped having his tie cut off by claiming, "It's my lucky tie, fellas." It probably was too. Any piece of apparel that Leo wore when the team won was lucky. And despite his fetish for neatness and constant clothes changes, he would wear the same clothes—down to the underwear—to the ballpark the next day after a victory.

Halfway through the trip, at New Haven, Durocher gathered everyone together and told them, "From now on, no more drinking. There's a mob waiting for us in Grand Central." Durocher took the players in for a steak dinner, hoping to sober them up. He kept hearing reports that many planned to leave the train at 125th Street to avoid the crowd at Grand Central.

Durocher didn't know about MacPhail.

So a conductor came by and asked if Durocher wanted the train to stop at 125th Street. That traditionally had been the first of only two stops the New York–New Haven Line made in Manhattan. "No, said Durocher, "I want everybody to stay on till we get to Grand Central, where those Brooklyn fans are waiting."

But MacPhail had taken a contingent of photographers and reporters to 125th Street, hoping to get photographed boarding the victorious train and then lead the departure as a sort of grand marshal at Grand Central. Instead, as cameramen got ready to start clicking, MacPhail had to hold on to his fedora as the train whipped past, sending up gusts of paper. MacPhail had never turned redder.

The victory train sped gloriously into Grand Central, where all outbound trains were delayed for an hour because of the crowds, numbering in the thousands.

A beaming Leo got off and immediately spotted Red Barber doing a "live remote" radio broadcast. But Durocher wondered, "Where's MacPhail? How could he be avoiding all the cameras and reporters?"

Later, MacPhail went to Durocher's hotel room. Durocher was waiting for the compliments. "You're fired!" MacPhail bellowed. He went on to rant and rave about his embarrassment and how Leo had disobeyed his order to stop. Leo, however, had never received it. This time Leo retaliated against a drunken tirade. He kicked his chair.

"When he left me that night," Durocher recalled, "I wasn't the manager of the Dodgers."

About 3:00 in the morning, McDonald, MacPhail's man, knocked on Leo's door. MacPhail wanted to see him. Durocher bellowed no and went back to sleep. At 7:30 in the morning, MacPhail called again and asked to see him. Durocher stopped by the office and MacPhail said to him, "Let's figure out how to beat those Yankees."

So Leo would be able to manage in a World Series after all.

It had been a remarkably successful collaboration between these two characters. The 1941 Dodgers had won 100 games for the first time in their history. Higbe, the acquisition, and Wyatt, shared league honors with 22 victories apiece. Reiser, a twenty-two-year-old, became the first rookie to win a batting title with a .343 average. He also led in slugging average (.558), runs (117), doubles (39), and triples (17). Camilli led in homers (34) and RBIs (120). Walker, restored to right field, swatted .311 and Medwick, Leo's old pal, hit .318.

* * *

It was quite an impressive array of talent, and Leo did the most with it. It had the fewest stolen bases in the league with 36—but then again, Leo used his players' talents. When he had the horses, baseball people were going to say about Leo, you couldn't beat him. The thing was, you had to keep his interest when the team was lousy.

Leo won with a team that struck a league-leading 101 homers. He didn't have to rely on the stolen base or the hit-and-run to get an edge. Reiser, for example, stole only 4 bases even though he would later set a steal-of-home record of 7 in a season. Because Durocher had the lead so often with this relatively powerful club, he didn't need to rely on the complete array of the baseball arsenal. Perhaps most important, his pitching staff had a league-leading 3.14 earned run average.

Herman still proved to be the best second baseman in the league. Walker had come through in the clutch; Pee Wee was described as "a bit overawed by his surroundings" in one analysis.

"And you can say it and say it again," as one writer put it, "that Durocher was the gent whose spirit and fight coordinated the talent of a scrambled ball club composed of oldsters, middle-aged big lea- guers, and kids hardly dry behind the ears."

In the newspaper business, the largest front-page headlines are called war banners. Presumably, they are saved for, well, wars.

Except when Brooklyn won the pennant.

And so on the front of Brooklyn's own paper, the *Eagle*, the banner headline proclaimed:

Million Roar Salute
To Parading Dodgers

The lead story began, "Dodgerville tossed aside its dignity."

It was a nice, ironic tone. For what Dodgerville and Leo and the Dodgers didn't need, or want—and certainly didn't have—was dignity. Perhaps that was Leo's secret in the Borough of Churches after all: that he was loud, that he was pushy, that he didn't say excuse me, that he fought for what he believed in, that he questioned au- thority, that he stuck up for family, that he was generous, that he owed money, that he had come up the hard way—in short, he was "like us."

It wasn't so surprising that other news was bumped to secondary space on the front page of the paper which sold for three cents: British planes bombed nine cities in Italy. Sixty thousand people marched behind the Dodgers motorcade from Grand Army Plaza; fans yelled, "Murder those Yankees!" Borough historians described it as Brooklyn's biggest parade since it honored returning Civil War veterans in 1865.

Monday, September 29, had been declared an official holiday. School let out in Brooklyn. Every youngster seemed to be on hand as the parade formed under the Heroes Arch at Eastern Parkway and Prospect Park Plaza.

A band of mounted policemen led the parade of Durocher and Reiser, Reese, Medwick, Wyatt, Higbe, of Camilli and Fitzsimmons, and Owen. They went past the densely packed mob of people at Flatbush Avenue and Fulton Street. The gathering defined a borough.

People deliriously burst the police lines—old men, young women, schoolchildren. They leapt in front of the police motorcycle escort, they ran alongside open limousines. They kissed the players' arms, slapped their backs. The car carrying MacPhail and Durocher was mobbed. People pressed forward to tell Lippy Leo whom to use against the Yankees. Policemen had to break the fans' grip on the car.

At Fulton Street near Boerum Place, a gray-haired woman broke past policemen at the curb, dashing for Leo's car. She wore a blue apron with the sign "HOORAY LEO DUROCHER." She tried to kiss Durocher's hand while policemen pulled her away.

Then, the business of the World Series was at hand. For the first time, the Dodgers faced the Yankees.

There was a convergence of sports fans coming to New York: for the Series, the Joe Louis–Lou Nova heavyweight title fight, opening football games, as well as the beginning of the nightclub season and the opening of Broadway shows. In rail terminals, fans arrived hourly from every section of country, including the West Coast. Four hundred visitors for the fight and the World Series checked in during one afternoon at the Waldorf-Astoria.

Leo was besieged by ticket requests. He tried to take care of everyone, as usual. But certain information came to Judge Landis that made the commissioner unhappy. He ordered Leo to take back the four tickets in his private box he planned to leave for the actor George Raft. Landis learned that Raft had won more than $100,000 betting on baseball.

On the eve of the Series, the Giants tried to have the last word. Their secretary, Eddie Brannick, was chagrined that the Dodgers had won. "They'll get murdered in the Series," he said.

To say the least, this sort of comment just wasn't customary coming from another National League team. At times like this—especially against the hated Yankees—the National League teams had to stick together. The idea was that your league's reputation was at stake in the World Series. But between the Giants and Dodgers, personal hatred overrode league matters. And to the Giants, Leo was the most visible object of that hatred.

The Yankees, meanwhile, had their own complaints about the Dodgers. Why was everybody paying so much attention to that bunch of Bums? The Yankees had won their pennant by 17 games, for crying out loud. What was all the fuss about?

Thirty-seven-year-old Curt Davis—a throw-in for the deal that brought Medwick to Brooklyn—started the Series opener against Red Ruffing.

But not before Commissioner Landis held an unusual meeting with Durocher and Yankee manager Joe McCarthy. Landis said there would be no time-consuming meetings at the mound, with the entire infield listening in as the manager spoke to the pitcher. He ruled that only two players besides the manager and pitcher could be at the mound. And, as an obvious restriction aimed at Durocher, Landis decreed only one visit per inning by the manager to his pitcher. There was also this warning by Landis: Players and managers were expected to behave "in a proper manner."

That final stern notice was probably the result of Brooklyn's final series of the year at St. Louis, in which Leo's incessant hounding of the umpires helped lead to the rule that forbids arguing over balls and strikes.

Undaunted, Leo was determined to mastermind this World Series as surely as the Dodgers were going to try to win it on the field. He thought he could trick the Yankees into thinking they were going to face one of his stars—either Wyatt or Higbe. He didn't announce his starter for the opening game, not even on game day, not even when the ballpark opened.

"What difference does it make?" replied McCarthy, whose team had finished first by 17 games, when asked about who the Yankees would face.

Perhaps Leo was thinking back to Connie Mack's trick before the 1929 Series, when he started a thirty-five-year-old named Howard Ehmke against the Chicago Cubs, also managed by McCarthy. Ehmke got the nod over Lefty Grove, who had won 20 games, as well as 24-game winner George Earnshaw and 18-game winner Rube Walberg. Ehmke had a 7–2 record. But he won the opener and then Mack came back with Grove in Game 2 against the flustered Cubs.

So Leo had Davis—and Wyatt and Higbe—warm up before facing the Yankees. Just before game time, he named Davis.

The Series opener was a tight game, both sides getting 6 hits, but the Yankees, and Red Ruffing, escaped with a 3–2 victory.

Still, something happened in that game that was a symbol of all the things that always happened to the Beloved Bums in World Series play. Sometimes, the Dodgers benefited. Not this time.

Down by 3–1 going into the seventh at the Stadium, the Dodgers staged a comeback. Lavagetto reached base on an error, Reese singled. Lew Riggs pinch-hit for Owen—who had tripled earlier off Ruffing. But Leo wanted the left-handed Riggs against the right-handed Ruffing. It was a good move as Riggs singled home Lavagetto. With two on and none out, the Yankees for the first time were in trouble, with Ruffing tiring. Leo pinch-hit for Casey, who had relieved Davis. Leo found Jimmy Wasdell on the bench and told him, "Get in there and hit."

Maybe those were a poor choice of words. What Leo really wanted him to do was bunt. Or at least, that's what Leo claimed afterward.

After the first pitch, Leo supposedly showed him the bunt sign. Instead, Wasdell swung and fouled to third baseman Red Rolfe, who made a nice running catch. Reese, on second, seeing third base uncovered, tagged after the catch and dashed for third. But Phil Rizzuto at shortstop saw what was happening and also ran for third. He got there ahead of Reese, took Rolfe's throw, and doubled up Pee Wee. The rally died when Walker grounded out.

"I didn't see any bunt sign," Wasdell said later. "But there must have been one because Durocher bawled hell out of me in the dugout. I can't blame him. It was my fault."

Maybe it was, and maybe it wasn't. Leo was protective, sort of, of Wasdell's blunder. "We blew our chance that inning," said Durocher. "That's when we should have come through, but we didn't. What the hell, it's just one of those things. It was a tough time to miss a bunt sign, but that's baseball. I'll take the responsibility. Don't blame Wasdell."

That magnanimous gesture did not mollify Wasdell's former manager, Bucky Harris. The Senators' skipper, who was at the game, said, "I managed Wasdell for three years. Jimmy wasn't a smart ballplayer, but he never missed a signal. I doubt if Durocher gave him one."

In Game 2 at Yankee Stadium, Leo quit fooling around with mind games. He pitched Whit Wyatt. The score was the same but the result was reversed. Even though the Dodgers won, Leo came in livid. Owen had broken up a double play by barreling into the smallish Rizzuto. Yankee second baseman Joe Gordon announced, "They're going to get some of that rough stuff, too."

"So they want to play rough, eh?" said Durocher. "Well, that suits us. That's when we play our best ball." And just what was he groaning about? In the first game, Reese had slid hard into Rizzuto. Yankee Johnny Sturm retaliated by sliding spikes-high into Herman. Johnny Allen then hit Sturm with a pitched ball. And then Owen followed this up in Game 2 by nearly spiking Rizzuto and knocking him down with a football block.

Game 2 also produced one of those instances in which Leo's instincts proved to be uncanny. Wyatt was in trouble in the first inning, then got Joe DiMaggio to end it with a double play, and was still shaky through four innings. He even told Leo he didn't feel right, that he had nothing. Leo stuck with him. He gave up only two singles after that.

The Dodgers had for the second time reached Yankee pitching for only 6 hits, leading MacPhail to complain that his pitcher, Wyatt, had "hit the hardest ball in the two games."

It was so hot for Game 3, at Ebbets Field, that one of the reporters in the press box was writing in his undershirt.

Fat Freddie Fitzsimmons, at thirty-nine the oldest pitcher ever to start a World Series game, hooked up with Marius Russo. It was a beautifully pitched game, scoreless through seven innings. The problem for the Dodgers, though, had come with two out in the top of the seventh. Russo, a good-hitting pitcher who batted .231 that season, was up with Joe Gordon on second. Russo nailed a liner that hit Fat Freddie, who couldn't bend easily, squarely on the left knee-cap. The ball bounced high in the air, and was caught by Reese, who threw to first. The umpire signaled safe, Russo beating the throw. But Fitzsimmons was down. He had to be helped to the dugout, cursing with each painful step, leaning on Dressen and Lavagetto. He could not continue.

The Yankees thought they had a rally going, runners on first and third. But only the umpires seemed to have realized what actually happened, even if the Yankees and Dodgers didn't. For Russo's shot never touched the ground. Instead, it sailed off Fitzsimmons's knee-cap to Reese on the fly. Thus, Pee Wee's catch had ended the inning.

Hence Hugh Casey, the top reliever, made the first of two appearances that again became the stuff of legendary Brooklyn discombobulation in the Series.

Casey warmed up—or tried to—for the eighth inning in a hurry when Fitzsimmons couldn't continue. Casey's body, and head, weren't in the game. The Yankees got a pair of tainted runs, with 4 straight hits, and won by 2–1. The second "hit" actually was a simple grounder between first and second on which Casey didn't cover the bag for Camilli. Bothered by this lapse, he pitched from the stretch with runners on first and second, looked to hold Red Rolfe, the man on second, and spotted Rolfe moving the wrong way. All Casey had to do was toss the ball to Coscarart at second and Rolfe was picked off. Instead, Casey froze. He pitched the ball to DiMaggio, who singled through the hole vacated by Coscarart.

"I wanted to throw it," Casey told Durocher later. The reliever who made a career of coming into every tight and pressure-filled situation failed to handle the Series pressure. After the game, Casey sat slumped at his locker with the "glazed look in his eyes that you see in Joe Louis's victims," one reporter noted.

Then came Game 4.

It is famous for the third strike missed by catcher Mickey Owen. And it should be. For that kept alive a ninth-inning Yankee rally, which won the game for the Bronx Bombers. It is less famous for Leo himself remaining immobile in the dugout when it was time to make a pitching change.

Actually, Leo could be second-guessed for quite a bit in this game. He finally decided to start Higbe—who had started a league-high 39 games that season. He had completed 19. His 298 innings were the second-highest total in the league. He thrived on work. He even relieved nine times. He had not, however, pitched in a week. And thrust into this situation, he didn't have his control.

Higbe was to remember, in a conversation with Peter Golenbock, author of *Bums*, that "[it was] the one time I got mad at Durocher. I'm 22–9, the winningest pitcher he has, and he doesn't start me until the fourth game of the Series. The first two wuz okay, but when he come to start Fitzsimmons in the third game, that's when I got mad. And when it came my turn to pitch in that fourth game, I just wasn't in shape to pitch. Really, I hadn't throwed a ball."

He yielded a walk with two out and a man on first in the first inning to keep the Yankees alive. Then he gave a base hit for the first Yankee run. He was saved in the third inning when Walker made a running catch on a drive by Henrich with a runner on. Then in the fourth, he loaded the bases with none out, put away the next two batters, but got touched for a single by Sturm that drove in two and the Yankees held a 3–0 lead.

Finally, Leo lifted him for Larry French, who escaped the inning helped by poor Yankee baserunning.

The Dodgers, though, came back with 2 runs in the bottom of the fourth. And in the top of the fifth they halted a Yankee rally when Casey came in to relieve Johnny Allen with the bases loaded and retired Joe Gordon, the Series' top hitter. This revived the Dodgers, who produced 2 runs in the bottom of the inning and took a 4–3 lead.

Now Casey was sailing. He yielded a 2-out single to Sturm in the sixth. Then DiMaggio beat out an infield hit in the seventh. No problem. And the eighth was a 1–2–3 inning.

This was not the era of the "closer." There was no $2 million man who hurled eighty innings a year and saved 40 games. So relief pitchers often would be middle relievers, as well as closers, going as long as they could pitch effectively.

It was the ninth inning, and Ebbets Field was poised for a spectacular thing: A victory would tie the series at 2 games apiece, with Game 5 to be played the next day in Brooklyn.

Sturm grounded out. Rolfe grounded out. Tommy Henrich—Old Reliable—loomed. Fans moved down to the box seats. The people in the box seats were poised to jump over the rail and onto the field.

Casey's first pitch was a ball. Then he put over two called strikes. Henrich fouled off the next one. Casey tried to get him to bite on a pitch off the plate and Henrich let it go. The count was 2–2. This time Hughie tried another outside pitch that fooled Henrich. He didn't move his bat. But it was wide. The count was 3 and 2.

The pitch that Hugh Casey delivered next has been speculated about and argued over since. Casey himself was to add to the legend by claiming it was a spitter and thus had a life of its own. A spitter would take Owen off the hook, especially if Hughie had thrown it without Owen's knowledge. Owen contended he called for a curve and that's what he got. Henrich claimed it was a curve.

It came up there looking like a fastball headed for the fat part of the bat. But Henrich couldn't do a thing with it. He started to swing but the ball swooped in a different direction. He missed with a chopping swing. Strike 3. As soon as he fanned, the crowd surged on the field. The Yankees headed for the clubhouse.

But Owen didn't have the ball. It broke so sharply that it slithered off his glove and bounded behind him. Owen was baseball's best-fielding catcher that summer. In fact, he had gone nearly an entire year, from September of 1940 to August 29, 1941, without making an error. He had amassed 508 putouts and assists without throwing a ball away trying to cut down a base runner, without dropping a third strike.

But he made an error at this moment in history.

"As soon as I missed it," Henrich recalled almost fifty years later, "I looked around to see where the ball was. It fooled me so much, I figured maybe it fooled Mickey, too. And it did."

At Henrich's 1988 induction into the Brooklyn Dodger Hall of Fame (how's that for irony?), he told Dave Anderson of the *Times*, "Spitballs drop down. I swung at a big breaking curveball."

And Owen was to explain that Casey had two types of curves: a big sweeping job, and a short, quick one. The short, quick one had been Casey's pitch all day. So when Owen signaled for a curve— there was only one "curve" sign—he figured Casey would give him the quickie.

Whatever it was, Owen chased it. Leo claimed later that the police who had immediately pounced on the field to halt the crowd from surging interfered with Owen's vision, preventing him from picking up the ball cleanly. In any event, Henrich scooted for first and made it.

"The big mistake I made," said Owen, "was not going out to the mound to tell Casey that I blew it. I just stood there behind the plate.

I should've gone out to tell Casey that I blew it and to settle him down. But all of us were in shock from what happened."

When Henrich got to first, he was somewhat surprised that Camilli didn't say a word, "not a word." "I couldn't believe what happened," he admitted. "None of us could."

The hardest hit, physically and emotionally, was Casey. Leo, though, stayed in the dugout, transfixed. The man who had spent a career controlling situations, or trying to, *of talking*, now was reduced to watching, to being a frozen spectator.

Here is how Leo himself remembered that moment: "It wasn't the pitch to Henrich that did it, anyway. There was still only a man on first with two out. It was what happened afterward. And right there is where I do think it is possible for a manager to second-guess himself. Considering Casey's actions within a very short period of time . . . throwing those beanballs at Magerkurth in Pittsburgh, and freezing twice within a matter of minutes [in Game 3], I should have called time and gone to the mound to remind him that he still only needed one out to end the ball game. To slow him down, in other words, until I was absolutely sure that he was in full control of himself."

Instead, Leo never took the ball out of Casey's hand, never gave him a few seconds to compose himself.

DiMaggio lined a hit to left, with Henrich stopping at second.

"And right here," Durocher recalled, "is where I have to really give it to myself. A legitimate second guess. The next batter was Charlie Keller, a left-handed hitter. I had Larry French, a veteran left-hander . . . warming up in the bullpen . . . the situation screamed for me to replace Casey with French. I did nothing. I froze."

Keller, though, swung and missed at the first two pitches.

"My mistake was that for the first time in my life I was shell-shocked," Leo said. He was thinking, but not acting: Maybe he should have gone out and told Casey to brush Keller back with one or two pitches. This would have given Hughie some time to settle down. "I told myself, what was to be gained by going out and getting everybody jumpy?" said the man who always made everybody jumpy. "Defensive, timid thinking, it will kill you every time." Leo, not a master of the second guess, was also to recall how "I sat on my ass and didn't do anything."

Leo did whistle for Casey's attention, and signaled for a chest-high curve.

Keller drove it high off the screen in right. That scored Henrich easily to tie the game. But the ball, instead of coming down to the field, hit the angled wall below the screen, popped up for a second, and then came down. That extra bounce allowed DiMaggio to score from first with the go-ahead run. It was, said Owen, "as good a play as Enos Slaughter scoring from first base for the Cardinals in the 1946 Series."

Durocher still sat.

Casey walked Bill Dickey to put runners on first and second. Then Joe Gordon doubled over Wasdell's head in left field and two more runs scored.

Casey walked Rizzuto, but "Fireman" Johnny Murphy, the Yankees reliever, finally made the last out.

Twelve years later Leo wondered whether Casey had a "latent instability" that led to that blowup. He asked the question after Casey had committed suicide.

When the game ended, MacPhail, tears in his eyes, which were bleary anyway from his game-long drinking, looked for Owen in the clubhouse.

"I'm going to hear something now," Owen thought. Instead, MacPhail hugged and kissed Owen.

"I can't believe this," the catcher thought as the drunk, slobbering MacPhail wouldn't stop.

Over in the Yankees clubhouse, DiMaggio told Henrich, "They'll never recover from this one."

To this day, Reese believes that "Mr. Casey might have given Henrich the wet one at that time. It may have done a little more than he thought. Casey could throw a spitball and get it over at any time. He didn't throw hard, and it might have come over faster than Mickey realized. It might have crossed him up. I don't really remember Leo getting on Mickey Owen about that. There's nothing you can do about it. It's just part of the game."

Wyatt pitched credibly the next day on only three days' rest, a pattern that was to haunt Durocher, and other Dodger managers through the years: not enough front-line pitching. (Leo had gone into Series with only two pitchers with more than twenty starts—Wyatt and Higbe.)

He walked Henrich in the first, and on ball 4, the pitch eluded Owen. The crowd moaned with a shock of recognition. But when

Mickey came to bat in the second, he received a thirty-second stand-ing ovation.

Wyatt yielded a pair of runs in the second. But he had also accomplished something no one else had all year: In that season of DiMaggio's 56-game hitting streak, Joe had never struck out twice in a game. Wyatt got him his first two at-bats.

Leo stirred in the fourth, coming out to argue a called ball with home plate umpire Bill McGowan. In the fifth, a Wyatt pitch sent DiMaggio to the ground. The slugger then flied out but went back to the dugout by way of the pitcher's mound and said something to Wyatt, who snapped back. DiMaggio turned sharply toward him, and both benches poured out. But umpires got to the mound at the same time and quieted the milling crowd.

That was the only dramatic action of the final innings, and the Yankees, with their fifth starter of the Series, Tiny Bonham, scored a 3–1 victory.

A gloating Yankees coach, Art Fletcher, kept repeating in the clubhouse, "We moidered duh Bums, we moidered duh Bums!"

For the Dodgers, it was the beginning of the cry, "Wait till next year!" Their third World Series try, their third failure—while the Yankees won their ninth Series.

In the 1941 year-end roundup of baseball in *The New York Times*, the Dodgers' pennant was cited as the most significant story. Di-Maggio's 56-game streak? In the fourth paragraph.

CHAPTER VII

REUNION WITH RICKEY

LEO WAS OUT of control. The pennant had overshadowed MacPhail's disgust with Leo's gambling and host of unsavory locker room visitors. And so Leo's annual dance at the end of a rope was about to begin. Year in, year out, no matter how well the Dodgers had played, there was always some question whether Leo would be back the next year. And Leo himself seemed to put obstacles in the path, daring MacPhail—even while MacPhail was virtually threatening to fire him.

In negotiating his contract for the 1942 season, Durocher felt he was bargaining from strength. He insisted that MacPhail give him a player-manager contract. This would pay him more than just being a manager. Talks stalled. It was only a matter of weeks until training camp.

Bill Terry did his bit to diminish Leo's bargaining power. Terry was an ex-manager now, having been replaced by still another Giant hero, Mel Ott. Terry, installed as the Giants' farm director, said he didn't think much of the Dodgers' chances to repeat in 1942.

"Well that's the finest before-three-o'clock talk I ever heard," said a miffed Durocher.

By mid-February of 1942, Leo finally signed, to be player-manager part of the season. The same day Leo signed, though, Cookie Lavagetto told the team he had enlisted in the Navy Air Corps. The second baseman was the first Dodger to enlist. Brooklyn, and baseball, was going to war, and the following years would create a different kind of challenge for all managers. They would make do with minor leaguers, a one-armed outfielder, draft rejects, older, tired men.

As usual, MacPhail had been busy. To replace Lavagetto, he acquired Arky Vaughan from the Pirates and sent them pitcher Luke Hamlin and the "neurasthenic" Babe Phelps.

The Dodgers were prepared for spring training, in gay Havana once more. "I've got just the kind of club I've always wanted," Leo said after the first workout in Tropical Park Stadium. "They all love to play and they all want to win." Leo the Lip was always Leo the Optimist in camp. And this particular day, why shouldn't he be? He had a team that had captured a hundred games for the first time in club history. The squad was virtually intact. It had learned how to win. It would only get better. And he had young Pete Reiser returning from that remarkable rookie season.

"He was as good a player as Stan Musial," Reese recalled forty years later after Reiser's death. Reiser, who died of a respiratory ailment, had been a nonstop smoker who had survived five skull fractures and seven concussions as a player. It was his all-out crashes into the unyielding walls that led baseball to install warning tracks and padded fences.

If 1941 was a revelation, folks in baseball hadn't seen anything yet. In early July, with the Dodgers enjoying a big lead over the Cards, they visited St. Louis. Reiser was batting .380. "I was just starting to get warm," he recalled in a conversation with Donald Honig, the baseball historian. "I could've hit .400 that year. No doubt in my mind about that. And to make it all the sweeter, we had a 13½-game lead."

The Dodgers and Cards were locked in one of their traditional pitching duels in the second game of a double-header. It meant the sun was going down, the visibility quite different from what it had been earlier in the day. The Dodgers' Whitlow Wyatt and the Cards' Mort Cooper were turning in zeroes. Then it was extra innings. Like most clubs in baseball, the Cards would not turn on the lights to conclude a game. They would just call it on account of darkness.

Enos Slaughter led off the thirteenth with a line drive over Reiser's head. "My first thought was that it could be caught, which is pretty much the way I felt about any ball that was hit."

Reiser, knowing that if it fell it would probably be a triple and lead to the winning run, sped after it. He didn't see the flagpole in his path. With a sensational run and catch, he snared the ball. Then he spied the pole and grazed it—but his momentum brought him right into the wall on a dead run. He dropped the ball, picked it up, and instinctively—not realizing he had separated a shoulder—threw the ball to Reese. The relay just missed nipping Slaughter at the plate, where he slid for an inside-the-park home run.

When Durocher reached the stricken Reiser, he started to sob. Blood was streaming out of Reiser's ears. He lay with arms outstretched, face to the sky, not seeing anything.

Reiser woke up in a hospital. The Cards' team physician told him he had a concussion *and* a fractured skull. Don't play any more this season, he was told. He was back on the field in a few days.

Why did Reiser insist on coming back time after time? Why did he take those chances of always going for the impossible catch? "You slow up a half step, and it's the beginning of your last ball game," he once explained. "It might take a few years, but you're on your way out. That's how I look at it. You can't turn it on and off any time you want to. Not if you take pride in yourself."

Even though Reiser went on to lead the league in stolen bases that year with 20 (and in 1946 stole home an outlandish record seven times), he was never the same player. He wound up playing in 125 games in 1942, still batting .310. In 1946, following three years in the military, he returned to hit .277. In 1947, he batted over .300 for the last time. The Dodgers traded him to Boston after the 1948 season, then he retired in 1952 after stints with Pittsburgh and Cleveland. He was reunited with Leo on the Cubs in the 1960s as a coach, but he couldn't take any more of Leo's shenanigans, and asked the Cubs to allow him to scout. They agreed.

Perhaps Reiser's affinity for walls wouldn't have mattered in 1942. Perhaps it was just one of those years when all good intentions, and good talent, are overcome by a surging opponent—in this case, the Cardinals. They overcame a Dodger lead that as late as mid-August was 10½ games. The Cards won 43 of their final 51 games, a winning percentage of .843 over one third of the season.

But the on-field dramatics of Dodger life always had their off-field counterpoint. The day spring training ended, the boys were hanging around the Havana airport waiting for the flight to Miami. So naturally, they started playing cards, for money. A Cuban tapped Hugh Casey on the shoulder and started to bawl him out in Spanish. Hughie didn't understand, or so he let on. The stranger opened his

wallet and revealed a gold badge. "Scram," said Casey. Outfielder
Johnny Rizzo added, "Vamoose."

That, the plainclothes cop understood. He whipped out a pistol.
He waved away their teammates, who had started to converge, and
marched Casey and Rizzo off to the baggage room. He called for a
police van. Dodger secretary John McDonald, the club's palm
greaser, among his other talents, located the minister of Sport and
had the pair sprung.

The Dodgers' talent for trouble wasn't over even after they returned to the States. MacPhail was handed a report by a private
detective that detailed the after-hours shenanigans of several players
in Cuba. He immediately notified Leo that he was to take action.
The major culprit was Johnny Allen, the thirty-six-year-old right-
hander. No sooner had Allen put on his uniform for a workout at
Daytona Beach, than Leo announced he was suspended indefinitely
and ordered him to remove his uniform. The sin was "rules violation
in Cuba. And there're three other guys I've got to talk to."

The 1942 season was the first after America's entry into World
War II. On Opening Day, the Dodgers were at the Polo Grounds.
For the first time, the National Anthem was played at the ballpark.
America stood before games to honor its men and women in the
Armed Forces.

Along with the movie industry, baseball helped spearhead America's patriotic fervor. Someone sang "Any Bonds Today" and Mayor
LaGuardia called out Managers Ott and Durocher to home plate. He
gave them each bonds they had bought with 10 percent of their first
paychecks. In fact, all the players had earmarked 10 percent of their
salaries for defense bonds.

When the mayor mentioned Leo's name, booing cascaded from
the stands. "I see," said the mayor to Leo, "you brought your friends
along."

A fan was later booed for not throwing a foul ball back, while a
dozen others were cheered when they did. Before the game, Horace
Stoneham, the Giants president, had asked for an announcement that
fans return balls hit into the stands. These would be forwarded to
Army and Navy camps.

The season started so brightly for the Dodgers that soon a devil-
may-care attitude pervaded the club. Was it because of the war, with
its realization that these young, strong athletes soon would be risking

their lives overseas? Or was it because of the way they were playing, led by the ebullient, combative Durocher? It was a team almost saying: If this is the way the world is going, let's make the most of it.

So they gambled away money. Nothing like this unchecked activity had been seen in baseball in fifteen years, since the Yankees glory days when their wealthy players, led by the Babe, were throwing around money. These Dodgers played in parlor cars and in hotel rooms, and of course, even in airport waiting rooms. The limit was doubled to eight dollars in seven-card stud. These games weren't only for the players, though. Durocher and his top aide, Charlie Dressen, sat in and often took younger players for a considerable amount of their paychecks.

Leo was also running wild on the field. For the second time, he was suspended. This lasted three days after an incident in late June when Umpire Tom Dunn warned him not to leave the bench to protest a called strike. "What?" roared Leo after the ruling. "Bill McKechnie leaves the Reds bench all the time and nothing was done about it."

In that same series, he was kicked out of a game arguing Reese was safe on a bunt. After Dunn threw him out, he refused to leave. The other umps, Ziggy Sears and Bill Stewart, spent ten minutes in the dugout with him. Durocher had kicked dirt on Dunn a few times. From the dugout, he threw a towel in Dunn's face.

The suspension again put Durocher up against authority. It was supposed to start at Philadelphia. That night he went to Philadelphia and sat in a first-row box seat, ten feet from the Brooklyn dugout.

As the season sweated into the summer, the Dodgers and their rivals turned nasty. The Big, Bad Brooks were dominating everyone, and their pitchers, under Leo's orders, were aiming at the head. Everywhere the Dodgers went, there were beanball wars. Everyone hated Brooklyn.

After one series in Boston, Frick notified Durocher and his Braves counterpart, Casey Stengel, that each would be held responsible for beanballs and subject to automatic fines of two hundred dollars.

This followed a game in which Wyatt and the Braves' Manny Salvo were in a dusting duel. Wyatt even threw his bat at Salvo after the not-so-proper Bostonian had knocked him down.

Most of that season's beanball incidents involved the Dodgers. In one game, a Cub hurler, Hiram Bithorn, threw a ball at Durocher in the dugout in retaliation for Leo asking his pitchers to throw at the Cubs.

Durocher always had an unreasoning fear of—or respect for?—the Cardinals. Now, there was good reason. His hatred for the Cards began, of course, with his banishment from the team that had meant so much to him once upon a time. Now they were his chief rivals. The 1942 season was to bring out the worst in him when it came to playing his former team.

Despite Brooklyn's lead, MacPhail felt there was trouble in the clubhouse. It centered on Medwick and Durocher. Just as Ducky had done in St. Louis, he was more concerned with getting his base hits than seeing the team do well. Also, Leo was involved in high-stakes card games. That, coupled with his continual defense of Medwick, created a bad situation. But in baseball, that usually doesn't mean a thing if a manager is winning.

MacPhail, though, was no respecter of tradition and certainly not of Durocher's feelings. Before the Dodgers went into St. Louis for a 4-game series in August, bringing in a 7½-game lead, MacPhail called the players up to the Press Club for an informal get-together, and he started to hit the hard stuff. He was talkative. He told the team he was unhappy with the way they'd been playing lately and he was unhappy with the gambling. He said they had become smug. They weren't hustling. Their 10½-game lead had shrunk thanks to a poor home series against Philadelphia. And now they were headed for St. Louis.

"I'll bet you two hundred bucks right now we'll win this thing by eight games," blurted out Dixie Walker. It was an incredible statement. After all that MacPhail had railed against—the gambling, the smugness—here was Walker betting his own boss. MacPhail roared out of the clubhouse.

And the Dodgers got roaring drunk on their train ride to St. Louis, a party that lasted through the night.

In the Cardinals, Rickey had fashioned the club that was to dominate the 1940s: Not one regular—pitcher or player—was over the age of thirty. He had a trio of fine right-handers in Mort Cooper, Johnny Beazley, and Murry Dickson, and southpaws in Max Lanier and Howie Pollet. Walker Cooper was the catcher, rapidly becoming acknowledged as the best in the league. Marty Marion anchored the infield at shortstop. The outfield had the brilliant young man with the corkscrew stance, Musial, the gifted center fielder Terry Moore, and the hustling Enos Slaughter.

The Dodgers, meanwhile, were performing with a damaged Pistol Pete, although his good buddy and roommate, Pee Wee Reese, had turned into such a solid player that Leo, essentially, had retired as a player and never got into a game.

In the crucial August series between the two powers at St. Louis, the Cards won three of four. MacPhail was getting desperate. He paid $50,000 to the Senators and bought the well-traveled, thirty-four-year-old right-handed pitcher, Bobo Newsom.

With two weeks remaining, the Dodgers held a slim lead and were host to the Cards for the final two games between the teams. Wyatt and Cooper hooked up in another memorable pitching battle, won by Cardinal third baseman Whitey Kurowski's homer. The Cards came right back and won the next day too. For the first time that season, the Cards were in first. And there they stayed.

Yet, the Dodgers didn't collapse. Indeed, Leo got them cranked up again. They went into the final day of the season with 7 straight victories, trailing the Cards by 1½ games. If by some incredible set of circumstances—if they could win their finale, and the Cards drop their doubleheader—then the two teams would end up tied and meet in the first playoff in league history.

Well, it was nice to think so. The Dodgers did capture their game against the Phils. But the Cards won their pair over the Cubs.

When Walker, sitting in the clubhouse, heard that the Cardinals had won the opener to ice the pennant, he rattled his locker by tossing his spikes inside. "I declare," he said. "I didn't think it was possible."

The Dodgers and Cards each wound up the season with 8 straight victories. Brooklyn, with 104 for the season, had outdone themselves from the year before. But who could have guessed that the great 1942 season would end not only with MacPhail's last game in Brooklyn, but Rickey's last regular season in St. Louis?

The Dodgers money men were angry at MacPhail. All that spending—$50,000 for Bobo Newsom!—and what did they have to show. Sure, he was paying off the club's debt, and they had a contender, and Ebbets Field was spiffier than ever. But MacPhail also was paying himself a huge salary, thanks to an attendance clause. The more people came, the more money he took home. But the Dodgers' stockholders had decided a week before the season ended that he was gone. What would have happened if the Dodgers had somehow pulled out the pennant is anybody's guess.

The Redhead's five-year tenure had produced a winner and a break with Dodger daffiness. It had brought in Durocher. But with the stockholders not getting extra dividends, this meant little to them.

MacPhail announced he was accepting an Army officer's commission and would serve in the office of Service and Supplies. Tears streamed down his florid cheeks as he made the announcement.

Meanwhile, the Cards roared through the World Series. They toppled the Yankees in only five games, the only time the Bronx Bombers would fail to win a Series in a string of fifteen appearances.

Even as the Cards soared over the Yankees, and even as Brooklyn was trying to figure out who would replace MacPhail, Rickey and his parsimonious owner, Breadon, were finished. The old man was paying Rickey $75,000 a year. That had been okay, sort of, up to this point. But continue? With all that talent—Musial and the others—hanging around, and with the war effort diluting other clubs but not the Cardinals' far-flung empire, who needed Rickey anyhow? Breadon believed he had picked up enough knowledge about how to run a club so he could lop off Rickey. Besides saving his salary, and not having to cut him in on a percentage of cash realized from player sales, Breadon finally would get some credit for being a smart person himself. Twenty-four days after the Cards had taken their fourth straight from the Yankees, Rickey was out of a job.

Jim Mulvey, however, one of the Dodgers' owners, had wanted Rickey all along and so Rickey joined the Dodgers as general manager at the age of sixty-one, with a salary of $40,000 plus bonuses.

This made Leo's fate open to question. Rickey wanted Leo to stop gambling. He toyed with Leo, in a way, delaying signing him as manager even though he had led a team that won 104 games.

Rickey also called in Dressen and promptly fired him for betting on horses from the clubhouse. Dressen pleaded with Rickey to reconsider. "I'll stop, I really will," he promised Rickey, who would not relent. Finally, after Dressen, pleading, asked if he could stop and could prove it, would he take him back, Rickey agreed, and in fact eventually did rehire him.

But what to do about Leo? Actually, World War II would be taking care of that, or so Rickey figured. For Leo was about to become Sergeant Durocher. He was told by the draft board he would be called by June 1943. That meant the Dodgers would have to start the season with another manager.

Other facets of Dodgerdom consumed Rickey. In one of his first pronouncements, he was "definitely" taking them out of Havana as their spring training site for 1943. He also pointed out that the Dodgers had more ten-year players than any other team in the league, "and that isn't good." The Dodgers would learn that Rickey did not wax sentimental over older players. His well-worn philosophy was better to sell a star too early than too late.

And looking longingly at his old team, the Cardinals, he said, "They have eleven pitchers, all married and with children, to take South next spring."

Rickey by now was known as "the father of chain-store baseball." He was going to try to build another dynasty. But he still had to make a decision on Leo, Army or not. So when asked about Leo's future, he replied cryptically, with some faint praise, "An astute and fine tactician on the field." Rickey also said he would have to talk to Leo first before discussing the coming season. He said as well he had others in mind as possible replacements.

Leo's old friend, Sidney Weil, disclosed in his posthumous memoirs that Rickey had considered firing Leo after 1942. Weil had been in New York during the Cards-Yankees series. "I was in Rickey's room at the New Yorker. Branch said, 'Let me take you to the game.' He wanted to talk. He told me that 'on the field, Leo was the best,' but off the field, Durocher's habits were not to his liking. He related a lot of incidents and told me to think about it.

"When I arrived in St. Louis and went to Branch's house, I reminded him that he had admitted that Leo was a great manager on the field. I proposed that he make it a rule for Leo to come to see him every morning the team was in Brooklyn, and Branch might be able to correct some of the things he didn't like."

In other words, Leo would be on parole, with a daily meeting with his parole officer.

By late November, Rickey still hadn't told Leo his plans. He claimed publicly that Leo's draft status was not a consideration. Leo apparently hadn't sold himself to Rickey. When they met for five hours in Brooklyn, Rickey told him he was unhappy about the poker playing.

Both Mulvey and National League President Frick were worried about the Dodgers' behavior under Durocher. It was becoming tiresome, at the very least, to keep fining the guy for beanballs, for cursing umpires, for agitating the opposition. Worse, the locker room was an open sewer. Gambling of all sorts went on there: craps, card playing, and horse betting. Bookies roamed the clubhouse. Perhaps that was more because of Dressen, a lifelong horseplayer, than Durocher—but the manager did nothing about it.

One of the bookmakers was Memphis Engelberg, a well-known New York character. He not only touted horses to the players, he booked their bets. Red Barber recalled, "Clubhouse doors could be shut at times to newspapermen but never to Memphis, or George Raft or Danny Kaye or anybody else from Broadway or Hollywood. Leo gambled and therefore was in no position to stop gambling on the ball club."

It wasn't as if gambling was acceptable back then. In fact, Judge Landis made his name as commissioner by riding the Black Sox scandal. He suspended for life eight White Sox ballplayers—even though they had been cleared in a trial of fixing games. In his tenure, Landis suspended fourteen players for life for gambling.

After Rickey met with Leo, he was exceedingly blunt in a news conference about what he expected. "There is the matter of terms, also Durocher's possible playing condition, should we need him as a player, and general ideas which I have concerning a manager, such as discipline, both as applied to oneself and one's players," said Rickey. "I do not want to start with a manager and then have something come up that will be disputed later. I want to make all these adjustments and understandings now."

Rickey also made the point that he had not fired Leo previously from St. Louis. It was Frisch who had wanted him gone.

After Rickey and Durocher met, Leo was asked to smile for the cameras. "I'm not happy yet," he said, demurring.

In late November, though, Rickey signed Leo. It was an extraordinary contract, and a bitter pill for Leo—embarrassing, actually. Rickey was concerned not only with clubhouse gambling, but with players and Leo openly consorting with gamblers. And so he signed Leo not only for one year—but to a straight player contract. Thus, the club could dismiss him at any time, just as it could any player, and not pay the remainder of his manager's salary. Leo received the same amount of money, $25,000.

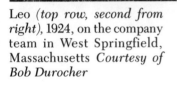

Leo *(top row, second from right)*, 1924, on the company team in West Springfield, Massachusetts *Courtesy of Bob Durocher*

The 1928 Yankee rookie shortstop *National Baseball Library, Cooperstown, N.Y.*

Yankee manager Miller Huggins, shortly before his death in 1929, and owner Colonel Jacob Ruppert *National Baseball Library, Cooperstown, N.Y.*

Pepper Martin, the heart of Leo's Gashouse Gang *National Baseball Library, Cooperstown, N.Y.*

Leo and Grace Dozier at their wedding on the eve of the 1934 World Series
National Baseball Library, Cooperstown, N.Y.

A pensive Durocher ten days after his 1933 trade to St. Louis *National Base-ball Library, Cooperstown, N.Y.*

Wild man Larry MacPhail with his pioneering artificats: an airline ticket and a microphone *National Baseball Library, Cooperstown, N.Y.*

Leo arguing with umpire Babe Pinelli at St. Louis during the Dodgers' frantic 1941 stretch drive *UPI/Bettmann*

Joe McCarthy and Leo, rival managers, before the 1942 All-Star Game held at the Polo Grounds *UPI/ Bettmann*

Havana, 1947, with a happier Branch Rickey looking things over with Leo, before his suspension *UPI/Bettmann*

Suspended, but still dapper, Leo says good-bye in 1947 to Pete Reiser. Pee Wee
Reese, standing between them, watches. Hugh Casey is also standing, while Dixie
Walker is seated *(far right)* next to Gene Hermanski *Wide World Photos (AP)*

Durocher's typical mode, 1950 Giants *Photo by Carl Kidwiler*

Leo and his adopted son Chris, 1950 *National Baseball Library, Cooperstown, N.Y.*

Leo, shaved and showered, congratulating Casey Stengel on his 1951 Series victory *World Wide Photos*

Laraine Day and retired Leo posing before a 1957 TV visit from Ed Murrow on *Person to Person* *National Baseball Library, Cooperstown, N.Y.*

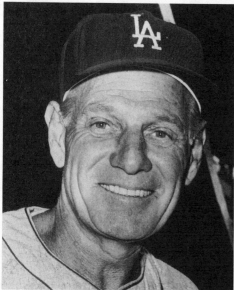

Back in baseball, and controversy, as a Dodgers' coach in 1962 *National Baseball Library, Cooperstown, N.Y.*

Brain trust of the 1954 world champions: Leo and *(left to right)* Herman Franks, Fred Fitzsimmons, and pitching coach Frank Shellenback *Photo courtesy of Giants Alumni Association*

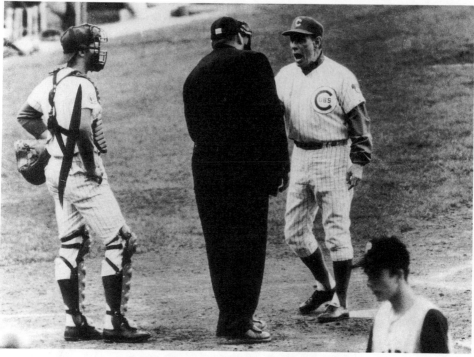

Managing again, kicked out again. Umpire Stan Landes heard Leo's voice from Cubs dugout in this 1968 game and gave him the thumb. *Chicago Sun-Times*

Joined by Don Gutteridge, his former Cards teammate, as opposing managers in a 1969 Chicago intracity game *Photo courtesy of Don Gutteridge*

LEO DUROCHER

"I wear 'em and I'm as much of a man as you are!"

JOCKEY COLOR UNDERWEAR

In a 1970 Jockey ad campaign to show that real men wore colored shorts *Photo courtesy of Jockey Underwear*

Frank Sinatra commissioned LeRoy Neiman to paint Leo in 1972 for a housewarming
present *Photo courtesy of LeRoy Neiman*

In his last managerial job, Leo and Astros' general manager Spec Richardson enjoy a laugh late in 1972 *UPI/Bettmann*

At his last public event before his death in 1991, Leo, eighty-five years old, shaking hands with Joe DiMaggio at the New York Baseball Writers Dinner as Pirates manager Jim Leyland watches *Photo courtesy of Baseball Writers Association/Jack Pokress*

This was turning into a confession. For Leo then admitted he and his players had been involved in high-stakes card gambling. He said from then on there would be a fifteen-cent limit in poker. Leo again made the claim that, even though many players lost considerable amounts of money, "I never took any of that money." He said he would tell the player to owe it to him, and then Leo would turn it back in the form of a bonus when the player did good work on the field.

Speaking of Leo, and playing, Rickey said, "I do expect him to get in perfect playing condition, mentally, physically, socially, and every other conceivable way necessary." Too, Rickey said some players, "including Leo," would report to training camp earlier. He was talking about Leo as if he were some out-of-control teenager. And Leo, who wanted the job, took the public flogging.

There would be no Havana and its open city under Rickey. There would not even be a Florida, for baseball was under wartime constraints. Landis decreed that spring training was to be restricted to the frozen North, more or less. Because of train travel restrictions, clubs had to hold their camps north of the Potomac and Ohio Rivers and east of the Mississippi.

As it turned out, Durocher didn't go into the Army after all. It seems that thirty-seven-year-old Leo had a perforated eardrum, and the Army was rejecting anyone with such a condition. (Ironically, just a few days before, he had visited the Mayo Clinic to get a checkup.) Leo claimed that at the draft board on Montague Street when he asked the chief medical officer why they turned him down, they showed him the rule book. There in black and white, put in not six weeks before, was the rule saying someone with a perforated eardrum was unacceptable for military duty. The reason the Army gave was that if there was a gas attack, gas would go through the eardrum. Actually, Leo was not alone. Thousands of American men were ruled 4-F because of perforated eardrums.

Leo was going to the Army anyway. Sort of. Earlier in the year, Rickey had arranged for him to become the baseball coach at West Point if he were not drafted. Rickey had a wonderfully old-fashioned sense of redemption. And Leo, he felt, could be saved by giving him a sense of responsibility. It also wouldn't hurt his image—and anyway, the Dodgers were going to have spring training at Bear Mountain because of wartime travel restrictions. Six years earlier, when Rickey was with the Cardinals, he had done the same thing with Leo at the United States Naval Academy in Annapolis. "He did a bang-up job then," the crafty Rickey observed.

While West Point—the United States Military Academy— enjoyed playing host to the Dodgers, the team also was warned that "this is the capital of the Army." Thus, if cadets needed training fields for any sort of maneuvers, they would have priority over the Dodgers.

For much of spring training, the weather was nasty. So the Dodgers usually worked out in the immense field house at West Point, where the click of bat against ball, the thud of ball against wood floor, the whack of ball off the wall reverberated for many hours.

This was a confining way to live. Fresh mountain air and Leo Durocher weren't meant for each other, so Leo would steal away to New York City, just an hour or so down the road. There it was more to his liking than the snow-covered mountains, and for the time being, Rickey put up with his footloose manager.

The war years were a test as well as a demonstration of Leo's managerial skills. Before the 1943 season started, Reiser, Reese, Casey, Lew Riggs, Johnny Rizzo, and Larry French had all entered the military. Three of his four big winners that season were pitchers thirty-five years or older. His entire infield and outfield was at least thirty-one years old.

Fat Freddie Fitzsimmons, who was forty-one years old, was considered a starter. So was the thirty-seven-year-old Johnny Allen. By contrast, everyone in the Cardinals lineup was under thirty. And only one pitcher—just one—was over thirty. No wonder the Cards won the pennant by a whopping 18 games over the Reds, with the Dodgers finishing third, 23½ games behind. Leo's club slumped to 81 victories. And he had to contend with a bunch of no-names, so for the first time, he regularly platooned players, that way getting the most out of them. He would bring in a lefty pitcher for a lefty batter, figuring that, among bad players, it's better to have the best matchup possible. Not too many years later, Casey Stengel rode to the Hall of Fame with his platooning of the Yankees—although Casey was blessed with players with skills from both sides of the plates, and with *good* left-handed and right-handed pitchers.

Leo made an uncharacteristic foray into social politics at the height of war fervor. He told a reporter that there was a "gentleman's agreement" among the owners not to hire black ballplayers.

This was too much for Judge Landis. He immediately called in

Durocher and then issued a statement that no such agreement or understanding existed. Leo's sense of fair play—really, just human decency—in this controversial sphere was to surface again after some years. It's easy from another perspective to say, "What's the big deal? Of course baseball should be integrated." But it wasn't so easy for the people whose salaries were being paid to be outspoken about it—especially since they had been brought up in a society that kept black and white from playing together. Indeed, it was against the law in many of the places Durocher had played and managed. But Leo's sense of social justice seemed paradoxical for a man who could be against the right to join a union.

In 1943, Leo faced the most serious player conflagration of his young managerial career: a team revolt. By July of that season, tempers were becoming worn. There was no heat of a pennant race—just summer heat. The Dodgers were out of it. This wasn't the same team. Camilli was slumping and was about to be traded to the Giants. Medwick already had been sold to the Giants. Making deals with those guys across the East River indicated that Rickey had given up on the season and was doing his traditional trading of aged stars.

Anger had been bubbling to the surface easily. There was the time Billy Herman was batting as the cleanup hitter because there was no one else. Herman's days as a long-ball hitter were over, even though he hit for average. In a game against the Giants, he came up with the bases loaded, Dodgers trailing. He got to 2–0 in the count, a perfect hitter's situation. Dressen, coaching third, flashed the "take" sign. Herman was stunned, but took the pitch, a strike. Then the count went to 3–1 and again Dressen flashed the "take" sign, presumably sent from the dugout by Leo. At 3–2 Herman swung and whacked a line drive to third that was converted into a double play that ended the inning.

Seething, Herman went back to his position at second base. Before the Giants got up, the ball was tossed around for infield practice. When it rolled to him, Herman snapped. He looked in the Dodger dugout and saw Leo there, looking at the dugout steps. Herman took the ball and flung it toward the dugout. It bounced once—and caromed off Leo's head. Al Glossop (whose .171 average was the lowest of any batter with two hundred appearances that season) looked over from shortstop and said to Herman, "Goddamn, you hit Leo between the eyes."

"That's just what I wanted to do," shot back Herman.

Herman was certain he'd be fined. But Leo never said a word.

The midsummer revolt had typical Leo overtones: confusion, denial, charges, countercharges, and ass covering. First, Leo suspended pitcher Bobo Newsom for three days because Bobo had blown up and popped off about a missed third strike by part-time catcher Bobby Bragan, who was one of Leo's favorites. Newsom had thrown a spitter that Bragan couldn't handle. After the game, with Newsom complaining, Leo claimed that he was trying to show up Bragan.

The story was written up by Tom Meany of the *Telegram*, but Durocher claimed it wasn't true, insisting he suspended Newsom for not following his orders on how to pitch to Vince DiMaggio. Leo had told Newsom "high and inside," but DiMaggio had doubled to left. Durocher yelled it wasn't inside enough. Newsom called Durocher a liar.

The day after the suspension, the players threatened to walk out before the game at Ebbets Field against the Pirates. In a remarkable scene, Durocher invited the reporters to a locker room meeting with his team. The club had come unraveled when Arky Vaughan appeared in the doorway of Durocher's clubhouse office thirty minutes before the game was to start. "Here's another uniform you can have," he said. Durocher leapt to his feet and began shouting at Vaughan. "I don't know what this is about," Leo insisted, "but if you feel that way about it, keep it off!"

Durocher was shocked when his old Gashouse Gang buddy, Medwick, sided with Vaughan. Within weeks, Leo got rid of Medwick. He went to the Giants, and in 1944 punched out a .337 average.

Durocher, trying to quell the rebellion, brought in his players from infield practice and called newspapermen inside. Meany wasn't there. He was off that day because the paper didn't print a Sunday edition, so he couldn't defend his Bobo Newsom story.

Vaughan interrupted Leo's explanation. "But you said you were suspending Bobo indefinitely and that it would be for the season if you could make it stick."

In fact, Leo had said to reporters that Newsom "seemed to think he had become Judge Landis, Mr. Baseball himself," and that Bobo had persistently ignored his instructions on how to pitch to certain batters. Durocher said, "The suspension resulted from my questioning him on how he had pitched to Vince DiMaggio yesterday when DiMaggio doubled to left. Nobody can talk to me like that and get away with it," said Leo.

Dixie Walker was the first player to speak up in favor of Newsom and Vaughan. "If what was printed in the papers is true," he said quietly, "here's another uniform you can have."

"That makes two men!" Durocher barked, as if daring others to come forth.

"I don't see why this boy," said Walker, nodding toward Vaughan, "should suffer, and if he's out, I guess I'm out, too."

Durocher then heatedly denied he had suspended Vaughan, although he had in fact said, "You're suspended too," when Vaughan left his office. Durocher yelled at Walker, "He quit! He turned in his uniform and told me what I could do with it. I didn't suspend him."

In this incredible scene, Leo was once again denying what everybody else knew was the truth. And once again, it was other people who were lying. Not Leo. Never Leo.

Outside, the umpires were looking for the Dodgers to get on the field, as was everyone else in the park. The umps sent a clubhouse assistant in to get them out. The assistant told Durocher the umpires were on the field and that it was game time. Durocher announced: "Well, let's see if we've got nine men to put on the field. If we haven't we'll just forfeit the game."

Then he took out the lineup card and began, from the top, asking each man, before checking his name off, if he wanted to play. When Leo got to Vaughan, who already was in his street clothes, the player said no. Everyone else said yes. Vaughan and Newsom watched the game from the right field stands near the bullpen. Later in the game Vaughan returned to the locker room and suited up after Rickey went out to talk to him. The Dodgers overwhelmed the Pirates, 23–6.

The next day, the players upheld Meany, who had returned to the park. At another team meeting, with eleven baseball writers present, Durocher sat on a trunk, his arms folded defiantly, "kicking his heels against the side of the trunk," it was described. Durocher admitted the real reasons behind the suspension. That day, at a secret meeting, he also told players he was considering resigning. He had lost control of the team. But some of the older players, and coaches, got him to change his mind.

Two days later, Newsom—with his 9–4 record in half a season—was traded to the Browns. Rickey had sided with Leo in the first serious crisis for his manager. It was a vote of confidence. (It seemed an odd coincidence that no one else in the National League was interested in Newsom and that he was waived without a nibble. The good old "gentleman's agreement" among the club owners appeared to be in effect.)

After the deal was done, Rickey was at home in bed with indigestion, but he called the reporters around him to hold a bedside press conference. "Durocher has not resigned, won't resign, in my opinion, and, if he did, I would not accept his resignation." And he added, "Nobody can run a club for a manager, no president, no public."

The oddity of the situation wasn't over.

While Rickey was at it, he told the assembled reporters at his bedside that better things were ahead for the Dodgers. "We are at the moment engaged in the development of a vast, expensive farm system," he intoned. "Twenty-thousand letters have been sent to high school coaches all over the country, and ten percent have answered, with recommendations of young players. It's a tremendous undertaking. Yes, we're building for the future and if the war is over within two years, we expect wonderful results."

On Leo's home front, marriage number two was ending. He and Grace separated in August. It wasn't his only legal battle. A federal court in Missouri was trying to get back income tax payments from Leo for 1938 and 1939. Grace, meanwhile, filed suit in St. Louis, alleging Leo was "constantly of a nagging disposition; was possessed of a very uneven temperament and has grown very cold and indifferent." Also, she charged, he denounced her in "profane and abusive language." Further, Durocher was squandering his earnings in long-distance automobile and airplane trips. She later learned these "business" trips were "pleasure jaunts." Leo filed a general denial of the charges. The divorce was granted in October; she asked for no alimony, and securities were jointly divided. The couple had no children.

Grace Dozier died in 1987 at the age of eighty-five. Her obituary said she retired in 1976, when she was almost seventy-five years old. Her only survivor was Nellie, a daughter from a marriage before her one to Leo.

That same year, 1943, was Leo's first miserable wartime season. Camilli slumped late in the campaign, was traded to the Giants, and refused the deal. He went home to California to sulk. Leo mopped up the year with Rickey-acquired retreads such as Paul Waner,

Johnny Cooney, and Frenchy Bordagaray, the latter two remembrances from Stengel's Dodger era.

And then, coinciding with his marital divorce, came his first divorce from the Dodgers: He was unconditionally released. This was as much a bookkeeping move as a slap in the face, for salary cutting was behind Rickey's double-talk. And Leo had his defenders. "Branch Rickey believes," said the wonderfully cynical Dan Parker in the *Mirror*, "there should be no limit on salaries—provided they are paid to a club president."

Not at all, contended Rickey: "My reason for this move is to give Durocher an opportunity to accept any other position, in the movie industry or other managerial berth that might be tendered him."

"Leo knows his number is up," speculated sportswriter Tim Cohane. And there was speculation that Burt Shotton might take over, even though Shotton was more than sixty years old.

No, Leo was indeed coming back. Still, the *Times* cautioned that despite a new contract, "it may not be quite the Leo of old." Perhaps he would be chastened now, and perhaps that would inhibit his daring managerial style.

Instead of an odd player contract, Leo was given a manager's contract. But this new deal was in its way just as unusual: Either side could terminate it at any time. If so, his salary would immediately stop. Once more Leo was not even guaranteed his full year's salary, a security blanket every other manager in baseball enjoyed.

The new deal was estimated at $30,000, but matters "far more serious" weighed in the negotiations, according to Rickey. The most significant was Leo's loss of control of players during the summer. Leo said he didn't think he'd have any problems "except for one man." That was an allusion to Dixie Walker. But there were other players who also didn't like Leo, notably Herman, Vaughan, Owen, and outfielder Augie Galan.

It was not a secret that Rickey was concerned about professional gamblers associating with players and Leo. At this point, though, Leo apparently was marching the straight and narrow. And anyway, Rickey knew with this collection of performers, no one could do much with the Dodgers. They weren't going to catch his old Cardinals. In fact, they were to catch no one except the last-place Phillies, now managed by Leo's old pal, Freddie Fitzsimmons.

Leo was facing the 1944 season without pitching. The big winner, forty-year-old Curt Davis, produced 10 triumphs. It was to be Leo's first losing season in his managerial career. Things were going to be so bad this year, Rickey knew, that the old man asked Leo, who would be thirty-nine years old in July, to play at short once in a while. Pee Wee Reese was in the Navy and Kirby Higbe and Billy Herman also were in the armed forces.

No matter. This was war and everybody had to do his bit without complaining. Leo invited a bunch of writers and photographers to his apartment at 46 East Sixty-first Street, just off Madison Avenue. There, attired in baby blue silk pajamas and a white dressing gown, he announced the Dodgers would try their best this season. "I could play a dozen games at short," he announced. When Rickey saw the story, he called Leo and told him that wasn't enough.

Leo was to use half a dozen players at short. He had gargantuan Howie Schultz at first, he had starters named Rube Melton and Hal Gregg. The pitching staff issued 660 walks, an average of more than 4 a game, and almost 100 more than the second worst team. That number ranked as the greatest walk total in league history until the Dodgers of 1946 broke the mark by 11.

The big addition to the club was a fellow named Eddie Stanky, obtained after the season from the Cubs. His teammates included Bordagaray, described as playing third base like Al Schacht ("the Clown Prince of Baseball"), and Ben Chapman, once an American League outfield star who went to the minors and returned to the majors—as a pitcher. Then there was sixteen-year-old Tommy Brown, another shortstop. He wanted to be DiMaggio. He stood at the plate with a similar wide stance and held the bat back and high. He even wore number 5. Brown also had been a Flatbush legend by belting 60 "homers" over screens at a batting range.

The kid hit a home run the next year and, as was the custom, Red Barber rolled a carton of the sponsor's cigarettes, Old Gold, down the screen for the lucky batter. Durocher quickly took it away, explaining, "He's too young to smoke."

This was all down the road, so to speak, when the Dodgers assembled once again at Bear Mountain early in 1944. The big break— you might say the only break—from the regime was going to the movies in nearby Highland Falls. A team official stood at the entrance along with the theater manager and told him which ones were Dodgers. The players got in for free, but one young player complained, "we ought to get a dime for candy too."

This was the kind of season it was. On April 30, the Dodgers faced the Giants. The Giants won, 26–8, in the first game of a doubleheader as the Brooks issued seventeen walks—the most in the league in forty-one years. Mel Ott walked his first five times up, while in the second inning the Dodgers issued six straight walks.

With all those balls called against his team, Durocher naturally was banished for arguing, but not until the sixth, with his club trailing, 16–7. To make the situation even more ludicrous, Leo argued with all three umpires. He was kicked out simultaneously by all three. Fans booed, pelting him with oranges and apples. And when the game ended, they did the same to the players, though one fan threw a pop bottle that hit Medwick in the groin. He hit the ground and couldn't come out for the second game.

A few days later, Durocher was fined a hundred dollars. Now, this was really too much. He argued with Frick for two and a half hours, bellowing he would not pay the fine.

Late in the season he did more than argue with the umps. He charged their dressing room. That led to a five-day suspension and a hundred-dollar fine. He had been upset after a game in Cincinnati and wanted to chew out Ump Lee Ballanfant.

The next day, Leo attended the game as a "spectator." He sat in a box at field level, four steps from the Brooklyn dugout. Several times he waved his players to different defensive positions. In the ninth, he leaned over the railing so that Stretch Schultz at first would see him waving where he wanted him to play. This enraged manager Bill McKechnie of the Reds, who said after the game that a suspended manager was barred from any directing. The Dodgers had produced a 3–2 victory, which made Leo's directorial moves even more odious.

Leo, of course, begged to differ with McKechnie. Leo, after all, knew the rules. "There is no rule that says a manager has to leave the park when chased by an umpire," contended Leo. Thus, it made perfect sense to him to sit in the stands and manage from there. And when Frick sent him a telegram demanding that he not sit near the dugout, he merely moved down to the third base line to a box seat opposite the dugout.

There were few other lighthearted moments during the season. The bright spot was Walker's league-leading .357 batting average. And he was the guy Leo had wanted to get rid of. There were brief, spotty relief appearances by an eighteen-year-old college boy named Ralph Branca. But the staff overall was perhaps the worst since the bad old Dodger days. Its earned run average of 4.68 was by far the most horrendous in the majors.

As if the off-season wasn't bad enough—what memories were there to reflect on?—District Attorney Frank S. Hogan made a blockbuster announcement that he was investigating a charge that Leo's apartment had been used for a crooked dice game by none other than actor George Raft. The charges came to light in November, but the deed had been done on March 24. Supposedly, a wealthy airplane parts manufacturer was victimized at Leo's apartment when Raft rolled thirteen consecutive passes—an astronomical number of successful rolls. The loser was one Martin Shurin, Jr., president of Hudson Aircraft Company.

Shurin didn't learn about the supposed crooked dice scam until almost eight months later, and only because the wife of one of the players got angry at her husband, whom she found embracing a blonde. She called Shurin and told him that the dice had been loaded and that her husband had been in on the scheme. Raft reportedly rolled four 4s, four 10s, and five 9s.

Leo, however, wasn't in the apartment at the time; he was at West Point supervising the team's spring training. But he had lent a friend the key to the apartment. That friend probably was Raft, for Durocher virtually lived in Raft's place whenever he visited Los Angeles. The D.A.'s people, while investigating Raft, claimed Leo didn't know about any crooked game, or even that his apartment had been used for crap shooting.

According to the D.A., the evening had begun at Raft's apartment in the Sherry-Netherland Hotel at Fifty-ninth Street and Fifth Avenue. Raft had invited over nine men and three women. They had dinner at the hotel, then Raft said they would hold the game at Durocher's apartment, where the group would be less conspicuous than in a hotel. A couple of Raft's buddies, Broadway characters who were gamblers and racetrack touts, brought the dice and handed them to Raft.

At Leo's apartment, the suave Raft from Hell's Kitchen, known for his slicked-back hair, mobster looks, and mobster clothes, rolled first. Shurin never even got a chance to touch the dice. Within half an hour, Raft had unburdened the sucker of $18,500. Shurin and some of the other men, including the man who cheated on his wife, were "fading" Raft—that is, betting he couldn't make his point.

Raft's first roll produced Little Joe—a 4. That is a hard point to
make and the odds are 2–1 against. But Raft rolled two of the 4s the
most unlikely way—with a pair of deuces. Then Raft rolled Big Dick—
a 10. The odds against repeating also were 2–1. He made them, too,
including a pair the hard way, with paired 5s.

Shurin had $3,500 in cash. He forked it over to Raft but still was
$15,000 short, so he wrote the actor a check. Some of the other
gamblers ostensibly turned over their money to Raft as well, including
the blonde's husband, who said he lost $8,600. All this losing put a
damper on the evening, and the game broke up.

Shurin, who lived on Park Avenue, didn't hear anything more
about the game until the shill's angry wife called him in October.
"You thought it was a straight game, but the dice were loaded," she
told him. She explained she was suing for divorce and wanted to set
Shurin straight. She added that when the game was over, her husband
had handed her $600 and said, " 'Go buy yourself a fur coat or some-
thing.' And then I found him with that blonde!"

Leo always maintained he knew nothing about the gambling
in his place, and soon he no longer was the focus of the criminal
investigation. But baseball didn't forget, especially the new commissioner, Happy Chandler, who had taken over following the death
of Judge Landis. Chandler had been in the job only a few months
when the Raft-Durocher gambling story broke. Gambling was the
dirty word that had brought Landis to baseball. It was why there
even was a commissioner. And now, the most visible manager
in the game was connected with the dirty deed. For Leo, it was
Strike One according to Chandler, whose arm was poised to signal
Strike Two.

Not too long before the crap game in his apartment, Leo was
engaged in a somewhat more altruistic activity. He was on a USO
tour with another Hollywood buddy and one of his best friends, Danny
Kaye. (How might Leo have reacted almost fifty years later when
Kaye, the antic actor–comedian from Brooklyn, was revealed as Sir
Laurence Olivier's lover?) It was a three-week tour for the troops just
before springtime. At McDill Field in Tampa, five thousand soldiers
jammed into a makeshift open-air theater. For two and a half hours
the pair entertained them. While Leo was resting, soldiers started
to chant, "We want Durocher! We want Durocher!"

They visited seventeen camps in three weeks, doing from two
to five shows a day. They also appeared at hospitals. Leo was nervous

about these visits. "What can I ask these kids, 'How ya feelin?' " he said to the commanding officer at one hospital.

Also before the 1945 season, Leo, Medwick (then of the Giants), and Nick Etten (the Yankees' catcher) toured Italy for the USO. They met ten thousand troops at a racetrack below Naples built by Mussolini. Tom Meany, the writer, was on the tour and described Leo having the soldiers "roaring with laughter" at his umpire stories. Meany also marveled at Leo's quick-learning intelligence. In Italy, Durocher told an officer he'd like to take home a Beretta pistol as a souvenir. The lieutenant showed Leo how to strip it. Leo asked him to do it again, and then promptly repeated the difficult process himself without a hitch.

Leo still had the show business itch when he returned to New York. From his Bear Mountain spring training retreat, he once escaped after two innings of a game to keep a commitment on New York radio. Leo was heard regularly on such shows as the immensely popular *Duffy's Tavern*. Ed Garner, who played Archie the manager, described himself and Leo as "ham and tongue." Leo also was characterized by one of the characters, Miss Duffy, as "a very verbose guy who besides talks too much." Everyone in the national radio audience knew exactly what the allusions were—everyone knew Durocher.

Rickey continually admonished Leo on these extra activities. But one night, when Leo had gone to a rehearsal for a radio show, Branch snapped. He was looking for Leo on an important matter and discovered he wasn't around. Immediately, Rickey surrounded himself with the writers and said of Leo, in a frigid tone, "There must be an election of activities."

An election of activities. Had any manager before or since ever been told in quite this way to stop fooling around?

Before the Dodgers' next exhibition, Leo issued this statement: "I will not make any more radio commitments that interfere with managing the Dodgers. The next time I appear on a radio program it will probably be only after approval by Branch Rickey."

Branch Rickey, Jr., said, "Leo is Dad's favorite reclamation project." Branch sought to humanize Leo, to acculturate him, to soften him. Branch even taught card-shark Leo how to play the more civilized game of bridge, and since there was little else to do in the Bear Mountain evenings except go to the free movie in town (and slip into New York to do a radio show or the town), Leo and his mentor often played the game. But Leo didn't like to play by the rules, or at least the conventions. He simply refused to accede to his partners' bids or responses, which are mandatory.

In one memorable game with Rickey as his partner, the Mahatma bid "four no-trump," the famed Blackwood Convention. It called for Leo to indicate how many aces he had. A response was mandatory.

"I pass," said Leo. "Judas Priest," bellowed Rickey. "You can't."

They argued, and called in an expert, who upheld Rickey.

"What do you know about bridge anyway," growled Leo to the expert.

"You shouldn't be allowed to play bridge," groaned Rickey. "You should *not* be allowed to play bridge."

The 1945 season may have been the bottom of the barrel for finding players in baseball. One of Leo's coaches, Clyde Sukeforth, even caught a few games at the age of forty-three. He had not caught since 1939.

Rickey was so distressed at the talent that he saw in training camp, he offered Leo a thousand dollars if he played the first fifteen games, just to get the season started. The thing was, Rickey wanted him at second. He was contemplating trading Stanky to pick up a catcher and had just been stunned to learn that Owen had suddenly sold all his cattle and enlisted in the service. Meanwhile, Bobby Bragan was about to be inducted.

In these circumstances, with attention diverted overseas, Rickey thought the time might be ripe for giving black ballplayers a Dodger tryout. What was there to lose? So on April 7 at Bear Mountain, a pitcher named Terris McDuffie, who was thirty-two, along with Claude Crocker, a nineteen-year-old rookie with Montreal, showed their stuff. "McDuffie has good control but he does not follow through on any delivery. It might take considerable time before he broke that habit," said Rickey.

And Leo added, "I would not be interested in a thirty-two-year-old player who never has played in professional baseball." The incident carried no significant weight in newspaper accounts. It was almost as if the Dodgers were announcing a new starting time. But events were heading toward something more than a workout for black ballplayers and Brooklyn.

That season also symbolized another change for Brooklyn: For the first time since 1924, the team was in the hands of club owners instead of executors. In 1944, Rickey, John L. Smith, head of the Pfizer Chemical Company, and Walter O'Malley, a corporation lawyer, purchased the stock from the Ed McKeever estate, which owned 25 percent. Then in 1945, the group bought 50 percent of the stock held by the Charles H. Ebbets estate. That sale—for half the Dodgers—went for $750,000.

About this time, Tom Meany, writing for the New York *Telegram*, popularized Rickey's nickname, the Mahatma. Meany got the idea from a best-selling book of the time, John Gunther's *Inside Asia*, in which Mahatma Gandhi was described as "a combination of God, your own father, and Tammany Hall." Meany did not, however, come up with a nickname for O'Malley, who would be called many names some years later when the unthinkable happened and the Dodgers left Brooklyn.

If Rickey sighed deeply and blustered over Leo's transgressions, O'Malley would not be so lenient. He was not amused by Leo's antics. The beginning of the end of Leo's Dodger career was about to unfold. Typically, it lasted years.

No one event defined Durocher's bullying—some would call it cowardice—as much as the famed assault case in 1945, when he ganged up with a beefy special cop on a young fan who had been heckling the Dodgers. It was early June, and Leo's boys were contenders following their seventh-place finish of the year before.

The fan, John Christian, had been a star athlete at Thomas Jefferson High School before the war. "Jeff" was a defining monument of the East New York section of Brooklyn, where immigrants and their children lived, often packed together in four-story walk-ups and attached two-family frame houses. It then was a beacon of the American dream—many of the students would go on to attend college.

Christian was a returning war veteran, who had suffered a knee injury in a glider accident and been medically discharged. The five-foot-eleven-inch two hundred pounder was sitting with another East New York hero, Dutch Garfinkel, a former Jefferson basketball star who had become a famed player at St. John's University (in fact, in 1992, he was inducted into the New York City Basketball Hall of Fame). The Dodgers were batting early in the game, and there was a close play that favored the Phillies. Durocher did his usual storming-out-of-the-dugout act. Sitting in the upper stands behind third base, Christian laughed and called down, "Leo, you're a crook." He also called him a bum and yelled that he was trying to steal the game. It was unclear whether Durocher could even hear him. But Joe Moore, a special cop, could.

Moore was a stereotype of a movie cop, and big and fat, maybe 280 pounds. He was famous for his enjoyment of catching kids sneaking into Ebbets Field and booting them out. He was, in fact, somewhat of a legend for his way of meting out immediate justice to trespassers.

Christian enjoyed the bantering, and then sat back to watch the game. He was surprised, though, at the end of the sixth inning when the burly Moore, who had been with the Dodgers more than twenty years, went over to his seat and asked him to come to the clubhouse.

His friend, Dutch Garfinkel, now a retired teacher still living in Brooklyn, recalls what happened: "I had a weekend pass, and a couple of the guys decided to go to the ball game. One of the guys was Johnny Christian. We were sitting upstairs in the grandstand behind third base. Johnny always had a strong voice—his voice could carry for two, three blocks. And he started to heckle the Dodgers. He was heckling the ballplayers and Durocher.

"The Dodgers dugout was behind first base, which was across from us, so we could see in the dugout. He was heckling the dugout and Durocher.

"But one thing I want you to know. He did not use any curse words, any profanity, because if he did I would have walked away from him. I would have been embarrassed.

"After a while I said to him, 'Johnny, why don't you cut it out and let's watch the game? It's not nice.' And he said, 'What do you mean, Dutch? I'm not using any profanity. I'm just heckling.'

"Meanwhile, Durocher sticks his head out of the dugout and Johnny really lets him have it. A couple of innings later a couple of security guards come walking to us and they ask him to come down, that Leo Durocher wants to talk to him.

"I said, 'Johnny, you better not go down. You don't know what will happen.'

"He said, 'What can happen? I'll meet Durocher.'

"I walked down with him. But then when I got to the gate where the players go in, I was kept outside. I remember going to a candy store after the game, across the street from the bleacher entrance. I was waiting there and Johnny came out and I said, 'What happened, Johnny?'

"He said, 'I'd better go to the hospital. I think he broke my jaw.'

" 'What do you mean?' I asked.

"He said, 'Durocher hit me. They punched me and Durocher broke my jaw.'

"He ended up in Kings County Hospital. His jaw was wired for a month or two."

Christian claimed that when he went downstairs with Moore, Durocher, scowling, met him in the areaway near the clubhouse and said, "You've got a mother, how'd you like to call her names?"

And then—wham—Moore whacked Christian with what was described as "a black weapon." In one report, Moore used brass knuckles, which then were used by Leo. Whatever happened, Christian was down and tried to get up, but Durocher took the "weapon" out of Moore's hand and smacked him with it.

The next day Durocher and Moore were brought before Christian's hospital bed, where he identified them. They were released on a thousand-dollar bail set by Judge Samuel S. Leibowitz, a celebrity judge who had become noted in the 1930s as the lawyer for the Scottsboro Boys, the Southern blacks accused of rape.

Naturally, Leo's version, which he was to offer in a magazine story many years later, was, of course, somewhat different. The way Leo told it, Christian had a booming voice "that could be heard all over the park." Worst of all, midway though the game, he started to yell, "Hey, Durocher, how much are they paying you to throw the game?"

Durocher claims he asked Moore to bring the young man around to meet him. Then Moore left the two of them alone. Durocher says he objected to being called a crook. When the lecture ended, claims Leo, he started to leave and walked up some steps to the dugout. But at that point, Christian said, "Leo, it still goes."

Leo says he jumped down the steps and headed for Christian. But Christian "slipped on some wet cement and broke his jaw."

In the *Post* of June 12, there was a familiar headline with a new twist: "DUROCHER'S BASEBALL CAREER JEOPARDIZED BY ASSAULT CASE."

Rickey kept mum, but his secretary said he was "satisfied" no blow was struck and the victim fell—the line put out by Durocher and Moore. If he fell, he suffered not only the broken jaw and head injuries, but somehow managed to give himself a black eye as well.

Two days later, Rickey was at a Rotary Club luncheon, one of those obligatory civic affairs that ballplayers used to routinely be part of before they separated themselves from the community. Rickey turned to the players and apologized for "any negligence on the part of the management in not protecting you from any unfair remarks from the stands."

In other words, Leo's actions were hardly the point. You just can't go around yelling at ballplayers and their manager. At least, that was the message the Mahatma proferred for his ongoing reclamation project.

The case never went to trial. Christian settled privately for about $7,000.

"As far as the settlement, Danny Kaye got involved," recalls Garfinkel. Danny Kaye was an East New York product himself, having grown up a few blocks from Jefferson. "Danny lived on Bradford and Sutter. He was a very close friend of Leo Durocher. He also knew Johnny Christian. Danny tried to iron things out. There was a settlement."

But that didn't mollify Happy Chandler. Years later, reflecting on the case, he said, "If ever there was a miscarriage of justice . . . this was it. They didn't fool me at all, of course. I knew how crazy they were in Brooklyn about their ball team."

The commissioner was right about them being crazy in Brooklyn about their team. This crazy:

On the Fourth of July, Babe Herman returned. Herman was such a piece of Dodger nostalgia he went back to Wilbert Robinson's day. Fourteen years after his last appearance in Brooklyn—and eight years removed from major league ball—the forty-two-year-old was back. In his first at-bat he brought back daffiness baseball: He hit a long single to right and, admiring it as he headed for first, tripped over the bag. He scrambled back on his hands and knees, barely beating the throw that would have tagged him out.

In that doubleheader against the Reds, the Dodgers retained a 3½-game first-place lead over the Cubs. It wasn't easy. In the opener, Brooklyn outfielder Luis Olmo was called out on strikes by Dusty Boggess. Olmo heaved his bat at the ump, which prompted Ump Conlan at third to toss out Olmo.

The next inning Leo argued violently with Boggess on a ball Leo claimed was foul. Seeing their Leo really getting into it, fans tossed bottles and fruit.

Fan behavior (after all, Leo was their model) also figured on a Ladies' Day in August against the Cubs, who were still battling the Dodgers for the pennant. It was a crucial game, and it had a dramatic ending. The Dodgers went into the bottom of the ninth trailing, 4–1. They produced 2 runs and the fans were standing and going nuts. With two out, Walker hit a slow grounder, sped for first and, in the opinion of everyone in the stands, beat the throw. But Umpire Tom Dunn called him out. Game over.

They streamed out of the stands. One newspaper report indicated "hundreds of fans" surrounded the ump. A dozen Dodgers certainly did, shouting and pleading. Walker flung his cap at the "out" call, as did Stanky, and Durocher charged from the dugout. When special cops finally got the crowd off the field and the Dodgers back into their dugout, Dunn stalked after Leo. But Leo, from the dugout steps and in full view of the crowd, took a wet towel and threw it into Dunn's face.

Outside the park, after Dunn made his exit, a woman ran up to a police car and told the officer to "arrest that umpire! He robbed the Dodgers!"

Dunn was too upset to appear at the park the next day. It began a chain of events that led to his resignation. Leo, who had been driven from so many games, had driven the umpire out of the league.

The Dodgers' turnaround wasn't good enough in 1945, although they did finish third. The Cubs, of all teams, won the pennant. They wouldn't finish first again for thirty-nine years, although under Leo, in 1969, they expected to.

A few weeks after the season ended, Jackie Robinson signed a contract to play for Montreal, the Dodgers' top farm team. Rickey said that if his play earned it, then the fleet Robinson would get a chance to play for the Dodgers.

Within days after the season ended, Durocher and his legal intermediary, Danny Kaye, left for Tokyo. The war hadn't been over for two months when they agreed to do a show for the troops. It was at the site that had been planned for the 1940 Olympic Games, which never took place.

A writer who accompanied Leo was impressed with the manager's habits. He observed that, to Durocher, "Cleanliness is an obsession. He never puts back on the underwear or socks he wears to the park. He is constantly hauling clean clothes back and forth. Soaks himself in toilet water. As soon as he enters a room, it smells. He favors pinstripe suits with roll collars. Loves silk. When he went to Japan on a USO trip after the season in 1945, he brought back bolts of silk to make into suits."

If this was a giddy time for America, baseball tried to be a bit more sober. At a meeting later that year, the major league owners turned down the Pacific Coast League's request to become a third major league. Westward expansion was stopping in St. Louis, as far as baseball was concerned. Even night baseball was described by the owners as "this ticklish matter."

But they did concede that the West Coast was "potential major league territory." Ultimately, the Pacific Coast League's request was rejected "for the best interests of the players, since the Coast teams couldn't match the salaries," said the owners. After all, how many people could you draw for a game in Los Angeles?

The Pacific Coast League president, Clarence Rowland, was startled at the reaction of big-time baseball. "The men who control major league baseball are merely postponing the inevitable," he said, and he was right.

With the end of the war, not only servicemen returned home. So did Larry MacPhail—and guess what? He was running the Yankees. Inevitably, as he had in Cincinnati and Brooklyn, he planned to put lights in Yankee Stadium in 1946 and led a fight to set a limit on night games, with no more than a dozen or so.

Baseball was returning to normal, and yet it would never be the same. And Leo? Of course, he was returning, or should be. He had weathered wartime back home and he had kept the Dodgers respectable, except for the lapse in 1944 when the team slumped to seventh.

Leo also had Reiser coming back, too. But the-greatest-player-who-might-have-been had been unable to avoid injury playing ball, even in the Army. During Christmas week, he returned to New York to consult doctors to see if he could return. He had missed three full seasons, and now had an arm injury. The Dodgers' other returning servicemen included people named Gil Hodges, Pee Wee Reese, Rex Barney, Kirby Higbe, Gene Mauch, Hugh Casey, Gene Hermanski, Cookie Lavagetto, Eddie Miksis.

Rickey not only was juggling all this newly returned talent in spring training in Daytona Beach, he and the rest of organized baseball were faced with a raid from South of the Border: the Mexican League. It claimed Mickey Owen—who promptly was banned from American baseball for five years by Commissioner Chandler. One afternoon at the park, Rickey confronted a scout for the Mexicans. "Assassin of careers!" Rickey bellowed.

Meanwhile, during spring training, Jackie Robinson had to stay at a nearby hotel, the only player in camp who did not live with the other ballplayers. He made the daily round-trip by himself.

Leo spent a minimal amount of time observing Robinson, who was not about to be coming to the major leagues in 1946. Indeed, in its now infamous editorial, *The Sporting News*—the baseball bible and, at the time, Establishment mouthpiece—claimed, "Robinson, at twenty-six, is reported to possess baseball abilities which, if he were white, would make him eligible for a trial with, let us say, the Brooklyn Dodgers' Class B farm at Newport News, if he were six years younger."

Leo did have a good firsthand look at a darkly handsome, strong-armed young outfielder named Carl Furillo. He was a brooding presence, rock-strong, and impressed Durocher with his all-round abilities. Still, Rickey believed the team was yet a season away from being a force in the pennant race.

In spring training, before more modern sensibilities, there were always the obligatory cheesecake photos of players' wives sitting around the pool. But the manager's girlfriend?

Leo is pictured in the sports pages of the defunct tabloid the *Mirror* for late March with one Edna Ryan of Brooklyn at spring training. The lovebirds had met in 1945 during his USO tour of Italy. She was variously described as a show girl and starlet. But there was nothing improper about this young woman in her early twenties seen cavorting with forty-year-old Leo. Why, she even brought her mother along to spring training.

Leo was also looking beyond baseball in other areas. He signed to do a radio show on Sunday afternoons once the season ended. This was no rookie entertainer. Leo had done more than make guest appearances as a loudmouthed umpire baiter. He had been on the prestigious *Information Please* and *The Fred Allen Show*. His new program was designed with a Q-and-A format, with Leo responding to write-in questions. The sponsor was Chimney Sweep, a soot remover.

Doing radio was almost easier than playing exhibition games against the Dodgers' top farm team, the Montreal Royals of the International League. The South was in a dither over Robinson's presence. Once, the Royals showed up for an exhibition game in Jacksonville and found the ballpark locked. Even the Giants, who trained in Miami, were distressed before a game. They feared the Dodgers would bring along Robinson. Not only was it illegal for blacks and whites to appear together, black spectators were forbidden to attend unless they sat in special sections.

In mid-March, Robinson and another black player, John Wright, on the Royals performed against the Dodgers. It was described as the first time blacks had played with whites in the South. It happened in Daytona Beach, and it was such a singular event that Commissioner Chandler attended. Of course, since it was a Sunday, Rickey was not present.

However, the story in the *Times* noted it was "unlikely" Robinson would make the Montreal team in 1946.

Spurred by Leo, the Dodgers generated a terrific 1946, with only one "stopper" on the pitching staff, no slugging, first base, third base, and catching being shared by whoever was hottest, and an attack based on drawing walks and stealing bases. Yet, the Brooks were to finish tied with the powerful Cardinals and force the first playoff in baseball history.

Oh yes. The Dodgers benefited mightily by the Mexican raids. For Max Lanier, a Dodger killer who also was 6–0 (all complete-game victories), suddenly jumped the Cards in June. So did Fred Martin, who was 2–1. Eddie Dyer, in his first year as manager, found he had a fight on his hands. This was not going to be a Cardinal walkover.

Leo had another nice surprise that month. The old hometown was honoring him. It was to be an all-day affair on June 17, feted by the West Springfield Lions Club. Everyone still remembers it. They named the ball field in his honor. Later he stood on the stage of the West Springfield Auditorium talking, telling baseball stories as only he could.

Then he shifted. "A lot of people claim credit for discovering me," he said. "But there was one man who forced me to become a baseball player. This man worked at the same bench with me at Wico Electric, making batteries. It was nice steady work, and for a young fellow, I thought I was doing pretty good. But not David Redd.

"I'd come to work on a Monday and he'd say, 'Leo, you're spending your life in a shop like this when you could be out playing ball for a living?'

"I'd come in on a Tuesday and he'd say, 'You play better ball than most of the shortstops in that Eastern League, but you're just afraid to try.'

"I'd come in on a Wednesday, and he'd say to me, 'Trouble with you Leo is that you just don't believe in yourself.'

"This went on day after day and week after week. He nagged me. And he encouraged me to believe that some day I'd be one of the greatest shortstops that ever lived. He challenged me to go out and prove that he was right in his judgment. And finally to keep my self-respect, I had to quit my job and play professional baseball because he forced me to."

Leo looked down at the huge assemblage and said, "So come on up here, Dave, and shake my hand."

Somewhat shyly, Redd, the amiable black co-worker, went up to the stage and Leo put his arms around him.

Going back to the roots obviously touched Leo. He called the naming of the field as "the greatest thrill of my life."

Back on the field, Leo was anything but humble. There was a pennant to be won.

Getting a complete game out of a pitcher in 1946 was not something Leo expected. In that era of the complete-game pitcher, the Dodgers had only 52, worst in the league except for the last-place Giants. In this particular game, Higbe was beating the Cubs, 2–0. But Higbe was tiring. It was getting dark as the Dodgers came to bat, and if the Cubs could be prevented from getting their turn, the Dodgers would win.

"I'm going to start a rhubarb!" Leo announced on the bench. He screamed toward the Cubs' catcher Mickey Livingston, as Stanky got up to bat, "Stay up there long enough, Eddie, and that bum Livingston will call for the wrong pitch."

Livingston looked over to Leo.

"Yeah, you!" snarled Durocher. "They didn't even use you until the race was over last year. They wouldn't take a chance with a bum like you."

Livingston tossed his mask away and charged the bench, but umpire Beans Reardon shouted at Livingston to get back. Then Livingston and Reardon were screaming at each other. That miffed Charlie Grimm, the Cubs' manager, who stalked out wanting to know why his guy was being berated when it was the Lip that had started it all.

They fought until dark. The game was called. The Dodgers won.

"The old man may not like my methods," Durocher said, speaking of Rickey to club secretary Harold Parrott later, "but he likes to win and we won the game, didn't we?"

It was moments like this that prompted an admiring Stanky to give his manager the nickname Leo the Lion. He was always roaring about something, right or wrong. His theory was speak faster and louder and the chances are good you'll get away with it.

Such as his run-ins with Bob Broeg. Broeg knew Leo for fifty years and almost came to blows with him twice. Not bad for a sports columnist and sports editor of the *St. Louis Post-Dispatch*. Broeg recalls the first time he almost got punched. It was 1939 and he had just started working for the Cardinals:

"I was a young PR kid out of college. I was a temporary, getting twenty dollars a week. I was hired the day after Bing Devine was appointed general manager, and he was getting sixty-five dollars a month.

"The Cards used to give free passes, and free broadcasting, in exchange for radio announcements about the game—who was going to pitch, who they were going to play. Who was going to pitch was very important in Dizzy Dean's era. Of course, he was gone by then. But for some reason or other Leo felt that Ray Blades, who succeeded Frisch as manager, was taking advantage of inside information. So I went to Leo to ask who was going to pitch for the Dodgers and Leo was in a huff and said he'd take it out on me, which was typical of Leo.

"Leo thought he had the upper hand. You had to learn to live with Leo. He wanted to fight you. He kind of jostled me with his spiked shoes, and he kind of bellied up to me so I pushed him away. And then he comes up to me and I made a fist and the trainer, I think his name was Doc White, he jumps in and says, 'Jesus, Leo, you can't fight this kid.' I was bigger than he was and we would have had a pretty good tussle."

By 1946, Broeg had moved to the newspaper and was covering the Cardinals regularly. "The Dodgers came in here, a pivotal series late in the season, and they split a Sunday doubleheader which, with them leading the league, was a plus for them. So I walk into their clubhouse with a couple of other guys and there, straight ahead of us, was Medwick, whom we hadn't seen for a while. So we started toward him and Leo said, his voice that growl, 'Outside you guys, outside.' "

In the next day's paper, one of the writers noted that Durocher had kicked out the Cardinals reporters from the Dodgers dugout but had allowed in one of his show business pals. "I thought they were autograph hounds," Leo lied, when asked why he kept the reporters out.

"So the next night, a Monday night, Leo came through the Cardinals dugout, a shortcut to the visitors dugout, and said to Vernon Tietjen, who was a terrific writer, a Red Smith–type with a lot of salty humor, 'Hey, Teej, where's Toomey?' " Leo was looking for Jim Toomey, one of the St. Louis writers.

"And Tietjen says sarcastically, 'You wouldn't know him, Leo, he's been in the Army four years.' "

Broeg laughs when he recounts that story, recalling the perforated eardrum. "A lot of the guys said he gave it to himself."

In any event, Leo told Tietjen he hadn't known who the writers were the previous evening. "They didn't identify themselves and I threw them out," claimed Leo.

"Well, I jumped up and I said, 'Leo, I was there.' And he said, 'No, you weren't.' I got angry and I said, 'Damnit, Leo, I was there and you threw me out.' He was mad because Toomey had mentioned in his notes that a 'red-haired stooge' allowed Jack Benny to come in after Leo had kicked out the press. The red-haired guy was Harold Parrott. I've got a picture of that argument."

Broeg also recalls Leo's hatred of the Cards: "They rode his butt. Wherever Leo was, he brought out the beast and the best in the Cardinals. He was like waving the red flag. He'd have his pitchers throw at them. He'd get in that dugout and yell, 'Stick it in his ear!' I remember hearing once during the war—I was away, but they told me about it—that pitcher Les Webber purposely knocked Musial down on four straight pitches! That's the only time Musial ever started to the mound. When Stan hit a home run to win the All-Star Game for Leo in the twelfth inning in 1955, Leo kept saying, 'He owed me that one, he owed me that one.' Leo had this fetish. He didn't want Musial to beat him."

By 1946, Musial had been given the nickname the Man by Brooklyn fans. Few superstars ever seemed as self-possessed as Musial. But there is also a side to him that is unforgiving when it comes to Durocher. Musial is one of the former ballplayers who votes for the old-timers in the Hall of Fame. The Man has consistently vetoed Leo's entrance. Ironically, Ted Williams—the great American League slugger to Stan's National League dominance in the same era—has always championed Durocher for the Hall.

Leo had some tools to battle Musial and Company in 1946. He was blessed with Reese's return from the Navy ("he left a boy but returned a man") and with Stanky, who led the league in walks. But the run-making potential wasn't as apparent, and so Leo gave Reiser the green light to try to steal home at will. As a result, Reiser set a major league record of 7 steals of home. Despite the small number of incomplete games—completing only a third of all starts in those days was a handicap—Leo went to his bullpen brilliantly. The relievers' 28 saves were the most in the majors. Remember, starters routinely worked the bullpen. So Higbe, who had made 29 starts, also appeared in relief thirteen times. Joe Hatten added twelve relief appearances to his team-high 30 starts, and Vic Lombardi came out of pen sixteen times while starting twenty-five times. Even the top reliever, Hugh Casey with forty-five appearances, started once.

Leo also employed the squeeze play more than anyone else in 1946. In Reese, he had a marvelous bunter. In Stanky, he had a maestro of bat control, with 137 walks and some at-bats that fans remember to this day. People swore they were there when he fouled off 12 pitches in one appearance. With daring and creativity, the Dodgers managed to score 701 runs, only 11 fewer than the league-leading Cards.

Leo, though, had no patience with youngsters and rookie mistakes. One night a reporter asked him if he planned any changes. Leo was unhappy with the play of Howie Schultz, the gangling first baseman. He went into a tirade against Schultz—who was standing near enough to hear and who went into an even worse slump.

Durocher also was hard on Luis Olmo, which might have prompted him to jump to the Mexican League. Bill Hart, a Southern League infielder, was another youngster who faltered under Leo's withering remarks.

What hurt Leo in 1946, though, were two events beyond his control: Owen's departure for Mexico, and Reiser's continued inability to stop crashing into fences.

Chandler had allowed some Mexican jumpers back in the league when they returned before the season started. The others, ruled Chandler, would be suspended for five years. Owen, though, began playing for the rival league when he was released from the service. The Mexicans were offering him more money than American baseball ever had—the Dodgers were offering him the same salary he had earned before going off to war four years earlier. By August, disappointed and realizing he was losing a major league career, Owen tried to return. Chandler declared that Owen and others who jumped contracts "or otherwise violated their obligations to professional baseball clubs" were suspended five years.

Durocher wouldn't comment on the suspension. But a contrite Owen said, to no avail, "Nothing could induce me to leave the United States again."

It was surprising—or was it?—that Leo should be so silent on the career of one of his players. It was almost as if Leo knew there were some boundaries regarding the commissioner's office he could not cross. Yet, just a few years before he had made headlines by complaining about baseball's policy of segregation.

That doesn't mean Leo wasn't vocal in other ways. In a late-season game, Leo was coaching at third. Dizzy Dean, by now a broadcaster, was doing the radio commentary. This is how Robert Gregory recorded Dean's play-by-play in the book *Diz:* "Leo's runnin' to the plate and he's gonna tell that fella off. Now he's kickin' the dirt and pointin' his finger. I don't know how them Dodgers get the nerve squawkin' about the umparrs the way they do. . . ."

Well, the nerve came from the Lip, of course.

Red Barber recalled that Leo once told him to be more like the Chicago broadcasters, who were out-and-out Cubs rooters. In retrospect, that was sort of funny, for when Leo eventually wound up as the Cubs' manager, what he didn't have were announcers who thought he was flawless.

In any event, the request outraged Barber, who had always thought of himself as an objective reporter. He told Rickey what Leo had asked, and Rickey responded, "If you start doing what Leo wants you to do, he'll get you in more trouble than the commissioner and I together can get you out of."

Leo had whipped his team into first place and it appeared they might actually upset the Cards for the pennant. But Reiser hurt himself badly with only a few days to go in the season. Reiser's hamstring was bothering him and it was heavily taped. He told Leo before the game, "I can play but I can't run." But Leo needed a victory.

Reiser walked in the opening inning against the Phillies' Charley Schanz and limped to first. And then Leo flashed the steal sign! Reiser had to take a longer lead than he would have liked, even against the right-hander. Schanz went into his stretch and then threw a routine pick-off toss to first. Reiser slid back. But his spike caught. "I could hear my ankle crack. Leo came running out. 'Get up,' he was screaming, 'You're all right.' "

Though Durocher put Reiser at risk more than once, Reiser went on to coach for him for years afterward until it became intolerable.

In the final days of the pennant race, the pressure got to both teams. The Dodgers stumbled, while the Cards dropped three of their last six. The Dodgers entered the last day of the season tied with St. Louis. Brooklyn was playing the Braves at Ebbets Field, with their old St. Louis nemesis, Mort Cooper, now pitching for Boston. The Cards were playing the Cubs. Cooper shut out the Dodgers. Listening in their clubhouse to the radio, the Dodgers heard the Cubs win and learned they were going to go into the first playoff in the seventy-one-year history of the National League.

In 1946, Ralph Branca had started 10 games but was used more in relief. "I used to sit on the bench listening to Leo. He used to yell, 'Stick it in his ear!' That was the thing that got the hitters riled. 'Stick it in his ear!' was his favorite expression.

"I used to throw at hitters. I was a lot like Leo. But my one disappointment with Leo was in the 1946 season. I had a 3–1 record, won my last few games [including a shutout over the Cardinals]. But I was hurt earlier in the season and Charlie Dressen, his pitching coach, wanted me to pitch batting practice. Now you've got to realize that back then we didn't have the screen to protect the pitcher. The guys would get eight pitches to hit and they'd say, 'Give me a fastball,' every time. Once in a while, the eighth pitch, they'd say, 'Give me a curve, or a change.' And they'd also whack the ball right back up the middle. Wouldn't think anything of it. I got hit on the butt, and the arm.

"So when I told Charlie I didn't want to pitch batting practice, he put me under his doghouse. I didn't call it being in his doghouse—I was *under* his doghouse. And Leo never said anything to change it.

"Why didn't I talk to Leo about it? In those days, management was God. You didn't argue about those things. You had your pitching coach and he was the guy you had to deal with.

"Down the stretch he started me as a decoy in St. Louis. They put in a left-handed lineup and then he took me out."

Branca, though, was going to be Leo's pitcher for the opening game of the playoffs, a best-of-three series. First, there was the matter of where the series would open. And what happened then may well have altered the course of history five years later.

"It was a mistake—the Dodgers won the coin toss and had the option. They wanted the final two games at home, but what they didn't realize was we had a twenty-two-hour ride to St. Louis by train. The Dodgers opened the series in St. Louis a tired team. They were afraid of playing two games there, so if they opened in St. Louis, they'd have to play only once. Except that trip was a killer, the longest trip we had in those days. You know, the funny thing is, when we won the coin toss for the playoff in 1951 against the Giants, someone reminded Chuck [Dressen was managing the Dodgers then] how we had played the first game on the road in 1946, so we decided to play the first game at home and the next two at the Polo Grounds. Except in 1951, it wasn't like we had to travel to St. Louis if we opened at the Polo Grounds. All you did was cross a river."

The Cards were favored amid a frenzied atmosphere. Leo wasn't doing any decoying this time: "It'll be Ralph Branca and we'll win," said Leo of Game 1.

A playoff was so unusual that no one quite knew how the money thing worked—that is, do the players get paid extra? So the Cards held a meeting the day before to determine payment. Breadon, the skinflint owner who had dismissed Rickey for making too much money, said he would pay them an extra full week's salary.

The Dodgers arrived in their hotel that afternoon, took no work-out, but were typically noisy and jaunty. If anything, they seemed confident. For they knew after the next day's game, they'd be heading back to Brooklyn.

Branca remembers the Cards won the game "on three dinky hits." The score was 4–2, and Joe Garagiola, a .237 batter, touched twenty-year-old Ralph for one of the dinks.

Schultz was the hero in defeat, having belted a homer off Howie Pollet, maybe the league's best pitcher. Schultz also batted in the top of the ninth, down 3 runs, two runners on, one out. He hit a liner to right center. Slaughter cut off the ball. It scored the runner from third, but when Bruce Edwards tried to go from first to third, he was out by plenty. Schultz wound up on second, but was stranded there.

Back in Brooklyn, it didn't go the Dodgers' way either. Leo elected to sit down Schultz because Red Munger, a right-hander, was pitching. Durocher started Joe Hatten.

The Dodgers played miserably. They were held to 1 run and 2 hits (which they had gotten in the first inning) for eight innings. Durocher used six pitchers, who yielded 13 hits. And then in the ninth they routed Cardinal reliever Murry Dickson. They got 3 runs across, loaded the bases, and the tying run was at the plate with Stanky batting. The score was 8–4. Eddie Dyer brought in Harry "the Cat" Brecheen. He struck out Stanky looking. And then with Dick Whitman, a left-handed batter, scheduled to hit, Leo called on his fourth pinch hitter of the day—Howie Schultz.

On a 3–2 pitch, Brecheen threw Schultz a slow screwball. Schultz turned himself into a corkscrew, swinging and missing.

Of course, it wasn't on their minds just then, but the Dodgers had become full-fledged players, and would be perennial contenders, if not pennant winners. They had fully transformed themselves from the Daffiness Boys of yore into a National League power.

As the press, and Rickey, waited outside the locker room, Leo sat inside on a trunk. He had been edgy through the two games, snapping at friends, surrounded by his cronies who seemed to be everywhere. Finally, he ordered the door opened. Rickey was the lead man in, but he was brushed aside by a sharply dressed little fellow who barked, "Just a minute, Pop. Stand back!" Then another man followed the little guy inside.

"Who were they?" Rickey asked his aide, Arthur Mann.

"The first fellow is Killer Gray. He's a bodyguard," said Mann.

And who was he guarding?

"Oh, George Raft," replied Mann.

"Very interesting," said Rickey.

CHAPTER VIII

LEO THE LIP

THE NEXT FEW MONTHS not only were the most turbulent in the life of Leo Durocher, they roiled the Dodgers more than any other off-season in their history. And somewhere out there, Larry MacPhail was part of the story.

MacPhail had seen the stodgy Yankees go through three managers in 1946, his first year back at the helm of a baseball team. First Joe McCarthy, maybe the greatest manager in Yankee history, begged off after 35 games. Then Bill Dickey, the finest catcher the Yankees had, quit with two weeks remaining. And finally Johnny Neun who replaced him, left. Could MacPhail have been the reason for this turmoil? Of course he was. MacPhail really wanted Leo.

Even during the hot pennant race, newspaper reporters continued to speculate that this was, finally, Leo's last fling with the Dodgers. MacPhail, though, continued to confound the experts. In the midst of his three-manager regime, he went ahead and hired Bucky Harris, a career major league manager—and announced Harris was going to look after the Yankees minor league teams. Harris was his future manager if Leo would not take the job. Harris even "scouted" Leo during the playoffs against the Cardinals and brought back a positive report for MacPhail.

Actually, Rickey also wanted Leo back, and before the season was over, he had a verbal agreement with Leo to return. He did the same with Leo's top, trusted aide, Dressen.

The Series was over, the Cards beat the Red Sox, and Dressen led a barnstorming troupe in Cuba. As soon as he returned, Dressen quit the Dodgers, saying he was signing as coach of the Yankees. This infuriated the Mahatma, who saw it as a prelude to Leo's going over to the Yankees as well. And for all we know, it might have been— despite Leo's telling sportswriters when the season ended, "I'll stay in Brooklyn until I die."

Although they had an agreement, Rickey was getting testy with Leo's contract demands. "I'm getting fed up," he said. "Somebody's going to be named manager of the Dodgers Monday. It may be Durocher and it might be somebody else."

After Rickey did, in fact, sign Leo, he was asked whether there were any clauses "having to do with Leo's private life." "If Leo's private life had given me any concern," said the Mahatma, "there would be no contract."

Perhaps. But once again, Leo was tethered to the job by a thin strand. Rickey had shot him down over a demand for a five-year deal. Although Leo's contract made him baseball's highest-paid manager, believed to be between $50,000 and $70,000, it was only for one season. Even the threat of going to the Yankees didn't enable Leo to pick up extra time.

In an extraordinary sidelight to the negotiations, MacPhail revealed much later, the Yankees held up officially announcing that Harris was their new manager in order for Leo to hold the threat of going to the Yankees over Rickey.

All these machinations prompted the *Times*'s conservative columnist, Arthur Daley, to write: "If Leo were permitted to follow all his natural bents, the Broadway and Hollywood crowd would overrun Ebbets Field along with even less welcome characters who hang around the fringes."

Within a day of rejoining the Dodgers, Leo broadcast the news, at a sports lunch hosted by Jack Benny, that MacPhail called him a month before the season ended. "I went over and he offered me the Yankee job. I told him I had a verbal agreement with Mr. Rickey and couldn't take it."

It was almost more fun having Durocher and MacPhail on two different clubs rather than the same team.

When MacPhail heard that Leo was bragging he had turned down the Yankees, he claimed, "Durocher sent word to me that he was interested in the Yankee job." Then he added, "I don't think Durocher would be a logical choice for the Yankee job. There are angles to the job here that change the picture." Was he talking about Yankee "class" perhaps? The kind of job that required a certain pin-striped attitude?

At the same conference, MacPhail produced another falsehood (if you believed Leo). He denied that he made an overture to the Red Sox for Ted Williams to come to New York in a trade for Joe DiMaggio. In fact, Tom Yawkey, the Sox owner, had agreed to the deal, which supposedly was signed on a cocktail napkin. After sleeping it off, Yawkey telephoned MacPhail and called off the deal. The Thumper was younger than DiMag, explained Yawkey, and there was no way he could explain the deal to Boston fans.

Shortly after signing for 1947, a jubilant Leo flew to Los Angeles, arriving after midnight. The tabloid *Mirror* dutifully reported that he was met by the actress Laraine Day. "She greeted him with hugs and kisses," the paper reported of the sparking couple. He was forty-one years old, she was twenty-six. Just a week before she had filed suit for divorce from Ray Hendricks, former band leader and manager of the Santa Monica airport.

Leo and Laraine had met briefly in 1942 at the Stork Club, before she had became a nationally known actress. Her most prominent movie roles were in the *Dr. Kildare* series.

She was born in Roosevelt, Utah, in 1920, and raised as a Mormon. This was yet another odd coupling for Leo. When Leo's longtime New York newspaper buddy, the late Barney Kremenko, was asked how Laraine—a Mormon who didn't drink or smoke—could be associated with Leo, Barney replied, "Two out of three ain't bad." That quip aside, the couple was really in love.

Leo had set himself up for the public reaction and tabloid headlines that followed. He had an unabashed penchant for radio appearances, his byline appeared in national magazines, and he refused to back down to authority. Mostly, he was fun to watch and listen to.

Two days before Christmas, Commissioner Chandler disclosed he was investigating the Lip. Happy had been chafing under Leo's various notorious actions for some time. And now the unrepentant one was coveting his neighbor's wife.

Just as scholars like to point out that the assassination of Archduke Ferdinand was the immediate cause of World War I, it may have been Westbrook Pegler's indomitable assassination of Leo's character that forced Chandler's hand. Pegler, a former sportswriter turned right-wing columnist, phoned Rickey in November, threatening that if Leo weren't fired, he (Pegler) would start to write a series of columns that would dredge up Leo's criminal associations, as well as detail a laundry list of Leo's infractions. Durocher had no business in America's game because of his morals, Pegler claimed. Rickey refused the request, insisting that Leo had the right to work and that there was hope for him. Well then, asked Pegler, why was Leo still living with Raft on the West Coast?

Rickey dispatched his troubleshooter, Arthur Mann, a former newspaperman, to ask Chandler for help. Mann told the commissioner that Rickey was perplexed over Leo's actions and friends, and that they could backfire. But if Chandler himself warned Leo to "sever connections with all kinds of people regarded as undesirables by baseball—gangsters, known gamblers, companions of known gamblers and racketeers—" then Leo might take the warnings seriously.

Chandler met with Leo, pulled out a list of undesirables, and told him to stop meeting with them immediately. They included Bugsy Siegel and Joe Adonis, two mobsters whom Leo insisted he had only "nodded to." Chandler also warned him about Memphis Engelberg and Connie Immerman. Immerman, who had run the Cotton Club in Harlem, now was running a gambling casino in Havana, presumably under the watchful eye of Lucky Luciano. Memphis was the bookie who was a special friend of Dressen's.

The commissioner got Leo to agree. Then he said, "I want you out of George Raft's house."

"I'll do it," said Leo. "I'll steer clear of all those guys you've mentioned. They'll call me a louse, but I'll do it."

Leo's name had been linked to the mob since even before his friendship with Raft, since the Cincinnati days in the early 1930s, when he went across the river to Kentucky in search of illicit gambling.

Chandler himself was a great, good friend of none other than J. Edgar Hoover. The pair dined together several nights a week for years when Chandler was a United States senator. Certainly, Hoover would have gotten the goods on Leo for his pal Happy—if there were goods to have gotten.

For despite the repeated rumors, often masquerading as fact, a search of the FBI files on Durocher under the Freedom of Information Act has turned up exactly one document—an old clipping from the *New York Post* in the 1960s. And that article played down rumors that Leo had mob ties. This document, in fact, virtually disclaims any shady dealings. It explains that the only information on Leo and criminals is peripheral, in which he may have been mentioned in the course of a conversation involving someone else, and that to bring up the names of the people involved would be simply hearsay.

Still, mention Leo's famous suspension of 1947, and the odds are someone will respond, "Oh yeah—Leo's suspension for gambling."

It never happened. For all the good it did him, it might as well have. What Leo said and what Leo did were not always on the same track. And Chandler knew that Leo's promise to behave himself wouldn't be so simple. Chandler still didn't believe Leo was honest with him and told Rickey so. That prompted Rickey to write a "personal and confidential" letter to the commissioner that was unearthed years later by Murray Polner in his book, *Branch Rickey: A Biography.*

"It is not easy for Leo to understand that he cannot say, 'Hello, George,' to a person he has known for many years and a person, too, who has never bet on a baseball game and does not frequent race tracks . . . and at the same time find that the President [MacPhail] of one of our great baseball clubs and other officials are in intimate relationships with men like Connie and Memphis. All this . . . without apparent criticism. It is my opinion that Leo has completely cut acquaintanceship with 'George' and he has avoided as best he could . . . I am sure, any contact . . . with such persons as Connie and Memphis . . ."

Not long after New Year's in 1947, the page-one headlines began. Not for stealing money from suckers in crap games. Ray Hendricks accused Leo of stealing the affections of Laraine Day. There's nothing juicier than a love triangle for the front page—and when, if ever, had a baseball personality made it there in a sex scandal? This was the stuff of Hollywood, merged with sports. Why, there was even an argument in the Hendricks' home involving Leo, Laraine, and Ray, with Hendricks shouting that Leo was stealing his wife—and if he had to steal her, what kind of financial settlement could they make?

But in a legal agreement soon drawn up, the parties reached a settlement. Miss Day received custody of their adopted child, thirteen-month-old Christopher. She also had three children in her home, who were not adopted, from The Cradle, a children's institution in Evanston, Illinois. There would be more regarding a girl, Michele.

According to court papers, Hendricks claimed that Durocher "clandestinely pursued the love" of Miss Day. "Durocher has not conducted himself as an honorable man or gentleman and is not a fit and proper person for her to associate with, for she is only a girl of 26 and he is over twice her age." Furthermore, charged Hendricks, these goings-on had left him "completely humiliated and over-whelmed beyond the description of words." Presumably, it also left him unable to add, for Leo was fifteen years older than Laraine, hardly twice her age.

If it was Leo just being Leo again, messing around with another man's wife, it might not have infuriated Chandler so much as what happened next. But then Leo and Laraine went ahead and got married, defying not only a court order, but the convention of the time.

"The trouble started when Laraine went to Juárez, Mexico, immediately after Judge George A. Dockweiler granted her an interlocutory decree, and got a 'quickie' divorce," the *Daily News* reported. Then Laraine recrossed the border and married Leo in El Paso the same day—even though her California decree would not be final for a year. The couple was—in the lexicon of the noir 1940s—living in sin.

The judge was furious at Leo and Laraine for trying to get around his ruling. But reporters were in heaven: "LARAINE, LIPPY HUM CUBAN LOVE SONG," blared the *News*.

The couple was planning a Havana honeymoon, she told United Press—assuming, that is, that her marriage was approved.

Laraine had testified that Hendricks had "generally" come home drunk. In addition, she said with a *Modern Screen* magazine sensitivity: "I have been in love with Leo all my life. He lived up to my ideals, an ideal all my life about the sort of man I'd like to marry. He came along and I realize he's the man."

Leo's former girlfriend, Edna Ryan (the one whose mother accompanied her to spring training), asked about this marriage to another woman, described Leo as "a Dodger all right—an artful Dodger."

Faced with an ultimate authority—a judge—Leo reacted in his Leo fashion. "LIPPY BLASTS JUDGE, VOWS LARAINE'S HIS" said a *News* headline in late January. The article had Durocher describing Judge Dockweiler as "a most unethical and publicity conscious servant of the people."

Within a day, the Brooklyn *Eagle* reported that Chandler would soon ask Leo to explain his private life.

Leo's longevity in baseball didn't cut it with Judge Dockweiler, who was known as someone who was seldom riled, and pleasant. A Catholic, he did not approve personally of the divorces that made up the bulk of the docket in his Superior Court. Still, he presided even-handedly. However, he was outraged when Leo and Laraine pulled their cross-the-border stunt on him.

Leo soon was making waves clear across the country as well—from as far away as Havana, in fact. It was a memorable spring training in which Leo played a central role in a historic event: Jackie Robinson's becoming a big leaguer. And it was also historic for Leo in that his big mouth got him shouted clear out of baseball while Robinson was being shoehorned in.

Even before Leo got himself in trouble, he had to contend with a possible insurrection by the team's Southern faction. Rickey had arranged for the Dodgers to meet their Montreal farm team in seven exhibition games in Havana, where it was acceptable for blacks to play with whites. Robinson stole the show, batting more than .600 and stealing bases like crazy. It was obvious he was going to be called to the big club.

Dixie Walker wrote Rickey a letter. He wanted to be traded, he said, "for reasons I don't care to go into." The reason could be explained by his nickname.

Walker tried to ally himself with other Southerners on the team, including Bragan, Stanky, and Higbe. Finally, Walker drew up a petition. He asked the Dodgers not to bring up Robinson. Reese refused to sign. So did others. Branca doesn't even recall seeing the petition "because I guess they figured only the Southern guys would sign it."

One night over dinner, while the club was in Panama, Higbe broke the details to Parrott. As soon as Parrott returned to the hotel, he went up to Durocher's room and told him about the petition. Although it was then midnight, Durocher immediately hopped out of bed and ordered Parrott to round up the players and meet him in the barracks that served as a meeting room.

In his yellow bathrobe, in the early hours of the morning, in another country, Leo explained to the recalcitrant Brooklyn Dodgers that integration in baseball was going to happen, whether they liked it or not. He was furious. "I don't care if the guy is yellow or black," he said, punching out the words for emphasis. "I'm the manager of this team, and I say he plays." Then he delivered the clincher that has helped more than one minority member join an organization. "I say he can make us rich. And if any of you can't use the money, I'll see that you're traded."

Leo's historic stand meant nothing for the next round of Durocher vs. the World. The Dodgers were training in Havana and they were meeting the Yankees there for three exhibition games. Leo's old pal, MacPhail, was there too, this time as the top-ranking Yankee.

Leo's cronies, Memphis Engelberg and Connie Immerman, were in Havana as well—Immerman managing the casino at the Hotel Nacional, where the Dodgers stayed, and Engelberg . . . well, Havana was that kind of place. Just a few weeks before the Brooklyns arrived, there had been a scandal at the hotel, where it was discovered Lucky Luciano had a luxurious suite. The Cuban government kicked him out of the country.

Imagine Leo's chagrin when, before a Yankee game, he spotted Engelberg and Immerman sitting in box seats—but not just in any box. The Yankees' box! Those guys—those shady characters Commissioner Chandler wanted Durocher to steer clear of—were guests of MacPhail! At least, that's the way Leo saw it from his vantage point in the dugout, knowing where MacPhail's box was and seeing the pair sitting in it.

As Leo reddened, two New York writers—Dick Young of the *News* and Milton Gross of the *Post*—happened by and started to talk to Leo. "Look at that," he fumed. "If I had those guys in my box, I'd be kicked out of baseball."

Young, a dogged reporter, went over to MacPhail and asked whether the two gamblers were, in fact, his guests. "They're not in my box. They're in the box across the aisle," said MacPhail. Young asked, Was he being technical? Wasn't the box across the aisle his as well? Weren't they actually his guests?

"What are you—the goddamn FBI?" shouted MacPhail.

MacPhail should have been more generous with his answers to the newspapermen though—especially to Leo. For Leo had become a member of the Fourth Estate, in a manner of speaking. He had a column called "Durocher Says" in the Brooklyn *Eagle*, detailing the goings-on in the exhibition season. Actually, the column was written by Parrott, but Leo gave Parrott carte blanche.

By the time the Dodgers traveled to Venezuela a few days later for more exhibitions, Leo/Parrott was ready to strike. Columnist Leo accused MacPhail of entertaining gamblers. "MacPhail was flaunting his company with known gamblers right in the players' faces," he wrote. "If I even said 'Hello' to one of those guys, I'd be called before Commissioner Chandler and probably barred."

Leo the writer had the gloves off: It was a declared war against MacPhail. Leo still claimed he was angry over MacPhail's theft of Dressen, his most trusted aide. He wrote in his March 3 column: "This is a declaration of war. . . . [MacPhail] tried to drive a wedge between myself and all those things I hold dear. When MacPhail found I couldn't be induced to manage his Yankees for any of his inducements, he resolved to knock me, and to make life as hard as possible for me. . . . But surely people must recognize that it is the same old MacPhail. About Dressen, I cannot help but feel bitterly. He was a valuable man. Yes, but he got in Brooklyn a lot of kindnesses and compensations which he will never get in Yankee Stadium. He must find that out for himself, of course, and the learning of it may be a hard lesson.

"When he decided to break his word, he never gave me the courtesy of a phone call. This from Dressen, who asked me to go to bat for him with Rickey on innumerable occasions. One thing should be remembered: Dressen's only [escape] as far as his Brooklyn contract was concerned was that he could sign to manage a major league club elsewhere.

"Has MacPhail promised Charlie this? What does this mean to Bucky Harris? Be sure I will ask the questions when we meet in Caracas tomorrow."

Not only Leo charged MacPhail with having gamblers in his box—so did Rickey. "A liar," MacPhail branded Durocher.

That wasn't all he did. He immediately filed a complaint with Chandler, charging Durocher with actions "detrimental to baseball"—airing dirty linen. That charge, formal and official, seemed to be the excuse Chandler was looking for to kick Leo out of baseball. He immediately scheduled hearings in Sarasota and St. Petersburg.

The commissioner's investigations began in the midst of gambling hysteria that focused on New York: the Brooklyn College basketball-fix scandal, charges that two football Giants stars had been approached by bookies to throw a game, and the suspension of Rocky Graziano for an alleged bribe attempt he didn't report.

In the public's mind, Leo was being investigated for gambling as well. What the public heard was "bookmakers," "private box," "Havana," "Luciano," "casino." Yet, not one of the gambling charges stemming from the Havana incident was against Leo—it was against MacPhail.

Still, Leo's history was dredged before the public, for whom the Laraine Day headlines were fresh. And new information kept coming to light. Dan Daniel, the eminent baseball writer for the *Telegram*, claimed that Chandler borrowed some FBI people from J. Edgar Hoover to investigate the Dodgers. And the Braves felt they were being spied on by the FBI when they played the Dodgers in Havana. Furthermore, the FBI, spurred by Leo's associations, was preparing a list of undesirables to give to baseball teams.

During Chandler's hearings, Rickey called the Dodgers' front office staff together in Brooklyn and told them, "Leo is down. But we are going to stick by Leo. We are going to stick by Leo until hell freezes over!" After all Rickey had seen Leo go through, after the player revolt, the fight with the fan, various suspensions for fighting and arguing, the George Raft scandal, Rickey remained his protector.

According to Red Barber: "Rickey appreciated Leo's quick decisions, his courage, his willingness to do anything to win, his baseball savvy, his personal charm, his handling of his players, his fan appeal—and Rickey knew that Durocher would support him without question with Jackie Robinson. Leo would play anybody who, or do anything that, could help him win a ball game. Rickey knew Durocher would fight for Robinson, and Rickey knew he would need everybody and everything when Robinson took the field at Brooklyn. The rest of the league would be against the black man. Leo relished such a fight."

Rickey was battling for Leo on several fronts. While the divorce case was roiling through the courts, the Dodgers were hit with another blockbuster: On March 1, the Catholic Youth Organization of Brooklyn announced that its membership of 125,000 boys was withdrawing affiliation with the Knothole Club—a group that sponsored Brooklyn Baseball.

The Reverend Vincent J. Powell, director of the CYO's Brooklyn Diocese, personally wrote to the Knothole Club resigning. He said, "The present manager of the Brooklyn Baseball team is not the kind of leader we want for your youth to idealize and imitate."

Rickey invited Reverend Powell to his office and sat him down. "Father," cooed Rickey, "you are devoting your life to caring for boys. I applaud your work and I am devoted to the same thing you are. Now you and I are experienced talkers . . . convincers, perhaps, Father. However, if you and I both got into a ring at Madison Square

Garden and took turns talking, and if Leo Durocher was talking at the other end of the arena, and if the place was jammed with juvenile delinquents, nobody would listen to us. Father, you are playing for big stakes. This fellow Durocher has a tremendous influence on youth, for good or evil."

Then Rickey hit him with what he hoped was the clincher: "Why not get him on our side?" Redemption, in other words.

Powell, impressed, agreed. He went back to his bishop.

"No," the bishop said. And the CYO pulled its boys out of Ebbets Field.

Chandler was spending his time fielding phone calls from people who targeted Leo for a number of offenses. Chandler once called Rickey, with Polner reporting the following conversation: "Can you handle Leo Durocher?" Chandler asked rhetorically. "Well, I don't believe you can." Still, Rickey pleaded, but Chandler told him, "I've given you your chance, Branch. Now I'll handle him."

Later, at one of the hearings in Florida to decide what to do about Leo, Chandler ushered everyone out of the room except O'Malley, Rickey, and Mann. Chandler closed the door. Then, Mann recalled, Chandler looked at them and said, "How much would it hurt you folks to have your fellow out of baseball?"

This was the first time the brain trust realized that Leo was in danger of being kicked out of baseball. Rickey, for once almost at a loss for words, composed himself finally and said, "Happy, what on earth is the matter with you?"

Chandler reached inside his breast pocket. He pulled out a folded letter, but did not display its contents. "It's from a big man in Washington. He wants Durocher out of baseball," said Chandler. In later years, that man would be revealed as United States Senator (and eventual Supreme Court Justice) Frank Murphy, who was a friend of the commissioner's.

But Chandler said he was not doing anything about Durocher just yet. He was just feeling them out.

And the Dodgers felt much better about things when Durocher and MacPhail actually appeared in front of Chandler at a hearing. Leo apologized to MacPhail, claiming it was "just baseball talk."

MacPhail even put his arms around Leo and said, "Oh, forget it." To Happy he said, "As far as I'm concerned, it's over."

We will never know all the ingredients that went into making the decision to suspend Leo. Even after it happened, there was so much reckless speculation that it has become a truth: Leo Durocher was suspended for 1947 for gambling, or for his associates, or for marrying a divorced woman before she was free.

But it's important to understand Chandler's mind as well. While he was ruminating on what to do, Bert Bell, the National Football League president, suspended indefinitely two Giants—Merle Hapes and Frank Filchock—for failing to immediately report a bribe offer the previous season. Six days after Bell's decision—and on the eve of the opening of the baseball season—Chandler made his decision: Leo was out! He was suspended for all of 1947.

The news of Durocher's suspension arrived in Brooklyn while Rickey was engaged in an even more momentous discussion. For at that moment at the Dodgers offices at 215 Montague Street, he and Durocher, along with Coaches Clyde Sukeforth, Ray Blades, and Jake Pitler, were talking about Jackie Robinson's imminent arrival. The operator buzzed Rickey's office and described the call as "long-distance emergency" from Cincinnati.

Durocher was dejected and confused when he received the news in Rickey's office. "For what?" Durocher shouted at Rickey. It sounded almost like a plea as well. The man who had always squirmed out when caught with his hand in the cookie jar, now was defensive—and dumbstruck.

With that stunned "For what?" Durocher, for one of the few times in his life, was to react honestly. He repeated those two words through the day when anyone asked him for a reaction.

Someone asked Rickey if there would be an appeal. "To whom?" Rickey replied solemnly, with the air of a man who knows the governor would not heed a death-row plea.

When the decision was handed down, there was not one specific charge cited by Chandler. Instead, the operative phrase was "accumulation of unpleasant incidents detrimental to baseball."

"Unpleasant incidents?" Like spitting on the field? Like sneaking a cigarette behind the dugout? Like saying "Fuck you"?

After all he had done—after all the really bad accumulation of awful incidents—Leo's one-year suspension never was spelled out. And still hasn't been.

Chandler later told Peter Golenbock that he had repeatedly tried to get Rickey, without success, to straighten out Leo. "I had exhausted my patience with him," he said. "Hey, do you think I became commissioner to punish ballplayers?"

Forty-five years later, his son, A. B. Chandler II, publisher of *The Woodford Sun* of Versailles, Kentucky, was asked to reflect on that time and what his late father had done: "Time and again there were reports of George Raft and his connections. And people told Dad stories. Bill Robinson—Bojangles, the dancer—called once to complain. It was just an unsavory reputation," recalled the younger Chandler.

"Leo's first wife [actually his second, Grace] on two occasions defended him to my dad when they were married—and after he left she started talking against Leo.

"She told my dad he was a son of a bitch and my dad said, 'You said that, I didn't.'

"My dad was trying to make a big statement on the gambling. That was why there was a baseball commissioner to start with. It was unpopular to bar all ballplayers from the racetracks.

"Leo was known for being a hustler—people are more known for their transgressions. He was known as a troublemaker and my dad as governor twice had to put down trouble—he had to send in the State Police and he always believed you stop trouble immediately and forcefully.

"Dad didn't have trouble with his conscience over suspending Leo. My dad signed thirty-four death warrants while he was governor. *That's* something you lose sleep over."

It is likely that the Durocher ruling was a key factor in Chandler losing his job, even though there was virtually no movement by other teams to get him to rescind the order. He was ousted when his contract was up in 1951. Why?

"The New York writers thought of him as a Senator Claghorn [a hayseed bombast], and they didn't like the idea that the office moved to the South," said the younger Chandler. "His office was in Cincinnati. And then Leo's suspension was the last straw. In 1948 when they had the special day for Babe Ruth at Yankee Stadium, Dad was introduced and they booed.

"The people who voted Dad out included Fred Saigh of the Cardinals. He went to prison [for income tax evasion]. But Dad was always proud that the baseball people—Connie Mack, Griffith, and Briggs—voted for him. This was in 1951. When it came to renewing his contract he got eleven votes and you needed twelve."

He believes there might have been another reason his father was not reelected. "The owners met and voted 15–1 not to have Robinson come into the big leagues. Dad opposed that vote."

Take all of this as part of the reason to make such a remarkably punitive decision. Read Happy Chandler's suspension order and it has to do with the perception of baseball as the great game, and the game that must be kept in high esteem: "Durocher has not measured up to the standards expected or required of managers of our baseball teams," he wrote. "This incident in Havana, which brought considerable unfavorable comment to baseball generally, was one of a series of publicity-producing affairs [an interesting choice of words] in which Manager Durocher has been involved in the last few months.

"Managers of baseball teams are responsible for the conduct of players on the field. Good managers are able to ensure the good conduct of the players on the field and frequently their example can influence players to be of good conduct off the field.

"As a result of the accumulation of unpleasant incidents detrimental to baseball, Manager Durocher is hereby suspended from participating in professional baseball for the 1947 season."

Chandler also lashed out at others in the affair.

Dressen was suspended because he had broken a verbal agreement to remain with the Dodgers as a Durocher lieutenant. Instead, perhaps thinking he could succeed Bucky Harris as Yankees pilot, or realizing Durocher was about to be booted, Dressen went to the Yankees.

Parrott, the ex-baseball writer for the *Eagle,* was fined as Durocher's ghostwriter. Chandler also ordered Parrott to stop writing the column immediately. (Leo, to his credit, never backed down on anything Parrott wrote—even though Leo never actually read what was written under his own name.)

In the decision, Chandler also noted: "Evidence clearly shows that MacPhail did not offer Durocher a job as manager of the New York Yankees for the 1947 season and that statements quoting Durocher in this regard are untrue." According to Chandler, though, MacPhail did hold up signing Harris to a contract, leaving the impression he was interested in hiring Durocher, which raised Durocher's value with the Dodgers.

A $2,000 fine was levied against each club because "their officials engaged in a public controversy damaging to baseball."

Rickey wouldn't say whether he would pay the suspended Durocher's salary for 1947, and he wouldn't talk about Durocher's status for 1948. Durocher sat quietly in an adjacent office while Rickey spoke with the press. Durocher kept repeating, "For what?" but consented to pose with Rickey for photographers.

The suspension had come a week before the season, with four exhibition games yet to be played (including one with Montreal that very afternoon), and Sukeforth was hastily named manager for the day. The names of a Durocher successor that were tossed in the air were Blades, Dixie Walker, Bill Terry, Frankie Frisch, and Joe McCarthy.

Not even Judge Landis, who had died two years before after serving as baseball's first commissioner following the Black Sox scandal, had ever dealt so harshly with anyone other than those he perceived as fixers or gamblers. He had, of course, banned White Sox players for life. And he had suspended the Babe and Bob Meusel for forty days back in 1921. But with no proof of betting, and certainly no hint of fixing games, Chandler's punishment of Leo was considered the harshest ever meted out in sports.

Unless, of course, there was something he knew that the public didn't. Were there others besides Bojangles Robinson who had called the commissioner to complain about Leo's bum checks or refusal to honor a debt? Of course there were. There were even people who called the commissioner and threatened to seriously hurt Leo because of his deadbeat attitude. Chandler even told some people he was suspending Leo to protect him, that if Leo continued the course he was on, seeing the people he saw, his life was in danger.

Shortly after he was voted out as commissioner, Chandler spoke for the first time about Leo's suspension: "I would do it exactly the same way because I had to keep him from killing somebody," he explained. "I think Leo will be the first to tell me that the year suspension made a new man out of him and made him a credit to baseball instead of a detriment. But the way things were then in 1947, he was in such a mood that no one knew what he would attempt to do next.

"I knew that Durocher and Charles Dressen, who was a Yankee coach at the time, were associating with known gamblers. Durocher told me he had hit the fan at the park for taunting and insulting remarks that he made. With all of those things on his mind he was on the defensive every minute, against the fans, the umpires, and practically everybody. I was afraid at any moment there might be a new and far more serious incident and I certainly didn't want him to wind up by killing somebody."

The suspension without doubt cost Leo a timely entrance into the Hall of Fame.

Bob Broeg of St. Louis, a man with insight into baseball's workings and lore, is one of the Veterans Committee members whose repeated votes for Durocher fall short.

"You know, Buzzie Bavasi brought evidence to the committee that Memphis Engelberg was MacPhail's guest, not Leo's," said Broeg. Interestingly, there are committee members who believed that Leo was suspended for having gamblers in *his* box—and that Bavasi, the Dodgers' former general manager, had to bring "proof" this wasn't so.

Broeg, like many other people in the business, also believes that Rickey was involved in Leo's suspension, although this is hardly clear cut, and there is much evidence to the contrary.

"I said this to Leo one time and he said, 'You know, you might be right.' As devious as Rickey was, with the hot potato he had in his hand, with Leo marrying Laraine, and the Catholic Youth Organization threatening to withdraw their kids from the Knothole Gang, and O'Malley leaning on the Catholic Church guys to do that, I can see Rickey going before the commissioner and saying, 'Oh, this is a grievous situation, Commissioner, I don't know what to do. But I'll tell you, it wouldn't offend me too much if you were to suspend him, and I'll take care of the young man's contract.'

"So that whole thing might not have been black and white, meaning the Yankees black and the Dodgers lily-white, because then Rickey eased him out of there the following summer."

Even sweet Laraine said of Rickey, once the suspension was announced, "Leo, this man is not your friend."

This is how the *Times* described the reaction to the ban: "Every candy store in Brooklyn was an angry forum." The suspension brought people out to the streets, it united them as awesome events do every so often, it brought them to the town hall/cracker-barrel/hot stove/candy store to have a shared reaction.

People discussed the escapades of John McGraw and Babe Ruth and wondered, "Why Leo?" just as some fans today say that Pete Rose didn't do anything as bad as other members of the Hall of Fame.

The odds on the Dodgers to win pennant rose from 2½–1 to 3–1.

As Harold Driscoll of Clinton Street told the *Eagle*, "It's a rotten deal for Brooklyn. There's no future for the team without our Leo."

On April 10, the day after the ban, Leo met with his players. The Dodgers were playing an exhibition with Montreal. After batting practice, the Dodgers went into the clubhouse, followed by the writers. Sukeforth was running the show until Rickey could name his new manager. Suddenly, the door to the locker room opened and there stood Leo. He wore a dark blue suit, bright white shirt, and a dark tie. A white handkerchief, folded just so, as always, protruded from his coat pocket. One of his brothers was along. Leo looked at the writers and said, "Fellows, I want to talk to my players."

Inside the quiet room, Leo didn't speak about the bad break he had been handed. He didn't talk about himself, in fact. He spoke about the team. "You're a good club," he said. "You can beat the Cardinals. But you've got to work together—and remember, I'll be pulling for you."

The players wanted to know who would replace him. "Don't worry," Durocher told them. "Mr. Rickey will get the best guy available. You've got to trust him."

Ten minutes later, the Durocher brothers walked out.

Dixie Walker followed, turned to Red Barber, and said, "You know, I've never liked the fellow. But I'll tell you this: He can get you to play better than you ever thought you could."

And Stanky added, "The way he went out, he's bound to come back."

The exhibition game between the Dodgers and Royals soon began. Robinson made his Ebbets Field debut wearing a Montreal uniform.

Rickey had other things on his mind that day. During the sixth inning, the writers were handed a prepared statement from him: "The Brooklyn Dodgers today purchased the contract of Jackie Roosevelt Robinson from the Montreal Royals. He will report immediately.

The announcement was so stark, and yet it was the final moment of a two-year labor, much of it undercover, by Rickey and his staff. He had spoken to sociologists, to black leaders, and he had worked up a profile of six essential points to be considered: (1) The man had to be right *off* the field. (2) He had to be right on the field. If he turned out to be a lemon, our efforts would fail for that reason alone. (3) The reaction of his own race had to be right. (4) The reaction of press and public had to be right. (5) We had to have a place to put him. (6) The reaction of his fellow players had to be right. (Luckily, at Montreal, the Dodgers had the perfect farm club.)

Rickey, too, had told black leaders what he expected when Robinson finally came up to the big leagues: no demonstrations, no testimonials, no traveling circus between cities following him.

And Leo the innovator, the agitator, whose presence had helped make Jackie Robinson's debut possible, was not even to be around for that moment. For the team at large, though, Leo's presence still was felt, and so was his absence.

That night, he and Laraine attended the annual welcome-home dinner sponsored by the Knothole Club at the St. George Hotel in Brooklyn. Red Barber was the master of ceremonies and introduced Leo.

"Although I can't be with the team physically," Leo said is an uncharacteristically maudlin speech, "I'll be dreaming of them in my heart." He and Laraine stood and waved. The ballroom was packed with more than a thousand people, who got to their feet and cheered.

Someone asked Frick, the National League president who was at the dinner, about the Durocher suspension. "Let he who is without sin cast the first stone," Frick intoned.

Speaking of sin, by the end of the month, Leo's marriage still hadn't been sanctioned. On April 30, Leo and Laraine contended in court papers that they paid Hendricks $10,500 and gave him a car to sign a waiver to the Mexican divorce—and also to adopt Michele.

Most of Leo and Laraine's year away from baseball was spent away from baseball. They lived in California, and if Leo had been a show biz type of guy before, now he really was going Hollywood.

More important, he said later, was a change in his attitude. "Laraine taught me three things—responsibility, courtesy, and kindness. The lug Laraine took for better or worse was thoughtless, and maybe a bit hard-boiled and cynical." Leo soon learned about antiques, paintings, furniture, and collecting things. He was proud of showing off pieces of sculpture, other works of art, and beautiful furniture he had helped select.

While Leo headed West, Brooklyn was trying to sort things out. If this had been all a plot hatched (or at least artificially inseminated) by Rickey, then the Mahatma hadn't planned for it that well. For he had no manager to take over. He convinced his old friend, Burt Shotton, that he was the man for the job. But the Dodgers started the season with Sukeforth as manager.

In the opener, they beat the Braves, 5–3. Reiser was described as "almost completely recovered" from the many injuries that had plagued him. He won the game in the seventh inning when he capped a perfect day with a 2-run double off Johnny Sain.

In the same inning, Robinson bunted with Stanky on first and reached first safely on a wild throw. Jackie was 0–3 in his debut, scored a run, made 11 putouts at first, and was credited with a sacrifice. He batted second between Stanky and Schultz.

There was only a terse announcement of Durocher's successor: "Burton Edwin Shotton has accepted the management of the Brooklyn Dodgers and will take charge of the team today."

Shotton had been Rickey's designated Sunday replacement in the old Cardinal days. On the Sabbath, when Rickey wouldn't attend baseball, Shotton took over. But Shotton by now was sixty-two years old and somewhat weary. He liked to claim he didn't even realize he was being considered as the Dodgers' manager and learned about it only ninety minutes before he was named, before a Giants game at the Polo Grounds. He hadn't managed in fourteen years, after having led the Phillies from 1928 to 1933.

Part of Shotton's deal with Rickey specified that he did not have to put on a uniform. He had put his away two years earlier, when he coached at Cleveland. The only other big league manager who did not suit up was Connie Mack, the octagenarian pilot, and owner, of the Philadelphia A's.

Shotton didn't really know many of the players, and he was content for a while to observe them through his gold-rimmed glasses. What a difference from Leo!

Shotton had been tossed out of only two ball games in a thirty-nine-year baseball career. That included a stint as a St. Louis Browns outfielder, then at Washington, then with the Cards from 1909 to 1923. He had been a crack leadoff hitter. Rickey, who had known him since 1913, brought him to the Dodgers as a scout in 1946, and in the spring of 1947 Shotton ran the minor league camp.

There was this footnote to Shotton's taking over. It's a story that both men used to tell on the banquet circuit, so it may actually be true.

After Rickey convinced Shotton to come back to the bench, Rickey drove with Shotton to Manhattan after meeting him at the airport. They spoke about the team, the situation, and with no promises for the future. No one was quite sure if Leo was coming back the next year, if Rickey wanted him back, or if Chandler would allow him back.

Finally, Rickey got out for a haircut and said, "Burt, you know the way to the Polo Grounds," and left Shotton in the car alone.

Actually, Shotton had forgotten. He got lost on the way there, arriving just before game time.

His insistence on not wearing a uniform struck Dodger fans as odd. They had taken to calling "Leo!" whenever a call went against them, certain that their manager would charge out of the dugout immediately to argue the call. But Shotton just sat there, waggling a finger at his coaches, not really planning ahead, frustrating players like Branca, who were accustomed to a lively bench with plenty of cerebral baseball as well.

Within a few weeks, MacPhail was called into Chandler's office. It was hardly a surprise: MacPhail had violated the commissioner's no-talking-about-the-suspension rule he had imposed on all parties.

In an interview, MacPhail claimed that Leo wouldn't have been suspended if Rickey hadn't wanted him to be. MacPhail denied he had said that. And he also claimed that Shotton had done a good job in handling the Dodgers. Then MacPhail was asked whether he thought Durocher would be back. "I'll take a little bet at a hundred to one he won't be." MacPhail blasted Chandler's suspension of Leo as marking "the first time that a baseball commissioner had fined or suspended a man without stating in writing specific charges against him."

What transpired in their six-and-a-half-hour conversation? No one said, although MacPhail conceded, "I guess the commissioner's charging me with insubordination."

MacPhail immediately went down and took a drink. It was May 1. He had bet Dan Topping, the Yankees' owner, he could go on the wagon until May 1. He won. But what would have happened if Chandler had called him in on April 30?

In early May, the Cardinals visited Ebbets Field. The Cards, who had won the pennant and Series the year before, now were struggling. Who also came along? Durocher, making his first Ebbets Field appearance since the suspension. He sat with Laraine behind the Dodgers' dugout, even had himself photographed shaking hands with Shotton, and waved to the Dodgers.

Leo had come in for a meeting with Rickey over salary. Even suspended, Leo still had battles over his contract. In the past, when players were suspended, it also meant loss of pay. But Rickey buttressed his verbal support of Leo by paying him his full 1947 salary.

Well, the Leo-less Dodgers won the pennant in 1947. Shotton, given life and Dodger bodies, was at the helm (loosely speaking) as they toppled the Cardinals, Branca won 21 games. Robinson was rookie of the year. Furillo, Walker, and Reiser patrolled the outfield.

Leo and Laraine returned to town on the eve of the World Series—shortly after he announced he wanted to come back. But Leo stayed in the background during the Dodgers' pennant-victory celebration, remaining in his hotel room.

It was a marvelous series—Gionfriddo going "back, back, back," in Barber's immortal words, to flag down DiMaggio's homer-bound drive to left; Berra hit the first pinch-homer in Series history; the Dodgers bounced back to make it a 7-game contest after dropping the first 2, and Lavagetto broke up Bill Bevans's no-hitter in the ninth inning with a double off the Ebbets Field wall to produce a victory.

Leo and Laraine saw all seven games. As Bruce Edwards of the Dodgers bounced into a Series-ending double play, MacPhail pounded a table and shouted, "That's it. I'm through. I've got what I wanted." He had resigned.

A few minutes after it was over, MacPhail ran into Rickey, still disconsolate, and offered him his hand. "I am taking your hand," said Rickey, "only because people are watching us." As MacPhail beamed, Rickey added, "Don't you ever speak to me again."

A few hours later at the Yankees victory party, MacPhail, although he had announced his retirement, promptly fired George Weiss, the Yankees' general manager. Roaring Red also punched his old Brooklyn aide, John McDonald, closing his eye. He fought bitterly and loudly with Topping. Then MacPhail retired to his farm outside of Bel Air, Maryland, where he bred horses and cattle and became head of Bowie Race Course. He never hired, or fired, Leo again.

Chandler may have been lenient in allowing Leo to draw his full 1947 salary. But when he learned that the Dodgers voted the Lip a full Series share, the commissioner said no.

As soon as the season ended, Rickey met with Chandler, demanding to know Leo's status. Chandler did not like having to make a decision on Durocher's future. He had hoped that Rickey wouldn't bother him, would make it easier on him by just getting rid of Leo himself. Instead, Rickey now was asking him to bring back Leo into baseball's family. "Do what you damn please," a perturbed Chandler told Rickey.

On December 6, Rickey set up a press conference on Montague Street. When reporters got there, they received the following handout:

The 1947 contract of Leo Durocher has been renewed for 1948 by the Brooklyn Baseball Club.

                 Branch Rickey

"I'm giving Durocher his job back," the gracious Shotton said with a smile.

It was typical Brooklyn melodrama. Reporters were given a typed statement, but Rickey was absent. His daughter was ill with pneumonia in Philadelphia and he had rushed to her bedside. Leo wasn't at Montague Street either ("I have to be in California because I'm late for some appointments").

So who was there in Brooklyn? Burt Shotton.

He seemed happy. "I'm right back to where I was before," he said. "I'm going back to Bartow, Florida, as soon as I can leave here. I didn't expect to manage last season, nor did I expect to manage the Dodgers next year."

Chandler issued a statement from Cleveland: "The commissioner neither approves nor disapproves the appointment. It is solely a matter between Mr. Durocher and the Brooklyn Baseball Club. The baseball fans of the country are fair and will accept Leo Durocher's return in true American style." He added that since "the suspension order was lifted Leo Durocher has done nothing to aggravate or complicate the situation. If Durocher emulates the conduct of his predecessor he will have no cause to worry."

That didn't calm the Knights of Columbus. The group opposed his reinstatement. Perhaps they remembered that earlier that year, Leo's ex-girlfriend, Edna, wound up dating Laraine's ex-husband, Ray Hendricks. "I guess," said Miss Ryan, "you could say we have a lot in common."

But relations between Durocher and Rickey weren't the same, couldn't be the same—and never were the same. Now Leo was wary, wondering if at some level Rickey indeed had been responsible for his ouster from baseball, the most demeaning and—to Leo—unfair event of his life.

Leo fumed that the old codger, Shotton, had won the pennant with *his* boys, the ones Leo had developed and positioned. And now, by God, Leo would win it on his own. Nothing would stand in his way this year. It was to foreshadow behavior that was aberrant even for him as he tried mightily, overreacted strongly, to try to turn the Dodgers' bad 1948 start around.

CHAPTER
IX
THE
UNTHINKABLE

THE 1948 SEASON began with training camp in the Dominican Republic, and with an angry Durocher looking at a fat Jackie Robinson.

For the first time as manager, Leo had to equal what someone else—even the frumpy Shotton—had accomplished. And Leo was smart enough to know that it's difficult enough to repeat, even if everything stays in place. On this team, things weren't in place, not the manager, not who was playing where, not the pitching staff. Dick Young, the outspoken baseball writer, told readers Leo was "afraid of losing his job," a man who was managing in "fear." Leo promptly barred Young from the clubhouse.

Robinson arrived late for spring training after traveling two days by plane from Hollywood, where they were making a movie about his life, starring him. He admitted he was fifteen pounds overweight, but actually it was more like twenty-five. It started his problems with Leo.

And while Leo was miffed at Jackie, Branch Rickey was dagger-eyed at Durocher.

Leo's problems with Rickey intensified not long after spring training started. Jane Rickey, Branch's wife, was shocked to learn that Leo boasted of how he won three hundred dollars playing cards. That was bad—had his year away taught him nothing? Then Rickey found out

222 ◇ GERALD ESKENAZI

Leo was talking behind his back, criticizing the so-called Dodgertown training base *and* Rickey's teaching techniques.

"Outsiders," said the shocked Mahatma, "were still sitting on the team bench during warm-ups, a practice I had expressly forbidden so as to deter hustlers and touts from hanging about."

Meanwhile, Leo refused to stay in the regular hotel rooms assigned to him. Instead, he opted for a suite. And each day Leo criticized Rickey's choice of a training camp, as well as Rickey's friend, Coach Ray Blades. Then another coach, Sukeforth, went to Rickey and told him he was unhappy with Durocher too.

By then, after all their years together at St. Louis and Brooklyn, Rickey had come to realize there was, really, nothing to be done about Leo—accept him as he was or fire him. All the cute words about Leo being a "reclamation project" now sounded hollow, and not as disarming as they once had. Fifteen years later, in Rickey's final stint with a ball club, he returned to the Cardinals. When asked whether he had considered hiring Leo, who was available, he said, "Even in my most incoherent dreams, I would never advocate that Durocher be hired as manager. Given twenty-five good players, Leo can produce a winner. At two o'clock in the afternoon, he's a great manager. But there's more to managing than just a ball game."

Stanky was not yet aboard. He was a holdout, which bothered Rickey. This was no way to begin defense of a pennant. There was another sign, too, that repeating would not be so easy. Gionfriddo was injured when he was drilled in batting practice by Johnny Van Cuyk. And Lavagetto, who had one of the most dramatic hits in World Series history the year before, had retired because of shoulder and foot injuries. Reiser was . . . well, a shell. Bruce Edwards, the catcher who had driven in 80 runs at the age of twenty-three for Shotton, injured his arm in an off-season game against Folsom Prison inmates. Spider Jorgensen, the third baseman, had also suffered a shoulder injury while quail hunting—the repeated recoils of the shotgun had torn muscles in his right shoulder.

But the most wrenching blow to Leo came when Stanky was shipped out.

It was inevitable because Rickey, from the moment he had signed Robinson, had planned to use him at second base. Rickey had chosen not to start the rookie there because he believed that as a second baseman, the first black ballplayer in the majors would be targeted repeatedly by barreling base runners. Now, after a year, Jackie could move to second. Of course, that meant the Dodgers needed a first baseman and they needed a catcher. Eventually, fellows named Hodges and Campanella would do the jobs at those positions. But when camp began, Leo was fiddling around with Reiser at first; Campanella wasn't slated for the majors just yet. Rickey, wheels turning, looking at the big picture, had decided Campanella would integrate the American Association with the Dodgers St. Paul farm team.

But Leo had other plans for Campy. In Vero Beach, he told Rickey, "I'd like to switch Hodges to first and have Campy open as my catcher."

"I've got other plans for him," Rickey said mysteriously. "I want him in St. Paul."

"The hell with St. Paul," said Leo. "I'm thinking about my club."

Leo had a control mania that was always on the explosive edge, given the single-minded bosses he had. But Rickey would not waver on this one. Although Campy actually began the season in Brooklyn, the plan was for him to be sent to St. Paul after a month, then be recalled in mid-season if he were needed.

Second was set with Robinson. Stanky, the Brat, was gone. Stanky was so shaken when he learned of his trade to Boston that he immediately got sick and refused to leave his room.

Durocher later claimed that his downfall in Brooklyn began when he interceded on Stanky's behalf during his holdout, getting him a $2,500 raise that Rickey would not forgive, or forget.

Then Leo supposedly found out the old man wanted to trade Stanky and argued over the deal. However, this is at odds with Stanky's account, in which he roared, "My pal. He tells everybody he wouldn't trade me for two second basemen and now, when I am arguing with Rickey, he stabs me in the back!"

There was hardly a dull moment during that training camp. The federal police were called during an exhibition game with the Dominican all-stars. The home plate ump had signaled a Dodger safe to tie the score in the eighth. Fans begged to differ and threw bottles. As if that wasn't distressing enough to Leo, he raged because photographers dashed onto the field and positioned themselves behind the catcher whenever there was a play at the plate.

Leo's role in Robinson's rookie season had ended after spring training, but now, in 1948, there was a new aspect: The Dodgers were playing exhibitions in the South, which Rickey had avoided the year before. It meant that in some cities, a black would share a ball field with white men for the first time.

Since Jackie was the only black ballplayer with the club, the Dodgers would import local black businessmen to room with him or join him for dinner. When the Dodgers played in Macon, Georgia, Sam Lacy, the sports editor of the Afro-American newspaper of Baltimore, was there also. The team bus arrived at the entrance to the ballpark at about the same time Lacy and Robinson drove up by car. The players started to walk through, and Robinson got in step with them.

"You can't come in here. Can't you read?" said a policeman, pointing to a sign that said "WHITES ONLY."

"He can't go in this entrance?" said Leo, bellying up to the cop.

"No, he can't," came the reply.

"Well, we're not going in there. You know what that means, don't you?" said Durocher.

The cop, mindful that this game had been sold out, backed down. The Brooklyn Dodgers, helped by Leo's forceful stance, integrated Georgia. It was also typical of Durocher: He drove his players crazy, but then he'd stick up for them in ways they never expected.

Of course, we'll never know what life would have been like for Leo and Jackie if Leo had remained the Dodger manager. Certainly, there was a paternalistic way that Durocher later treated Willie Mays—a style that Robinson never would have accepted, nor would Leo have been dumb enough to try. What we do know is that, essentially, the pair hated each other—Jackie with his ego that remembered every slight, Leo with his ego that could not abide anyone who didn't slobber over his genius.

Throughout spring training, the Dodgers attracted thousands of black fans. There was a game in Fort Worth with a sea of black faces in the stands, people lined up behind ropes that stretched from foul line to foul line. That was not so unusual, because not only did this club have Jackie Robinson, it was, on paper, a powerful squad.

On the eve of spring training, Rickey called it "the best Dodger squad I've ever taken south." And in an ultimate tribute, he added, "It's taking on a Gashouse Gang aspect."

Leo's handling of the team when the season began indicated impatience and desperation. It was so obvious he was doomed in

Brooklyn that his pal, Toots Shor, told him late one night, "What are you waiting for? I'll name you manager of the Giants right now."

Even one of the writers who covered the Dodgers, Harold C. Burr, had told the retired Shotton at an off-season party at Shor's, "This farewell party isn't necessary. We'll see you back at Ebbets Field in July."

So it was in the air. There was no question that Leo would be in deep trouble with anything less than a smashing start. And then there was the ownership issue.

O'Malley and Smith didn't agree with Rickey on some of his personnel moves, and they didn't like the way he spent their money. They were unhappy over Stanky's trade. But most important they didn't agree with his decision to bring back Durocher. Then attendance flagged with a poor start in 1948.

Campanella remembered Durocher quickly got into a foul mood early in the season. The Dodgers had been picked to repeat—after all, if they could finish first under Shotton, why not again under Leo? But the Brooks lost four of their first seven games, and not one Dodger pitcher went the distance. Leo started to get on Robinson and Reiser over their weight. Jackie complained that his arm was sore, but Leo wouldn't hear of it. "I'll get him in shape or else," vowed Durocher.

The next day, Durocher commanded Sukeforth to hit grounders at Robinson. For one hour, Sukeforth pounded one after the other to Robinson. Robinson struggled, in pain, but said nothing.

Jackie was out of the lineup then; Gene Mauch took over at second. Leo was so miffed at Robinson that he was even thinking of moving Billy Cox, maybe the best-fielding third baseman of his time, to second, and putting the injured Spider Jorgensen at third. Cox got so upset that he jumped the club and went home to Harrisburg, Pennsylvania. There was more than a sensitive infielder at play with Cox. He had taken an emotional beating during World War II. Some of his teammates described him as being shell-shocked.

The team lost four in a row, and Durocher turned to Campanella. "You're catching tomorrow," he said.

Campy caught for the erratic Rex Barney, one of those wild, promising fastball hurlers that clubs hate to give up on (like Sandy Koufax and Nolan Ryan), and he caught him for a complete game. But the next day, Campy was relegated to the bullpen. If Campy did too well, it would mess up Rickey's plan.

Campanella recalled that because of this, "the feeling between the two men became strained. Looking back, I think that started the rift between Durocher and Mr. Rickey that finally ended with Leo being fired."

Finally, on May 15—cut-down day—Leo got his orders and had to tell Campanella he was being sent down. But not before Durocher marched into Rickey's office and demanded Campanella get a raise and a big league salary.

At the end of June, the sixth-place Dodgers recalled Campanella from St. Paul, where he was batting. 325. Leo was ecstatic, and when Campy showed up, Leo said, "Hah, fat as ever!" He returned against the Giants in Ebbets Field. The Dodgers had lost five straight. They lost again and fell into last place. During the Dodgers' fall into the second division, Leo tried everything. He started fights. He picked pitchers on hunches. He damned Rex Barney, saying he'd never pitch for him again.

One sports fan was Harry Markson, a raconteur, fight promoter, and all-round good guy. In the summer of 1948, he was the assistant to Mike Jacobs, the famed Madison Square Garden matchmaker. During a long drive home to Flatbush from Pompton Lakes, New Jersey, where Joe Louis was in training, Markson heard dire reports on the radio about Israel's future. The Arab nations were massing on the borders of the new country.

When Markson got out of his car, he spied his rabbi, who lived in the same apartment house. "It's terrible, what's going on," said the rabbi. "It's just one bad thing after the other."

"Frightful," agreed Markson, thinking they were talking about the Arab-Israeli situation.

"And do you know," the rabbi added, "I think it's all Durocher's fault. He's moving the players around too much."

With last place a sad reality, O'Malley and Smith wanted Rickey to move on Durocher. But they waited a day too long to dump Leo. For the Dodgers recovered and went on to win 16 of 19. Leo kept pushing back. He had to know he was a goner. He certainly knew Rickey was about to be unloaded himself.

On July 4, the Dodgers met the Giants in Brooklyn. Leo was thrown out of the game and was in the clubhouse when Parrott came down with a message: "Mr. Rickey wants you to resign." Leo stormed around and demanded Rickey call him himself.

Campy pulled the game out with a bottom-of-the-ninth homer, and the club embarked on a winning road trip. Recharged, Leo let it be known to his friend, Bill Corum, the *Journal-American* columnist, that there was front-office turmoil on the Dodgers. Leo got all his gripes against Rickey and O'Malley off his chest, but Corum wrote the piece as if all this was coming not from Leo, but from the writer.

Meanwhile, Giant president Horace Stoneham had come to a reluctant decision: Manager Mel Ott had to go. This was a wrenching moment for Stoneham, for Ott was one of the three Giant managers that defined the team in the twentieth century, following John McGraw and Bill Terry. It was a terrific legacy, and Ott had been a terrific player, the National League career home run leader, the final symbol of the great days of the Giants. But they weren't so great anymore. In 1947, even with a record 221 home runs, the Giants had finished fourth, making the first division for the second time since 1939. They had become perpetual losers.

Stoneham approached Rickey. The pair met in Ford Frick's office in New York. Down through the years the story has been that Stoneham actually wanted to talk to Rickey about Shotton. "No," Rickey answered, "I may need him at any moment myself."

Stoneham, who had always admired Durocher, asked, incredulous, "Does that mean Durocher will be available?"

"You may talk to him," replied Rickey.

That is what actually may have happened—Stoneham went fishing for Shotton and wound up with Durocher. Rickey, though, told it with a slightly different angle. And so did Leo.

The way Rickey remembered breaking the news to Leo was this way: Durocher, accompanied by Laraine, walked into Rickey's office and asked what his status was in Brooklyn if he refused the Giants job. "Your future," Rickey replied, "lies over the river, Leo."

Finally, there is Leo's version. This much is certain. The Dodgers were in St. Louis after the All-Star break. Leo was told by Rickey to go on a scouting expedition to Montreal. Leo saw that as an excuse to get rid of him and announce a coaching change. Rickey, according to Leo, said he could still be the manager in Brooklyn, although he had been offered the Giants job. "I wouldn't work for you another day after all that's happened," Leo said in his book.

It seemed inconceivable that Leo could become a Giant. It was like oil and water. There was Manhattan and there was Brooklyn. There were the Dodgers and the Giants. But what there never could be was a manager of the Dodgers actually managing the Giants.

"That was a little hard to believe," recalls Reese. "The skirmishes we had with the Giants—a lot of times it was war. If you could play well against the Giants, and you had a good year against the Giants, you were successful, whatever the ball club did. There'll never be another rivalry like the Giants and the Dodgers."

Back in late January 1934, Bill Terry, then manager of the champion Giants, had returned to New York for a hot-stove league conversation with the writers. When asked which teams would give the Giants the most trouble, he said, "Pittsburgh, St. Louis, and Chicago will be the teams to beat."

"Do you fear Brooklyn?" he was asked, a facetious question since the Giants had finished 26½ games ahead of the Bums.

"Is Brooklyn still in the league?" he replied, in the same spirit.

With whatever distinction there was between Manhattan and Brooklyn, that remark, which came back to haunt Terry, widened the gulf between them.

Did they hate each other? Passionately is a mild word. The fans couldn't stand one another either. There was that July in the 1930s, when a Dodger fan was drinking at Pat Diamond's bar on Ninth Street, not far from Flatbush. The bartender began to taunt the fan, calling the Dodgers bums. Another patron got on the guy, too, but all in fun.

The Dodger fan was unhappy. He ran out of the saloon. He went to the post office, where he was a trusted employee, unlocked the gun cabinet and took out two revolvers. He returned to the bar and shot both his tormenters. When the police picked him up fifteen minutes later, he told them he had been taking a razzing about his team far too long.

Branca was also shocked because he believed the Dodgers were on their way. "We had started to turn it around. It wasn't because of our record. I just think Mr. Rickey had enough of Leo. He couldn't handle him. I'm not talking off the field. Rickey wanted it his way. He wanted Leo to play the lineup he wanted. He was always interfering."

And so Leo was gone, replacing the "nice guy" whom he had referred to with disdain.

Leo, as usual, claimed that he really didn't mean that nice guys finish last. It's just that nice guys. . . . Well, how this most famous of sports quotes worked its way into the lexicon began at the batting cage one afternoon before a Dodgers-Giants game.

It was July 5, 1946. Red Barber was needling Leo about the home runs the Giants had hit the day before. Some of Leo's writer friends were around him, including Frank Graham, the respected columnist.

Barber's barbs irritated Leo. Durocher looked over at the ponderous Giant hitters and their amiable manager, who had a virtual lifetime mandate from the hero-worshipping Stoneham, who had inherited the team from his father eight years earlier. "Home runs?" snorted Leo, as if anyone could think the mere act of hitting the ball out of a park was enough to make you a finished ballplayer.

"But Ott's a nice guy," continued Barber.

"A nice guy!" barked Leo. "I've been in baseball a long time. Do you know a nicer guy in the world than Mel Ott? He's a nice guy. In last place. Where am I? In first place. I'm in first place. The nice guys are over there in last place, not in this dugout."

And so, the back-page headlines the next day screamed: "NICE GUYS FINISH LAST—LEO." A new expression was born. Leo contended that only Graham got it right, but it was too late. Evermore, Leo was to be connected with that phrase which, unfortunately, had a ring of truth to it. And what if Ott had said it? It would have been forgotten. But coming from Leo, the guy who *could* have said it, and did in fact say something very close to it—well then, it took on an added dimension, even truth.

Recalling Leo's "nice guy" statement, Branca concluded, "It's not true. Nice guys finish first. You couldn't be a bad guy and get your team to play for you well enough consistently to finish first." To Branca, Leo *was* a nice guy, at least not a bad guy. A guy the Dodgers would have won repeated championships for if he hadn't moved to the Giants. Instead, the Dodgers failed to repeat in 1948, won in 1949, but not again until 1952. And that was the team of Duke and Jackie and Campy and Skoonj and Newk and Preacher and Oisk and Gillie and Pee Wee. But not of Leo.

In 1950, Shotton was still managing the Dodgers. The next year— the Bobby Thomson–Ralph Branca playoff year—Dressen managed the Dodgers. "When Leo moved over to the Giants, and Charlie became our manager and we played the Giants, I think Charlie managed against Durocher, not the Giants. I think it was like the pupil trying to outdo the professor," said Branca.

Stoneham and Carl Hubbell, the director of the Giants' farm system, went to Leo's Manahattan apartment to meet with him. Leo wasn't home yet, and they barged in on Laraine. She was listening to the Dodgers game on the radio. "I don't know whether Leo has had a chance to tell you, Mrs. Durocher," said Stoneham, "but he is going to start managing the Giants in Pittsburgh tomorrow."

"Then why," she asked, "am I listening to the Dodgers?" And she turned off the radio.

"Durocher is out, Shotton is in," Rickey told the press. This was something more than page-one headlines. This was a social revolution. And for at least two new immigrants to America, the change was profound. George Freeman, the senior legal counsel for *The New York Times*, explains:

"In 1948 my parents came over from Hungary. They had just got off Ellis Island and they were proud that they knew all about American politics. They had studied hard. They knew about Washington and Jefferson and the election coming up with Truman and Dewey. And then they see on the newsstands every paper has this story on page one—'Durocher Quits,' and here's a name they never heard of. Durocher. They were so upset because they had never heard of him and they had never studied about him. And they thought they were Americans."

The Dodgers were 37–38 under Leo. Many of them still had confidence he would have gotten them in the chase. Others, though, implied they were happy he was gone. All of them seemed as stunned as the Freemans.

As Jackie Robinson waited in the visitors locker room in Cincinnati for Shotton to rejoin the club and replace Leo, he said, "I sure do like to play for that man. I can hardly wait."

Pee Wee was honest: "I'm a Durocher man myself. But Leo was on the spot. He had to win or quit, and he never would have quit. But I'll play my head off for Shotton."

Furillo, volatile, and no friend of Leo's, added, "May the best man win has always been my motto."

CHAPTER
X

STARTING OVER

"**W**ITH DUROCHER GONE, the Dodgers won't be the same," said one fan to the Brooklyn *Eagle*. While another suggested, "It'll be good for the team's morale. Now we'll have peace and quiet."

Both were right. The Dodgers would never be the same, but they'd never have the same exquisite turmoil either. The Brooklyn Dodgers as many knew them ceased to exist when Leo went up the river.

The Dodger players realized something the owners didn't: The rival Giants would be harder to beat now with Leo as their manager. They were 8–4 against them until Leo went over. Now the Dodgers would be the hated enemy for Leo's guys, and there'd be no coasting. When Leo went to the Giants, they were 27–38. They were a dispirited club, heavy-handed, heavy-footed, patsies for the Dodgers. The Giants won 7 of their 10 remaining meetings with Brooklyn.

Leo took over the Giants on July 17 in Pittsburgh. "I want to get a little life in this club," he announced. "Maybe we'll make a few changes that might provide the spark we need."

Durocher didn't actually have a Giants uniform, so he took Coach Red Kress's and borrowed the shoes from one of his pitchers.

Mize slugged his twentieth homer, Whitey Lockman went 5 for 5. But Leo needed a pinch hitter in the eighth with his boys trailing. There were men on second and third, two out, and he needed a hit.

Thomson, whom Durocher had watched in batting practice, was on the bench. Leo called for Bobby, and Bobby hit a single to knock in 2 runs. The Giants won the opener of the Durocher Era, 6–5.

Ten days later, in a pennant-race atmosphere between two clubs having disappointing seasons, he returned to Brooklyn. Shotton considered the game important enough to have Preacher Roe skip his regular turn to be able to start against the Giants.

At 8:00 A.M. that day lines began forming, even though this was a night game, twelve hours away. More than sixty policemen, on foot and on horseback, kept the milling crowds in some sort of Brooklyn order. Frick anticipated even more problems inside the park. He ordered Bill Klem, supervisor of umpires, to talk to Durocher and warn him against unnecessary arguing. "I'll manage my club the same as always," Durocher shot back.

Klem also spoke to Shotton, telling him, "You know these Brooklyn fans, Barney. Mr. Frick doesn't want any trouble tonight."

The amused Shotton replied, "I don't plan to do anything I'd be ashamed of."

A record Ebbets Field night crowd of 33,932 turned out, all to see a manager in the dugout. Just after the lineups were announced, the loudspeaker carried a special message that any fan on the field would be ejected.

People turned surly immediately when the Giants knocked Roe out with a 5-run first inning.

In the sixth, New York pitcher Sheldon Jones was rocked for 3 runs and fans looked to the Giant dugout to see if Leo would make his entrance or signal a pitcher to warm up in the bullpen. But Leo wasn't making himself visible to the fans. Instead, he relayed his signals through a coach.

The Giants hammered 17 hits, won, 13–4, and knocked the Dodgers from second to third place. Within a month, the Giants were in contention, even though this was not a team that Leo liked.

In a game at Boston three weeks later, Durocher sent his lumbering sluggers bunting in the seventh inning after they managed only 2 hits off Nelson Potter in six innings.

First the 215-pound Mize laid down a bunt along third. Then 205-pound Willard Marshall followed with another. Walker Cooper doubled, scoring Mize, and a 4-run rally was on. The Giants won the game.

In the Giants' first few appearances in the Polo Grounds, the fans had been hostile to Leo, booing when he brought out the lineup card, hooting when he made an appearance on the top of the dugout steps. But a few days after the odd array of bunts, the New York fans sensed that maybe, just maybe, this hated son of a bitch could really do something with their collection of slow power-hitters. He may have been a bastard, but now he was their bastard.

So for the first time, Polo Grounds fans rallied behind Leo as their boys beat the Cubs twice to move into second place past the Dodgers. The Giants amassed 19 hits in a 14–9 first-game victory. Their winning streak reached 7 games, the longest in the league that season. They had won 13 of 18 under Leo.

This didn't mean that Leo was happy at the way life was treating him. He noted Robinson's sudden resurgence at the plate: "He hit for Shotton and he wouldn't hit for me," grumped Leo. Once again, he was taking it personally.

There was also another ex-Dodger he was not in perfect sync with: Stanky, now with the Boston Braves. After a game in Boston, when the Brat refused to pose with the Lip for photographers, Leo blurted, "I need Stanky like I need a third eye."

This was actually a bit more sophisticated than Leo's ordinary "Go fuck yourself in the head," and certainly up there with this one from his playing days: When a guy would try to spike him at second he yelled, "I'll spit in your right eye and twist my spikes in it."

The Giants were rolling. Leo turned around a team that had been 27–38 under Ott, and it played 51–38 for Durocher, a .573 clip. It wouldn't be good enough to catch the Braves or other first-division teams. But it was a start. Leo already was thinking about next year late in the season.

In a September game in Boston, he saw his old buddy and pitcher, Fitzsimmons, who was coaching the Braves. Fat Freddie asked Leo if he were planning changes in his coaching staff. Leo replied that he was, and asked Freddie if he would like to join them. Perhaps Leo shouldn't have said anything, for Fitzsimmons was under a Braves contract. Before next season began, it would result in tampering charges against Durocher.

True to his victimized nature, Leo recalled he had merely told Fitzsimmons the truth. "What else could I have done?" said Leo, when challenged. "Spit in his eye?"

That first season with the Giants ended with the team in fifth place. Despite the winning record, Leo wrote up a report for

Stoneham on what the club needed for 1949: "Back up the truck," was Leo's advice. Unload what you've got. Bring in something new.

Leo needed some pitching. But his efforts to acquire Branca from the Dodgers failed. He was also on the lookout for a shortstop to replace slow Buddy Kerr (even though Kerr had set a record for errorless chances) and he needed a replacement for slow, homer-hitting Mize. And that was just for starters.

In November, Leo brought Frisch back to the Polo Grounds. Hiring Frisch might have been a curious act for another manager, but not for Leo. Frisch, after all, was the guy who had him chased out of St. Louis ("Can't stand Durocher. Him or me," Frisch had told Rickey). Yet, after the 1948 season, when Frisch was dropped as a Giants announcer, Stoneham asked Leo to hire him as coach in 1949.

"I'd swim the East River to get that guy," said a gracious Leo. (Apparently, though, the broadcast sponsors thought differently. Gravel-voiced Frisch would grate on listeners with shopworn analysis—"Oh, those bases on balls!")

Also in November, Leo hired Fitzsimmons, another old Giant hero, as his pitching coach. Leo liked his pitching coach to be the one to change pitchers. That way, they couldn't argue with him. He didn't want to be standing on the mound while his pitchers were griping, "Hey, I'm all right, don't take me out." He didn't want anyone to waste his time.

Now with a pitching coach he respected, Leo was ready to return to the field. He said he was going to coach at third.

Barely after celebrating New Year's 1949, Leo wound up in hot water with Chandler again—because of Fitzsimmons.

Leo's actions had helped popularize a new term in baseball—tampering. "Manager Durocher professed ignorance of the tampering rule," said a stern Chandler. "Such ignorance is not excused now and will not be in the future."

What distressed Chandler was that Fitzsimmons had made the overture to Leo while with Boston, in the same league as Leo's Giants. "Enforcement of the tampering rule is so important to the good name of baseball. . . . Baseball players and coaches are under obligation to give their loyal services solely to the club with which they contract," claimed Chandler. "The American people might easily lose confidence in the integrity of baseball if they observed players and coaches of one club carrying on negotiations . . . with a rival . . . " he concluded.

Fitzsimmons was fined $500 and suspended thirty-one days,

March 1 to April 1, training season. In fact, Chandler said he had almost banished him for the year. The commissioner also was fining the Giants $2,000.

Stoneham, though, was relieved. He had feared the worst—that Leo was gone again, to be joined in exile with Fitzsimmons. Chandler noted, "except for the fact that Frederick Fitzsimmons has had long and honorable service in baseball, the commissioner would deprive the New York club of his services for the 1949 season."

Leo escaped being tied up in tampering. But he couldn't escape his proclivity for swatting fans. On April 28, he hit a fan. Again. For the second time in four years he was accused of assaulting an ex-serviceman.

This time it was in the Polo Grounds, in the late afternoon after the Dodgers had trounced the Giants, 15–2. A twenty-two-year-old former ice-cream company worker from Brooklyn, Fred Boysen, was hospitalized at Sydenham Hospital in Manhattan. "Leo knocked me down and kicked me when the game was over," he told hospital authorities.

"Nothing happened," said Leo. "Somebody tried to take my cap as I stepped out of the dugout. I shoved him, grabbed my cap back, and that was all there was to it."

There were, in fact, several versions, none agreeing. The police report said Boysen suffered abdominal contusions. His lawyer said he would file a complaint against Leo.

Every fan in the Polo Grounds had his own version of the incident, which apparently was seen by hundreds in the upper tier as they were leaving.

Though it's hard to believe today, after the games in the Polo Grounds, fans would walk toward the center field clubhouse—players often alongside. The players would go up the steps to the locker rooms while fans would go out the doors at field level to take the subway. Boysen and his cousin joined the crowd on the field and walked toward the clubhouse.

From his hospital bed, Boysen admitted he had kept up a "running raspberry" at Durocher. Shouting, "You're a bum, Durocher," and "Get another pitcher," Boysen waved a white handkerchief every time Leo strode to the mound to change pitchers. "After the game my cousin and I went on the field. We were passing first base. On our way over to talk to Jackie Robinson, Durocher came up behind me. He grabbed me and punched me."

An eyewitness confirmed that about one hundred feet past second base, Durocher came up behind them. Then Durocher suddenly punched Boysen from behind, hitting him in the neck and knocking him down. Durocher kicked him in the groin, the witness said.

Boysen recalled going down, and then "as I tried to get up—I was dizzy—he kicked me in the stomach. I didn't try to hit him."

Mize and Frisch pulled Durocher away and into the clubhouse. Boysen was hauled outside, where, he claimed, he collapsed.

The next day, Leo was suspended "indefinitely." This time, though, there were no shadowy hints of past criminal activity. He was suspended before trial for allegedly hitting a fan who had called him names.

This suspension, New York decided, was unsupportable. It led to editorials in the *Times* and *Daily Mirror*—the *Times* asked for "a public hearing" but no lynching. The *Mirror* asked for "the American principle of fair play."

What the fans and papers didn't know, however, was that Chandler was getting reports of potential violence in Harlem, because Boysen was Puerto Rican. Leo was on the verge of starting a race riot. At least, that's what Chandler believed.

For the public, Happy said he was keeping "an open and free mind" and wanted to be as "impartial as possible." But he suspended Leo anyway. The Lip was on the train to Boston when he learned of the suspension. "Ridiculous," he claimed, and appointed Frisch interim manager.

The writers following the team drafted a "unanimous expression of confidence" in Durocher. It was presented to the public by the *Mirror*'s Ken Smith, secretary-treasurer of the Baseball Writers Association.

Boysen, meanwhile, left the hospital and his lawyer quit the case because he said he was "a tax lawyer" and not expert in criminal or negligence suits.

Leo's story was that "it's one of those things that has happened a hundred times on ball fields when we rush to the clubhouse." He said that about the sixth inning, "I heard somebody riding me hard" and "using pretty vile language." It must have been for Leo to notice.

When he returned to the bench from the coaching lines, he asked players to try to spot the guy. "But after taking one look at him I decided to ignore him and that I did right up to the end of the game. With the last out I started from the coaching lines for the clubhouse.

Just as I was going past second base somebody rushed up to me and I thought he was trying to steal my cap, which frequently happens on ball fields. I didn't even know this was the same fellow who had been riding me from the stands."

Leo claims he "shook him off—and so help me that's all the attention I gave it until the newspapers kept calling me up as though I had murdered somebody."

A day after the suspension, a Giants fan came forward and announced he, and not Durocher, was the one who "accidentally kicked and tripped over" Boysen. A thirty-three-year-old railroad fireman, George Cronk, said he had submitted an affidavit to the Giants to this effect.

Cronk claimed he had seen Boysen lunge toward Durocher as the pair headed for center field. Leo then defensively swung his left elbow. Boysen fell. "I was so close behind him, I couldn't help myself. I tripped over him. I supposed I kicked him in the leg or some other place in so doing and then stepped over him. I apologized."

Following this unbelievable statement, Cronk added that he also had heard Boysen heckling Leo, "You're still the bum you were in Brooklyn."

It had all changed around now. Instead of it being a situation where an irate manager had slugged a wise-guy fan, it had become the manager and his players walking to their clubhouse in peril of crazy fans.

The players said that they referred to their postgame walk to the clubhouse as the "death march." Certainly, incidents were not uncommon: fighting between players and fans, with fans snatching gloves and caps.

Leo flew to Cincinnati for a hearing with Chandler, knowing that if he was found to have hit Boysen, his career would be over. The Giants worked furiously to discredit Boysen and to exonerate their man. The club sent Chandler more than one hundred affidavits. Meanwhile, Chandler's own investigator, a former FBI agent, also returned to Cincinnati to disclose his information.

Leo, meanwhile, was charged by Boysen's new attorney with assault.

Chandler finally made his decision: The evidence was "not sufficient." From then on, he added, teams must keep fans away from the players and off the field until players went to their clubhouses. Also, it was up to the stadium security to kick out anyone using objectionable language. A new era was beginning because Leo had beat up a fan again. The average fan's closeness to the athlete was about to end.

The Giants that night celebrated the end of Leo's suspension. With Frisch still managing, they broke a 3-game losing streak at the Polo Grounds against the Pirates. Even at Ebbets Field, where the Dodgers were playing the Reds, the fans cheered when the announcement of Leo's reinstatement was made over the P.A. system.

For the first time, Chandler explained the suspension "was preventive rather than punitive." And just what did this mean?

"Prominent representatives of the colored race" had called the commissioner, indicating further incidents.

When Leo returned to the Polo Grounds after his suspension ended, the vestigial fans who had never been in his corner since he had taken over now greeted him warmly. As he made the long walk from center field to the dugout, the public address system played "I Love You As I Never Loved Before." Leo tipped his cap. He had become a Giant.

"I felt wonderful," he told reporters in the dugout. "There are just no words for it."

A few minutes later, process servers delivered a summons to Durocher in the locker room. The summons was in regard to Boysen's civil suit.

Jauntily, Leo trotted out to third when the Giants got up in the first, again he received another round of applause. His boys won big, 11–4, over the Pirates.

Durocher arrived in court at 9:30 A.M. sharp on the appointed day to answer the summons. But Boysen wasn't there. And just when the case was about to be dismissed at 11:00, Boysen suddenly appeared, claiming, "I was lost in the subway." He apologized to Leo and said he was willing to "take it like a good sport and forget the whole thing." Then Boysen told Leo, "Sorry, Mr. Durocher, I hope you have luck." (Unbeknownst to Leo, Boysen had dropped the charge a few days earlier.)

A smiling Durocher grasped Boysen's hand and said, "Thanks very much."

Just as Boysen was leaving, a warrant officer arrested him. A registered nurse had accused Boysen of being one of three men who had stolen her pocketbook in Harlem. She said she recognized him because of his picture in the papers. He was released on five hundred dollars' bail.

The next day the robbery charge against Boysen was dismissed. A magistrate told the woman her story was a "figment of her imagination induced by newspaper publicity." The jurist also called her story "fantastic."

Leo had business to conduct during this brouhaha. Two days later, he signed a new contract extended through the 1951 season and got a $10,000 raise. The Boysen case was forgotten. Now, Leo was ensconced as the Giants manager, not merely a one-year stopgap for the old tradition. (A month later, Frisch left the team to become the Cubs' manager, succeeding Charlie Grimm.)

Durocher was back from his 4-game protective suspension about two months when he was suspended again. This was worse than belting some poor fan, though. This time Leo committed the ultimate baseball sin. He touched an umpire.

In a game at Wrigley Field on June 25, he stormed onto the field protesting umpire Lee Ballanfant's call of a close play at second. In the shouting that followed, he muscled dangerously close to Ballanfant, actually going chest-to-chest. Ballanfant summarily dismissed Leo from his sight, the second time in five days an ump had kicked Durocher out of a game.

Frick fined Leo $150. Worse, he suspended him for five days, saying he "bumped into the umpire and used abusive language." Leo insisted Ballanfant had been out of position when he called Hal Jeffcoat safe at second. Somehow, Frick wouldn't buy Leo's pleas. He was banished until the Dodgers played at the Polo Grounds five days later.

That day hardly is marked on calendars. But July 5, 1949, well may be—the day the Giants got their first black players. One story at the time described it as "the unprecedented spectacle of two Negroes in Giant uniforms."

Stoneham had bought an outfielder named Monte Irvin, and an infielder, Henry Thompson, from his Jersey City farm club in the International League. Irvin was leading the league in batting, apparently a prerequisite for a black to be called up in those days. That move left only the Yankees of the New York teams without black players—it would be another six years before they brought up Elston Howard. By the time they did, Jackie Robinson's ten-year major league career had nearly ended.

Irvin was familiar with the Polo Grounds. He had played there many times as a member of the Newark Eagles of the Negro National League.

"Hank Thompson and I reported at the same time," Irvin recalled of his Giants debut. "We were the first ones in the clubhouse and got there early.

"We were sitting on the stool. Leo came over and introduced himself to us, then he went off and got dressed. After the rest of the team put on uniforms, he introduced us to the entire squad.

"I remember he said, 'Glad to have you, hope you can help us.' And then he said, "I'm only going to say one thing about color: You can be green or be pink on this team. If you can play baseball and help this team you're welcome to play.'

"And it was true."

Late in 1949 the Giants were going nowhere except toward a fifth-place finish behind the pennant-winning Dodgers. Leo had gotten rid of Mize, who went on to become a celebrity pinch hitter with the Yankees. Walker Cooper was gone too. Then Joe Williams, an important New York newspaper voice with the *Telegram*, blasted the Giants.

He pointed out that the team's box office slump set in at about time the Leo was made manager. The Giants still hadn't had a pennant winner in eleven years. They had finished no higher than third since 1937 and eight other times were in the second division, twice finishing last. The blame rested with Stoneham, charged Williams, and it wasn't getting better under Leo.

After the dismal season, Laraine came to Leo's defense, writing in a movie fan magazine that Leo was

Chivalrous: "You cannot light your cigarette, open a door, pick up your handkerchief or pull out a chair when Leo is within arm's reach."

Sober: "Only eats steak and potatoes, drinks lots of milk."

Intellectual: "Every night of his life he reads one whodunit in addition to a more serious book."

Generous: "No one can pay for anything, from a bar of chocolate to a box at the Polo Grounds, when Leo is around."

Sensitive: "When he loses, he's like someone lost."

What Leo really wanted was a double-play combination, not nice words from his wife. He knew that 1949 had turned sour for the

Braves after their 1948 pennant. He knew that his old boy, Stanky, was feuding with his manager Southworth, who likewise wasn't getting along with his former rookie-of-the-year shortstop, Alvin Dark. Stanky and Dark, second and short—a double-play combination.

The problem was, Stoneham didn't want Stanky, and the owner certainly didn't want to lose more links to the Giants' past, a past that was getting dimmer and dimmer. It was bad enough that Ott was given a meaningless front-office title.

Then in December, Lou Perini, the Braves' owner, cornered Stoneham in the Hotel Commodore in Manhattan. Perini asked for Sid Gordon, Willard Marshall, and Buddy Kerr, and another player— and the Giants could get Stanky and Dark. No way, said Stoneham, but he felt obligated to inform Leo of the offer. Leo was insistent. He wanted Stanky and Dark.

So in mid-December the big deal was hatched for Marshall, Kerr, Gordon, and a rookie right-hander named Sam Webb. The movement of Leo's slow, power-hitting players was under way.

"I am now set at second base with a combination that can make the double play," said Leo.

This was the biggest Giants' deal in a dozen years, but Leo had thought this out pretty well. He knew he'd have Hank Thompson for third and he figured the fans would forget about the popular, Brooklyn-born Gordon once the team began winning. As for Braves manager Southworth, he was happy to get rid of two malcontents. They had grated on him so much that he had actually retired for a while in August.

As 1950 began, Leo was just as happy. He had gotten the players he wanted, gotten rid of the players he didn't. Of the players who helped the Giants set the home run record of 221 in 1947, only five remained. Finally, he had the kind of team he liked. No nice guys. Tough guys who could run.

"We won't need any bulldozers to push our men around the bases," he announced in Phoenix before the start of spring training. It was a club, he said, that can "hit and run, can get that extra base, can make those double plays, and can grab those bleeders in the outfield."

The erstwhile overweight Giants used to come to Phoenix and immediately head to the weight-reducing mineral baths at a nearby spa. "We've gotten rid of so much beef," said Leo, "that we won't need those baths. You won't see that old gang anymore."

His starters were going to be Dave Koslo, Larry Jansen, Sheldon Jones, and Monte Kennedy. There was a returnee from the Mexican League, Sal Maglie, but he just hung around the bullpen. Nobody really knew much about him. Leo also had four of baseball's fastest runners in Bobby Thomson, Whitey Lockman, Hank Thompson, and Alvin Dark. On the opening day of camp, he named Dark his captain. He had a "hustling catcher" in Wes Westrum. He felt pretty good about this club.

"Brooklyn," Leo proclaimed, "is the team to beat. Although you wonder with all that talent why they're not doing better." About the young Phillies he said, "They've got only Robin Roberts and Russ Meyer as reliable pitchers."

Leo didn't always make accurate predictions. But he knew his players. He moved Don Mueller to right field, where he would find a niche. Then Leo told Dark: Play where you're comfortable.

This was a key move. At Boston, Southworth had wanted Dark to play in certain areas. Dark had fought with him.

"It all goes back to what Miller Huggins used to tell me when I was with the Yankees," said Leo. "Hug would say, 'You can't be here and smell a play over there. You must be where the play will be.' " Dark will be playing his hunches on the hitters, said Durocher. Just like I did.

Meanwhile, Laraine was becoming one of the team's most popular adjuncts. With her wit and style, she was regularly asked for opinions. And for the 1950 season, she was landing her own television program. It would be a fifteen-minute pregame interview show over Channel 11, sponsored by Chesterfield cigarettes. Chesterfield had been a prominent sign in the stadium, its "h" signaling a hit, or one of its "e's" signifying an error.

Opening Day saw the most thoroughly revamped Giants squad since the days of Mr. McGraw. But Leo was booed. They didn't like his off-season trades. Ironically, the traded heroes were back, for it was the Giants vs. the Braves.

The Giants got off to a bad start, and someone remarked, "Laraine's running a better show from the Polo Grounds than her husband."

It was a refreshing television program. She admitted she had known nothing of the game until she married Leo. Because of her disarming style, she would get someone like the barrel-chested Fitzsimmons to concede he could square dance—she had him dance right on camera. She then said she planned to play marbles with Pee Wee Reese, whose nickname came from a type of marble, and who had been a marbles champ as a kid in Louisville. She also told Frisch, the Cubs' manager, "I'm sorry, Frank, that I can't wish you luck." Sweet Laraine.

Her not-so-sweet husband and his old nemesis, Jackie Robinson, finally brought their own feud out into the open. It was at a night game in Ebbets Field in late June. With Jackie at bat, Leo shouted to Jansen, "C'mon, Larry, get the manager out of there."

Robinson retaliated, "Are you wearing your wife's perfume tonight, Leo?"

"So you want to get personal?" Durocher shouted.

"You're damned right," Jackie retorted. "Let's get personal."

Leo was coaching at first base, which meant that every inning when he went into the coach's box, he'd be only forty or fifty feet from Robinson. They went at it all night. But after the game, Leo claimed he never said anything to Robinson, although Robinson admitted he spoke to Leo about the perfume.

Meanwhile, Leo had made the right move with one of his pitchers. Maglie was developing into one of the league's stars at the age of thirty-three. This forgotten expatriate handcuffed the Cardinals in his first start, moving Musial to say that Maglie had the best curve in the National League. Quickly, he became known as the Barber for the way he shaved the corners—not to mention the way he gave the enemy batters a little "chin music" if they stepped too close to the plate. And with his facial stubble he had a menacing glower.

Leo, though, nearly lost it on July 4. First, he almost fought with his old nemesis, Furillo, after Koslo had hit him with a pitch. The Giants were in sixth place, and by dropping the second game of the holiday doubleheader to the Dodgers, they finished a streak that had seen them lose 13 of 15 games—some atrociously, as in 16–4 and 18–4 losses.

"My type of ball club," he had said, and now Leo was becoming a joke in baseball. But he persevered. After hitting rock bottom, he told the Giants, "Forget everything, the record. Go out, have fun—just remember to come back to the ballpark tomorrow night."

This was his genius, too—knowing when to ease up. The Giants won the next night, 13–3, over the Cardinals, and started a 9-game winning streak. In all, they won 17 of 18 games.

It would not be good enough to overtake the Phillies, who for one year would be known as the Whiz Kids. Leo kept hopping, though. In August he wound up protesting a loss to the Phillies.

All that Leo's man Stanky had done was wave his arms behind second base while Andy Seminick was at bat. It distracted Seminick? So look in the rule book, Durocher demanded of umpire Lon Warneke, and tell me where it's forbidden to wave your arms in a batter's line of vision.

Stanky actually had done it four times against Seminick the game before. The umps met with Leo the next day. And Leo promised—cross his heart—that he would lay off until they got a ruling from Frick. Leo really meant to keep his promise, but then he got angry after Seminick flattened Thompson in a base path collision. So from the dugout, Leo ordered Stanky to wave his arms again.

Stanky, now becoming an expert arm waver, had first tried the gimmick a few days earlier against Bob Elliott in Boston. The idea came to Stanky when Elliott, at the plate, had asked the second base umpire to move out of his line of vision. When the ump, Al Barlick, moved out, Stanky moved in and began dancing.

That was fun and games. But the batter can be seriously distracted. And in the Phillies game, Maglie nicked Seminick while Stanky was dancing around. Elliott hit two doubles to beat the Giants and Seminick walked his three other times at bat.

Stanky continued his shenanigans the next day. Warneke was fed up. "You're out of here," Warneke said to Stanky. Pretty soon, there was a free-for-all. The Giants lost in eleven innings and Leo filed an official protest. The Phillies termed Durocher "bush."

Frick, who should have kept a memo pad just to deal with Leo's appointments, met with him. Frick conceded that it was not illegal, but added it was not sportsmanlike. "There are extremes and baloney and this was baloney," ruled Frick. It wasn't legalese, but it was valid. Stanky's arm waving, the umps had ruled, "constituted conduct detrimental to the best interests of the game." Leo was quite familiar with this catchall phrase.

Arm waving or no, Maglie, Stanky, and the other players helped the Giants to the best late-season mark in the league. They wound up winning 50 of their final 72 games. On the next-to-the-last day of the season, they beat the Braves to clinch third—their highest showing since 1942.

For Stanky and Dark, this was retribution, and they hugged each other. The team finished only 5 games behind the Phillies. Leo's deal was vindicated—the Stanky-Dark combination turned into the pivotal ingredient of the team, while in Boston Kerr slumped, Marshall was benched, and Gordon tailed off.

After the season, Ott was dropped entirely. He left the team that he had started with when he was a sixteen-year-old.

From top to bottom, in the field and the front office, this team was now Leo's. In a way, it was like the housecleaning he had done in Brooklyn a decade earlier, only this time there was no zany MacPhail in the way, or to share the limelight with.

The Dodgers still occupied a place in his mind, if not in his heart. With the season ended, he reflected on the Dodgers, who were managed by Shotton: "They've got a great bunch of players—everything—and sometimes you wonder why they didn't win by ten games."

Just after the World Series—the one the second-place Dodgers weren't in—Rickey was pushed out of Brooklyn in a struggle with O'Malley, who described Rickey's departure in painful terms. O'Malley, after all, had developed "the warmest possible feelings of affection" and was "terribly hurt and sorry."

Leo was still in New York, and now Rickey was gone.

CHAPTER
XI

SOLIDIFYING
THE LEGEND

I N 1951, Leo set forth the following hypothetical scenario in an interview, "Look, I'm playing third base. My mother's on second. The ball's hit to short center. As she goes by me on the way to third, I'll accidentally trip her up. I'll help her up, brush her off, tell her I'm sorry. But she doesn't get to third."

This was the sort of stuff the once "nice guys" Giants were fed. And they responded.

The 1951 Giants were no Whiz Kid team out of nowhere. They were not the 1969 Mets. People forget that in a preseason poll by *The Sporting News* more sportswriters picked the Giants to win the pennant than the Dodgers.

Spring training had arrived. Leo considered a strong, nervous young rookie from Birmingham. "Hey, kid! What are you going to show me today?" were the first words Willie Mays remembers Leo said to him.

Willie was the kind of player who caused others to stop and watch. But he was considered too inexperienced to make it to the big leagues just yet. At least, Leo remembered, that was the way Stoneham wanted it. Leo always claimed that Willie had been ready immediately—just as, a decade earlier, Pete Reiser had been ready but management hadn't agreed, and just as Campanella had been ready.

At the start of camp, Leo announced that the Giants needed a quick start because early in the season the four strong Eastern teams would be playing one another frequently. Leo got his wish, on Opening Day at any rate. Larry Jansen won at Boston—the Giants had not won an opening game since 1946. Bobby Thomson was in center field, and Hank Thompson was at third. But Monte Irvin, at first base in an experiment, committed 2 errors.

There weren't too many victories after Opening Day, though, and by mid-May the Giants were atrocious. They lost 11 straight games. "It would take a miracle for them to win the championship now," said the *Times*'s Arthur Daley.

True to form, when things got nasty, Leo blamed the umps. In late May, Leo got into a fight in the dugout with Lon Warneke after a game in St. Louis. Leo claimed that Warneke had picked on his boys, tossing Stanky out of the game when Red Schoendienst should have been dismissed as well. Perhaps because Warneke did some shoving of his own, Leo was only hit with a hundred-dollar fine.

There was another incident that spring involving Sal Maglie and Jackie Robinson. In this particular game, Maglie threw a duster at Robinson. In his next at-bat, Robinson bunted along the first base line, and when Maglie ran over to field it, Robinson barreled into him.

"This sort of thing has to stop," Frick pleaded the next day.

After 30 games, the Giants needed a shot. Dressen was now managing the Dodgers, who zoomed out to a big lead, winning 28 of their first 36 games. Down at the Minneapolis farm, Mays was hitting .477.

Willie, who would spend his entire career looking for ways to relax (he often collapsed out of sheer tension), was at a movie one off-day. About halfway through it, the house lights went on and a man came onstage to make an announcement. "If Willie Mays is in the audience, would he please report immediately to his manager at the hotel."

He returned to the hotel office and was told to call Durocher. "What for?" asked Willie.

When he was told the Giants wanted him, he panicked and refused to make the call. "I'm not ready to go yet," he pleaded. Then reluctantly, he picked up the phone after someone dialed Durocher. "I'm not coming," he told last-place Leo.

"*What!*" screamed Durocher, for starters. Then for two minutes he roared.

Finally, Willie got a chance to speak. He was scared, he didn't think he could hit big-league pitching, he didn't want to go to New York.

"What," asked a suddenly benign Durocher, "are you hitting now?"

Willie told him, "Four seventy-seven."

"Well," Durocher barked, barely containing his anger, "do you think you can hit two fucking fifty for me?"

That didn't seem so bad, so Willie went to join the Giants, who were in Philadelphia.

Willie would never forget the sight of Leo's hotel room. This was only a weekend series, but the closet was stuffed with Leo's clothes and shoes.

"Glad to see you, son," Leo said, adding, "glad you're hitting four seventy-seven."

Leo might have made players nervous with his style, but he made Mays feel comfortable right away. He simply buttered up the big rookie. "I wanted you to be here all along, from that first day I saw you in Sanford," he said. "But Mr. Stoneham said no. He said you needed some more seasoning, but I could see that you were a natural and only needed to play." He told Willie not to worry about a thing "but playing ball." He said the only problem the club had was being so far behind the Dodgers. What it needed was to get a big streak going.

Before Willie put on a uniform, Leo spoke to Irvin about the rookie. "Leo put us together," recalls Irvin, Willie's old friend from the Negro Leagues. "We roomed together. Leo said, 'Look after him, watch who he talks to, make sure he gets to the ballpark on time, make sure he doesn't have a lot of hangers-on, make sure he talks to the right people.' " Leo had plans for this kid.

A locker was waiting for Willie right next to Irvin's. Leo came over and spoke to Willie in a strangely fatherly way that Willie didn't see Leo use with other ballplayers. "Son, you're batting third and playing center field," Leo told him, setting him up for the next twenty or so years.

Willie went 0 for 5. His first at-bat, he took a third strike against Bubba Church. But the Giants won, and so his debut evoked only a few words in the next day's papers. That day, a Saturday afternoon, the Giants climbed to .500 for the first time all season as Larry Jansen pitched a 7-hitter. But against Robin Roberts the scared rookie went 0 for 3, although he walked twice. In the third game, on Sunday, the Giants moved over .500—but Willie was 0 for 4 against Russ Meyer.

He came to New York 0 for 12. And they were returning to the Polo Grounds to face the Braves and Warren Spahn, the best lefty in the business.

When Willie arrived he was confronted with a stadium that had confounded Leo's outfielders. It was 475 feet from home plate to dead center. It also troubled his catchers: Incredibly, there were 74 feet behind home plate to the backstop. Chasing a wild pitch was practically like running to first base. It was not unusual for a runner to advance from first to third on a wild pitch or passed ball. But this was the truly intriguing part of the place: It was only 258 feet—less than three times the distance from home to first—to the right field foul pole. And it was only 280 feet to the left field foul pole. You could hit a Chinese home run that didn't even go 260 feet—and you could hit a 450-foot ball for an out. Even the distances to left-center and right-center went far beyond the average hitter's abilities: 425 to left-center, 450 to right-center. This area would become Mays's bailiwick.

Spahn got the first two hitters in the first inning, and then Mays was up. Ask Willie what Spahn threw and he replies today, "All I know is I swung at it and hit it on top of the left field roof." It was a crusher of a shot, evoking gasps. But the slump still wasn't over.

After that home run against Spahn, Willie went 0 for 13. He was now 1 for 25. Coming in after this latest loss, Leo was so mad he kicked over a chair in the clubhouse and ran upstairs to his office. Willie sat next to his locker and cried. When Durocher emerged, "I saw Willie crying and I put my arm around him," he recalled. "What's the matter, son?" Leo asked.

"Mister Leo," Mays replied. "I can't hit up here." Willie was bawling that he was going to get sent back to the minors.

Leo pointed to his uniform and told him, "Willie, see this across my uniform? It says 'Giants.' As long as I'm the manager of the Giants, you're my center fielder."

And he was.

Leo might have been the all-American out, but he knew what you're supposed to do at the plate, even if he couldn't. He advised Mays to stop turning over his right hand, which forced him to pull the ball. Leo figured if he could get Willie to swing straight away, he had enough power to take the ball deep to right-center—even in that ballpark that drove hitters nuts.

What Leo told Willie worked. Leo also asked him to bat eighth. He explained that it was a dead spot in the batting order and he needed someone to spark it. Leo needed a winning streak and he needed to avoid any weak spots that could prevent a rally.

Willie's slump ended against Pittsburgh with a single. He went 2 for 4, his other hit a triple that landed over the sign in right-center. That big park wasn't going to hurt him, after all. Just as Leo had figured.

Leo had all the answers. When Roy Campanella, another pal from the old days, was behind the plate, he'd get on Willie. Campanella chattered constantly, first asking "How's the folks?" questions, then in a friendly way warning Willie that Newcombe was about to unload a pitch at his head. Willie would listen too.

Finally, one day, Willie realized what had been going on, how his answers to Campy's questions had been distracting him from batting. Willie stomped his feet. Then he motioned to Durocher in the coach's box.

"What's wrong, son?" asked Leo. Four-letter words didn't cross Leo's lips when talking to the impressionable, high-strung youngster.

"He's bothering me," said Willie.

"Pick up a handful of dirt and throw it in his face," barked Leo, and trotted back to third.

Leo nursed Willie along. In a sense, he had two kids with him. Chris Durocher used to copy Leo's attitudinal stance by standing in the dugout with his leg on the top step, jaunty, like Leo. Six-year-old Chris spent more time with Willie that summer than he did with his father. On road trips young Willie and young Chris would eat together, sleep together, have a catch. The pair went to a movie practically every night, then fell asleep in their room reading comic books.

"I grew up in Santa Monica," Chris recalls today. "But when baseball season began, I was with the club. I was a batboy. I rode the bus with them. I shagged balls in the outfield."

"Willie was almost like a son to Dad." And as a parent to his adopted son, Chris, "he was pretty much the way you'd see his public image—he was strict with me. You live with it. I will always be grateful for the things that I could see and do. It was a wonderful childhood. I wish I could bring it back today."

In addition to cajoling Willie, Leo kept the Giants' spirits up during their terrible start.

He got ammunition.

"The Giants is dead," announced Dressen one day in mid-season. It appeared to be true. It was so perfectly stated, so . . . so ungrammatically, or grammatically, pure.

Leo's so-called psychology often confounded his players. They never could be sure what tactic he was using, or why. In late July they dropped a Sunday doubleheader to the Cardinals in St. Louis, 10–1 and 11–2. On top of that, they had to play a night game on Monday. When they staggered into the clubhouse, Leo was waiting. He had remembered a tactic he had employed not too long before.

"Don't anybody get undressed," he began. "You looked like girls out there today. Now I'm giving each one of you an order. I don't want to see any of you until eight o'clock in the morning. You heard me right. Stay out all night, do whatever you want—but don't be back at the hotel until eight. If anybody does, I'll fine him two hundred dollars. Do I make myself clear?" Some of the players were so leery of crossing Leo that they stayed at a friend's, afraid to go to the hotel for fear Leo would spot them.

The next night, Leo was chipper and he smiled as he greeted them as they dragged themselves into the locker room. They won.

Still, on August 11, between games of a doubleheader, the Dodgers surged to their biggest lead of the season—13½ games. They reached that peak when they stopped Boston in the first game while the Giants were being shut out by the Phillies.

The insurmountable lead hardly diminished Leo's fame, even on the floors of Congress. In August, during a hearing before the House Judiciary Committee on exempting baseball from antitrust laws (which it would win), a Republican congressman asked Ford Frick, "Do you have Durocher under control now?"

"If this statement is to stand for posterity, I shouldn't have to answer that," quipped Frick.

At the same hearing, Representative Kenneth Keating asked Frick if Durocher's behavior had improved since leaving the Dodgers. Which led Brooklyn's most noted representative, Emanuel

Celler, to comment, "The Dodgers have improved since he left."
So there, Leo.

Though the Dodgers dropped the second game of their August
11 doubleheader, they still had a 13-game edge to carry them through
the season. And they could even increase that huge lead, for they
were about to square off against the Giants in a 3-game series.

The Giants had to start winning immediately or they could find
themselves 16 games out in just a few more days. This was Durocher's
lineup for the series that was to begin the miracle: first base—Whitey
Lockman; second base—Eddie Stanky; shortstop—Alvin Dark; third
base—Bobby Thomson; left field—Monte Irvin; center field—Willie
Mays; right field—Don Mueller; catcher—Wes Westrum; and pitchers—Sal Maglie, Larry Jansen, Dave Koslo, and Jim Hearn. Leo
honestly believed he could catch the Dodgers. He told his Giants
that they hadn't started to play their best ball yet. "Sweep the Dodgers, we can catch fire."

That is exactly what happened. The Giants swept them and began
a 16-game winning streak. Leo wheeled and encouraged, rarely
negative, always upbeat. The streak lasted from August 12 to August
27—the longest in the league since 1935, the longest for the Giants
in thirty-five years.

The Giants faced the Dodgers again in the middle of September
and were only 5½ games behind. Fans seem to remember that the
Dodgers collapsed after their 13½-game lead in August. But that isn't
what happened. The Dodgers weren't playing .600 ball anymore, but
they weren't playing losing ball either. In fact, when that September
series began at Ebbets Field, the Dodgers won the opener as Don
Newcombe pitched a 2-hit shutout. The next day, with Maglie, the
Giants spun a 2–1 victory.

As the season sped to its dizzying finale, with the Giants chopping
away, Durocher's philosophy kicked in. Win for the moment. This
was Leo with the horses, Leo living for now, Leo making the right
moves.

"He was an excellent tactician," recalls an old acquaintance,
Chub Feeney. He was the Giants' general manager then, sometimes
keeping rein on Leo, a job that continued after Feeney became
National League president. "He ran a ball game as well as anybody
you've ever seen. He was a much better manager when he had
good players, but I guess everybody is. He was not a very patient

manager, but when he had the horses, he knew how to make them run."

With a little more than two weeks remaining, Durocher announced he would use only three starters the rest of the way—Maglie, Jansen, and Hearn. With such a short staff, those who asked whom Leo might pitch tomorrow received the reply, "I want to win today. Tomorrow? It might rain."

What, Leo worry? He chortled with a week to go, "We'll win all our remaining games. The pressure's on them."

The Dodgers were in Boston the final week. There was a game Branca remembers as clearly as the one in which Thomson homered for the pennant. "There was a throw to home," says Branca, "Campy blocked the plate and tagged the guy out. But Frank Dascoli called him safe, Campy threw the glove in the air and he was out of the game. That was about the eighth inning. And then it's the ninth inning and the bases loaded, and who's hitting in Campanella's slot? Wayne Terwilliger. We lost the game, 3–2. That cost us the pennant. Nobody ever talks about it, but Dascoli's horseshit decision cost us the pennant. The guy was out."

After the loss, which cut their lead to half a game, the Dodgers splintered the door to the umps' dressing room. Campanella and Jackie Robinson were involved, reporters said, and maybe even Preacher Roe. Leo loved it. Durocher, the law-and-order guy, said that Robinson should be suspended if he kicked the door. Leo explained that his boy Westrum had been suspended three days for pushing an umpire.

With one day remaining the Giants tied it. "I'm glad they weren't suspended," Leo said of the Dodgers. "We don't want any stigmas on our pennant."

The teams went into Sunday, September 30, the last day of the regular season, tied for first. The Giants, with a 6-game winning streak, played the Braves in Boston while the Dodgers faced the Phillies in Philadelphia. What followed was one of the most dramatic afternoons in baseball history, an afternoon that seemingly could never be topped. But of course it was, just a few days later.

The Giants got it over with first. Larry Jansen pitched a clutch game, at one point retiring twenty-two straight batters. Jansen took a 3–1 lead into the bottom of the ninth, but almost lost it when the Braves scored once and put two runners on base following sloppy fielding by the Giants. But Jansen grimly collected the third out and the Giants produced a 3–2 victory. They also thought it had given them the pennant.

Brooklyn trailed, 6–1, and then, 8–5. The Giants got on their train for New York while the Dodgers were still playing, and losing. But the Dodgers tied it with a 3-run splurge in the eighth. Then the game dragged into extra innings—tenth, eleventh, twelfth. Finally, in the bottom of the twelfth, it was about to end. The Phillies loaded the bases with two out, and Eddie Waitkus faced Newcombe. Waitkus smoked a low line drive to the right of second base. Jackie Robinson raced over, dived, and clutched the ball just off the ground. Umpire Warneke shot his arm into the air, signaling "out." Robinson, groggy, fell hard on his shoulder and collapsed, couldn't get up for a few minutes, then rose and walked unsteadily to the dugout. But he remained in the game.

In the fourteenth, as fate would have it, Robinson came up with two out and Roberts pitching. Robinson crashed a home run into the upper left field stands, giving the Dodgers a 9–8 victory. That forced the second playoff in the seventy-five-year history of the National League.

On the train ride from Boston, the Giants needed to know how the Dodgers were doing. "They had a special phone on the train you could actually use as you went into the station," recalls Feeney. "Whenever we got to a station, I'd call the Dodgers radio station and get the score. I heard the Dodgers won and told the guys.

"A bunch of our guys were getting off in Stamford since they lived in Westchester and Connecticut, and Leo said to them as they were leaving, 'Okay, we'll get 'em tomorrow.'

"And Alvin Dark said, 'You've been saying that every day, Leo. How long can we keep that up?' "

New York City went nuts for this one. Two trains, one carrying the Giants, another carrying the Dodgers, were converging that night. Five thousand fans waited for the Giants when their delayed Merchants Limited train glided into Grand Central at 9:30 at night. Another two thousand Dodger fans waited for their heroes to arrive from Philadelphia.

"The Dodgers are like that every year," one man said of the finish. "They always drive everybody crazy."

The final regular-season standings showed, mute but dramatically, just what the Giants had done:

	W	L	PCT	GB
Dodgers	96	58	.623	—
Giants	96	58	.623	—

Over the last 44 games, the Giants had won 37, including their last 7, and 12 of their last 13. The Dodgers hadn't exactly collapsed. Since their 13½-game lead they played better than .500 ball. But no one had ever staged a finish like the Giants had. Ask the Giants today what held them together, and they'll still tell you Durocher.

Miracle finishes weren't over yet.

First, there was a coin toss to determine who got the opening game, which was to begin the next day. Stoneham lost the toss to Jack Collins, the Dodgers' business manager. If you played the first game of the best-of-three playoff at home, you played the last two away.

That decision still bugs Ralph Branca. "It was stupid," he says. "Someone remembered that in 1946 we had opened the playoffs on the road and we lost, and so they decided that in 1951 we'd open at home. But there was one exception. In 1946 the road trip for us was St. Louis. We were exhausted by the time we got there after a twenty-six-hour train ride. In 1951 it was Manhattan. Wouldn't you rather have your last two games, if you had to play two, at home?"

Instead, the Dodgers chose to open at home.

There was baseball frenzy all over New York, because whichever team won the playoff would immediately face the Yankees in the Series. Acting Mayor Joseph T. Sharkey proclaimed "Baseball Week in the World's Greatest City."

In a case of foreshadowing, the big blow in the opening playoff game was Bobby Thomson's 2-run shot off Branca. With Jim Hearn pitching, the Giants won, 3–1. Monte Irvin also starred, scoring on Thomson's home run, then belting one into the stands himself in the eighth inning, after making a great running catch on Andy Pafko to end the seventh.

Despite the victory, Durocher refused to pose for pictures, "not until this is over." He was edgy. And even though he had always been superstitious—wearing the same clothes if he won, which must have presented an intolerable burden to the dapper Leo—he rarely spoke about it.

His superstition made perfect sense the next day, when the

Dodgers, behind Clem Labine, shut out the Giants, 10–0. During the game, as Wall Street traders examined the stock ticker, they read, "Dow Jones 2 P.M. Stock Averages 30 indus 274.20 up 1.64 . . ." And then: "Baseball NY Giants—no runs two hits no errors . . ."

On Wednesday, October 3, 1951, the Dodgers and Giants met for the National League championship. Newcombe (20–9) started against Maglie (23–6).

The Dodgers got the first run but a bonehead running play by Thomson messed up a potential Giants rally. Brooklyn took a 4–1 lead with a 3-run splurge off Maglie in the eighth. Then Newcombe, tiring badly, tried to preserve it in the ninth. He had pitched more than fourteen innings over the weekend as the Dodgers pitching staff found itself desperately short. He told Dressen he was tired, but Dressen wouldn't make a move, even though he had been calling the bullpen since the sixth inning to see how Branca and Erskine were warming up. (Roe had a sore arm late in the season.)

Then, in the bottom of the ninth, Alvin Dark opened with a single off Gil Hodges's glove, only the fifth hit off Newcombe. Mueller then singled through the right side as Hodges, unaccountably, was holding Dark close to first. Irvin, though, popped out. Lockman rammed a double to left, with Mueller racing to third—but as he slid into the bag, he sprained his left ankle. He was carried off on a stretcher, prolonging the suspense. This was not a seamless rally as memory would have it. It was a rally of fits and starts, held together by Durocher's cajoling from the bench and coach's box. There was a lull on the field, but not at New York Telephone. Through the course of the day, it received more than seven hundred thousand phone calls at its special World Series number.

Dressen called his bullpen. Coach Clyde Sukeforth answered. What to do? Erskine, a sinker ball pitcher, was warming up. He could get a grounder, perhaps a double-play ball. Branca, who had tossed the homer in game one to Thomson, also was warming up. Just as the phone rang, Erskine unloaded a sinker that bounced.

"Erskine's sinker just hit the ground" came the report to Dressen from Sukeforth. Those six words meant Branca.

Ralph was glad to come in. "I liked the pressure," he recalls. "People remember me only as a starter. I had relieved fifteen times that year in addition to twenty-seven starts. There was nothing un- usual about me coming in to that situation, none at all."

There were runners on second and third, and the Dodgers led,

4–2. If Branca intentionally walked Thomson, that could set up a force play at the other bases and the experienced pitcher would face the nervous rookie. But that also went against the "book"—the unwritten set of rules, that included the tenet that you never intentionally put the potential winning run on first. Dressen wasn't a book manager, but he went by it this time.

"Dressen managed against Leo, not against the Dodgers," insists Branca. "Leo could do that to you."

Leo came down from the coach's box at third base to talk to Thomson. Thomson had hit a home run off Branca on Monday in the first game. Leo now asked Thomson if that pitch had been a slider. When Thomson, who had forgotten that it actually was a fastball, said it was a slider, Leo said, "Then look for a fastball this time. He remembers you hit a slider. He won't throw it again. Just be ready for the fastball."

Mays was on deck, practically quaking, praying to God for Thomson to hit a homer so that he didn't have to get up. Yet, Mays had never seen Leo so sure about anything—and in such a tough situation. Sure enough, the first pitch was a fastball, a called strike. Leo hollered down the line to Thomson, "C'mon, now, he'll come back with one." And sure enough he did. The Giants were about to win the pennant.

Up in one of the boxes, Toots Shor and Frank Sinatra watched the theatrics. They were both bombed on booze.

At least they saw it. Stoneham never saw the homer. He had gone down to the clubhouse to commiserate with Maglie.

What happened next everyone seems to remember—Thomson running around the bases, dancing. They remember Leo jumping up and down in the third base coach's box. But do they know why Stanky tackled the exuberant Leo? It was to prevent the hysterical manager from grabbing Thomson as he approached third. That could have made the homer illegal. Then Leo running with Thomson from third base on toward home plate . . . Robinson watching to make sure Thomson stepped on every base . . . On the radio, fans heard Russ Hodges screaming over and over, "The Giants win the pennant! The Giants win the pennant!" A young man, taping the Giants broadcast off the radio, wound up with the only recording of Hodges's historic call. Predictably, Red Barber's was less emotional, but no less poignant: "It's in there for the pennant." Barber always thought his was the more professional call.

Then the Giants had to run all the way to the center field clubhouse. Jumping would be more accurate. Even at this extraordinary moment in the history of baseball, Leo's wheels were turning. After he hugged Mays, he told his rookie he was surprised Dressen hadn't walked Thomson and pitched to Willie with the bases loaded.

Sinatra and Shor took a limo downtown. Shor threw up over Sinatra. As Frank tried to clean himself off as best he could, Shor bellowed, "God, you smell! Open the damned window."

Outside the clubhouse the Giants could hear fans shouting, "Thomson, Thomson," or "Stanky," or "Leo." A police official told Leo the players had better go onto the clubhouse steps, one by one, and wave to the crowd or the people would never leave. It was a series of curtain calls, as if Broadway had moved outdoors. No show ever had an improbable ending like this.

Fewer than twenty-four hours later, the Giants had to gird themselves for a World Series. "Just keep going," Durocher told them.

They did in the opener at Yankee Stadium, 5–1. Irvin tied a Series record with 4 hits in one game, and also became the first man in thirty years to steal home in the Series when he detected a flaw in Allie Reynolds's pitching rhythm.

"I had stolen home six times that year," Irvin recounts. "Leo and I had agreed that if I got a good jump, I could go. In that particular inning it was two out; Bob Thomson was at the plate. And we both noticed that Allie Reynolds was taking a long time to wind up. I softly whispered to Leo and said I thought I could steal. He whispered back, 'Get a good jump.' He didn't want McDougald to hear. So I inched off and as soon as he went into his windup I darted off. The throw was high and that's the reason I got in. I got in by a couple of inches, Thomson hung in there so that Yogi couldn't come up."

The Yankees came back to win the second game, 3–1, as Ed Lopat tossed a 5-hitter. With Lopat throwing his famous "junk"— screwballs, off-speed curves—the Giants were never in the game despite Irvin's 3 hits.

The teams moved to the Polo Grounds for Game 3, and this one produced a "field goal" by Stanky that still drives Phil Rizzuto crazy when he talks about it. In the fifth inning, when 5 unearned Giants runs crossed the plate to seal the game, Stanky and Rizzuto were involved in the play at second. It keyed the Giants rally. With one out, Stanky walked. Then he tore for second, attempting to steal the bag. Berra tossed a bullet to Rizzuto, waiting for Stanky, and Rizzuto applied the tag. Instead of being called out, though, Stanky kicked the ball out of Rizzuto's glove with his right shoe. While Rizzuto chased the ball, Stanky headed for third. Rizzuto and Stengel were outraged. They charged that Stanky never went for the bag with his foot, but instead aimed for Rizzuto's glove, which should have been interference. And anyway, said the excitable Rizzuto, "He never even touched second." The Giants won the game, 6–2, to take a 2-games-to-1 Series lead.

After Reynolds kept out of trouble the next game by getting Mays to hit into 3 double plays, the Series was then tied at 2 games apiece.

Durocher's manipulating, confidence building, and cajoling had taken the Giants this far against a team that would place four players in the Hall of Fame—DiMaggio, Mantle, Mize, and Berra—not to mention its manager, Casey Stengel, and general manager, George Weiss. Of all the Giants in the Series, on the field and in the front office, only Willie Mays would be voted into the Hall.

McDougald became the star of Game 5. In the history of the World Series, there had been only two grand-slam homers—Elmer Smith of the Cleveland Indians in 1920 against the Dodgers, and the Yankees' Tony Lazzeri in 1936 against the Giants in the Polo Grounds. This time, the twenty-three-year-old McDougald put the game out of reach in the third inning by slamming one into the seats. The Yankees went on to crush the Giants, 13–1, behind Lopat. DiMaggio went 3 for 5, driving in 3 runs, making the most of what would be his final Series.

The Yankees went for the clincher in the Stadium. And this game had overtones—if that were possible—of the great Giants-Dodgers finale of the week before. The Yankees, thanks to Hank Bauer's bases-loaded triple, took a 4–1 lead into the ninth inning. Stengel had been making all the right pitching moves, starting Vic Raschi, then relieving him with Johnny Sain when Raschi faltered. An era also ended that game. In the sixth inning, Stengel sent in a pinch runner for DiMaggio, who trotted off the field to a standing ovation. Somehow, the fans sensed that this was his last appearance on a field. And it was.

In the ninth, the Giants broke through. Stanky led off with a single and Dark outraced a bunt. Then Lockman drilled a single to right. The bases were filled with none out and Irvin, the right-handed slugger who had pounded 11 hits—one under the Series record— was coming to bat. Stengel then mystified just about everyone in the park by going against that famous "book"—he brought in Bob Kuzava, a left-hander, to face Irvin, a right-handed batter.

"The Negro star," as he was described, immediately blasted a tremendous fly to deep left-center. But Gene Woodling ran it down, Stanky tagged and scored, and the other runners moved up to second and third.

Then, incredibly, Thomson was up in the exact same setting—his team trailing, 4–2, two men on, first base open, ninth inning. And Stengel taunted fate by employing the same strategy that had backfired on Dressen.

What spelled disaster for the Dodgers worked well enough for old Casey, though. Thomson hit a towering fly to left-center. Woodling caught this one, even though it scored a runner. The Giants were down to their last out, and Durocher had virtually depleted his pinch hitters as the tying run got to second.

He sent up still another right-hander, Sal Yvars, Westrum's perennial backup. Yvars smacked the first pitch on a line toward right. It looked as if it would hit the grass. But Bauer, on a dead run, speared the ball while tumbling to the turf. He held it. The game and the Series were over.

In defeat, Leo was bigger than ever. Leo and Laraine were Mr. and Mrs. New York. He was becoming something of a fine arts collector, learning about paintings, antique silver, china, furniture, and sculpture. They traveled, and they collected.

He returned to New York to meet with Stoneham to discuss a future that looked so bright. Willie was to be his key man for the 1952 season. Meanwhile, the Giants turned down the Cards' offer for Stanky. St. Louis had been willing to give up Slaughter for him, but then reneged. "It was rejected," said Stoneham, "because the Cards said Slaughter was the club's last symbol of the Gashouse Gang."

Another symbol of the Gashouse Gang was still active, in a Giants uniform, and just about the most famous manager in baseball.

CHAPTER
XII

BLUE SKIES...
FOR A WHILE

WITH A SICKENING CRACK, Irvin broke his ankle in an exhibition game in Denver. This was the slugger who had led the league in RBIs with 121, had batted .312, and had kept Mays mellow. And Stanky did wind up as the Cards' player-manager, with Davey Williams becoming the new Giant second baseman.

No problem. The pitching was great. Jansen and Maglie started out almost perfect, and the Giants brought up a twenty-eight-year-old rookie knuckleballer named Hoyt Wilhelm who had a knack of winning games in relief.

Baseball was changing. For the first time, the Giants opened at home with a night game, which they won. Happy Chandler was gone as commissioner, replaced by Ford Frick.

The Giants started with a 16–2 tear through April. Then both Jansen and Maglie developed back trouble. Still, the Giants swept a 3-game series against the Dodgers in May. They had a 1½-game lead and were 26–8.

The next day, Willie Mays went into the Army.

Willie and the Giants fought his induction. He wanted a dependency hardship, claiming he was chief support of four of his nine brothers and sisters. He claimed his stepfather was unemployed. When Willie had originally taken the aptitude test he failed it. They made him take it again, and he was 1-A. He had to go.

When Leo learned Mays had lost his appeal, he said he "just

didn't know how" he would replace him in the outfield. "But I positively will not break up my infield again."

The Giants were never the same, and not even Leo could shore them up, the Leo whose new nickname had become "the Little Shepherd of Coogan's Bluff." It had been bestowed upon him by the writer Red Smith following the Miracle of 1951. The name had godlike connotations, but the shepherd had lost Willie, and from that point, his flock played 66–54 ball. After Maglie's 11–2 start, he was ineffective with his back injury. Thomson, who had anchored third, had to shift back to Willie's spot in center. The infield was broken up.

Leo, though, kept the same sort of spirit he had exhibited in 1951. He refused to give in. He believed he "had the horses," in Feeney's words, to win again. If Leo had confidence in his team, he battled like crazy. So Leo fought with the umps again, he fought with the enemy. He liked this club.

Early in the season he was kicked out of a game against the Braves by umpire Art Gore after protesting that Spahn had quick-pitched Mays. In late June, he was nailed by National League President Warren Giles with a four-day suspension for a run-in with ump Bill Stewart.

A few days after his return, he benched Mueller, Dark, and Thomson and called up one Dusty Rhodes from Nashville in the Southern Association. "If I'm going to lose, I'll lose with players who have some fire, players who are alert and act as if they want to play ball," shouted Durocher.

In August, Leo, dearly beloved of the Giants fans, was given a "night" at the Polo Grounds. Durocher Night took place before a game against—you guessed it—the Dodgers. He got a car; Laraine got wifely things, such as roses and a basket of candies. George Jessel, a New York fixture since his song-and-dance days of World War I, and who claimed he was a Giants batboy in 1909, was emcee.

That sweet moment came to a crash, though, when Leo was banned five days in mid-August because of his aggressive actions against umpire Augie Donatelli. The Braves were leading, 7–3, in the ninth. Durocher, changing pitchers, was rubbing the ball for the new hurler, Hal Gregg. Donatelli asked to see the ball, which sent Leo into a rage. Why, did Donatelli think Leo was doctoring the damn thing? How dare he. Durocher tossed the ball to Gregg, then grabbed it out of his hand and tossed it to Al Barlick, another ump. That angered Donatelli, who immediately raised his arm and kicked out Durocher. As soon as Leo saw the "you're out!" he raised his right fist and started to bring it crashing down, but stopped midway through as Giants, Braves, and other umps rushed out.

Giles knew of Leo's habit of managing from the stands with hand signals and he warned Durocher that during the suspension he was not to be anywhere near the dugout.

Interrupted by Leo's suspensions, the Giants just couldn't get going. At one point, they trailed the Dodgers by 10 games. Then Irvin returned. Things began to happen. In early September they got to within 4 games, beating the Dodgers, 6–4, taking three hours and thirty-eight minutes to play. It was the longest nine-inning game ever played in the majors. Then the Giants won the second game too. They had a 5-game winning streak, and had won 11 of 14. Could it happen again?

In the finale of the season series against the Dodgers, Jansen hit Brooklyn third baseman Billy Cox. This happened merely a month after Giles issued a "beanball directive," ruling that a manager is primarily responsible when beanball throwing escalates. Leo was kicked out, then suspended for 2 games. It was the third time that season he was suspended.

The Giants never caught the Dodgers, finishing second by 4½ games. Although Leo had seemed to burn with all the fire and passion of 1951, he made a strange announcement when the season was over. He said he would quit baseball after 1953 and try a career in the movies.

The placid Stoneham erupted. He gave Leo a directive: one month to decide, movies or Giants, in the future. If Leo indeed were quitting after 1953, he'd better not wait. He was gone now. "I thought at first it was a press agent's stunt," said Stoneham. "But Leo told me he [had] three offers he should examine."

Durocher explained he was getting to the stage where he wanted to spend more time with his children on the West Coast, where he preferred to live.

Pressured, Leo called a press conference in his New York apartment. He came out of his suite wearing a monogrammed white flannel bathrobe to announce that he would manage the Giants in 1953 and be available for the 1954 season. When asked about his future he replied, "Not movies necessarily. But that television is something else. There's big money there."

The Giants by now were full-blown members of the baseball

establishment. If the Dodgers had their own poet in Marianne Moore, the Giants had their own artiste in Tallulah Bankhead, the deep-voiced actress who did nothing by halves. The hard-drinking, dirty-talking Miss Bankhead was a wild-eyed Giants fan. To punctuate her rabid rooting at the Polo Grounds, she appeared at the annual Baseball Writers show, playing the Giants manager. She once remarked, "There have been two geniuses: Willie Mays and Willie Shakespeare."

With a vastly different lineup and without Willie Mays, Leo went to a two-platoon system in 1953. The club got off to a terrible start, and was in seventh place within three weeks. Irvin was wearing special footwear to protect his damaged ankle. Thomson, the symbol of that magical 1951 victory, was benched as Leo turned the lineup upside down.

Then Leo himself was threatened with an indefinite suspension for the suggestion the umpires in the National League were "ganging up" on him. It was early June, and he was frustrated by a team that would finish fifth, that didn't have Mays, and whose star pitchers were getting older. He was kicked out of 2 straight games. "Don't tell me they don't get together before the game and decide the first time a certain person says something he is going to be put out of the game," he complained.

"I was burning mad," said Leo, explaining later why he popped off. "There's one thing I want to stress. In all my years in baseball, I've never questioned the integrity of the umpires," he lied after Giles forced him to make a public apology.

Leo tried more shake-ups. He put Dark in left field. The club went on a streak and in mid-July, winning 10 of 11, it had risen to fourth. Then it went sour again.

Would Leo be back? Newspaper stories said no. To quash them, Stoneham suddenly signed Leo to a new contract extending through 1955. Leo was now the senior manager in the league in terms of continuous service. Of course, continuous didn't also mean uninterrupted. He was about to get kicked out again.

Beanball ruckuses always seemed to fuel Leo's problems. If only he didn't keep shouting to stick the ball you-know-where, then maybe those lousy umps wouldn't misconstrue his intentions. But whenever a Giant threw at anyone—usually a Dodger—Leo was getting the boot, and fined, and suspended.

In September, as the Giants were losing their eighth straight to the Dodgers, whose lead increased to 10 games, Brooklyn pitcher

Clem Labine low-bridged the Giants' Bobby Hofman. So the next inning, Jansen decked Duke Snider. The Duke promptly bunted toward first, beat out the hit, but missed any contact with Jansen. Then Jackie Robinson did the same thing. Again, there was no brushing down the baseline. Still, Jansen didn't like being intimidated, so he knocked down Campanella. You couldn't blame this on Leo, though, for he already had been kicked out for arguing with Bill Stewart over a called ball four.

So this was the sort of milieu the clubs met in at the Polo Grounds. It was late in the season, the Giants were a second-division club, and still more than twenty-five thousand fans showed up. The Dodgers were in.

The fans were not disappointed. Ruben Gomez enraged Carl Furillo by hitting him on the right wrist in the second inning. That was actually pretty normal retaliation, since two batters earlier, Campanella had homered. It was the old ethic that prevailed until ballplayers got so wealthy they felt they had to be protected from being skulled. Furillo, the league's leading hitter with a .344 average, strode to the mound and started yelling at Gomez. The umps came out and the incident appeared over when Furillo went on to first.

"Crybaby, crybaby," shouted Leo from the nearby dugout.

The count on Billy Cox went to 2–2, when Furillo pointed to the Giants dugout. Furillo called time. Then suddenly he veered off. Leo had stopped calling him names and challenged him. Furillo charged the Giants dugout.

Pee Wee Reese recalls, "I don't know what it was that got Furillo upset, but knowing Furillo I would not want to get him too upset, because Furillo would fight a buzz saw, and of course Leo never backed down from anyone. He could get to a ballplayer and get his mind off the game. That's what he did with Furillo. Furillo charged into the dugout. I guess Monte Irvin got Carl off of Leo. I wouldn't have liked to see Carl get to Leo."

And Irvin, who was, so to speak, right on top of it, remembers, "I was sitting on the bench. I had that bad ankle. Furillo left first base and started for the dugout. All I wanted to do was to keep Leo and Furillo from killing each other. But Furillo wrestled around me and got to Leo, and they both went down to the ground. Someone stepped on Furillo's finger and broke it."

Players from both benches jumped in trying to act as peacemakers. Hodges and Irvin attempted to restore order. Both Furillo and Leo were kicked out of the game. As Furillo mounted the clubhouse steps in center, a fan swiped at him with an umbrella, but missed.

Though it is hard to believe, Leo denied calling Furillo names. "I never called him anything. The first thing I saw was Furillo pointing and then charging, so I came out to meet him. I don't know why I was put out of the game. As for Carl saying he's going to get me, whenever or wherever he wants to try it I'll be ready."

Yes, Furillo had said he would get Leo. Their bad feeling probably started when Leo was with the Dodgers, but it escalated in 1949 when Furillo was hospitalized after being hit by Sheldon Jones. Furillo always blamed Leo for that one.

So after going to the clubhouse, he said, "I will get him. The first time I see him, the first time we come face-to-face, I will get him. He has crossed me once too often."

Ironically, Furillo seemed less distressed about his left hand. He said someone stepped on it during the fight. He didn't realize how seriously it had been injured. X rays revealed a fracture of the metacarpal. He was through for the season, but his average counted. He won the batting title by 2 points over Red Schoendienst.

Giles, of course, began an immediate investigation into all the statements. But since Furillo wasn't going to be in uniform again, it hardly mattered.

Leo, meanwhile, decided that with his club far out of it, he would start a four-man manager-of-the-day club, rotating Rigney, Westrum, Lockman, and Dark. Interestingly, those four all wound up as major league managers. It was a testament to Leo's influence on them, and his managing skills. How many other teams could ever boast of having four players go on to manage? Then again, how many teams had a Leo Durocher to learn from?

After the 1953 season, Leo toured Japan and Rhodes was one of his ballplayers. Up early one morning at 6:00, Leo was in the lobby when he spotted Dusty. Was he just getting in or had he been out all night?

"I went to see my sister," Rhodes said.

Now Leo had heard everything. A sister in Japan? He was so ticked off at Rhodes that later in the morning he went up to Stoneham's suite to complain. And who should open the door to Stoneham's room, with a drink in his hand? Dusty, drinking with the boss. But the funny thing was, Dusty was telling the truth. He did have a sister in Japan—she was married to a sailor.

Dusty didn't seem bothered by Durocher's rules. He would borrow money from Leo all the time. Durocher, the old St. Louis "C-note," always had a big roll of bills, and he could peel a fifty or a hundred off the top with the ease of dropping a quarter. Dusty would always be asking for a hundred. The next day, Leo, curious if his money had been well spent, would ask, "Dusty, what time did you get in last night?" And Dusty would tell the truth: 4:00 A.M., 6:00 A.M., whenever.

But the kind of guy Rhodes was also said something about the kind of guy Leo was. Leo, the ex-altar boy, wasn't looking for altar boys. Could you play for him? That was what Leo wanted to know above everything else. So Leo had no beef with Rhodes because he was always one of the first in the clubhouse ready to play. "I'm your man, Skip, if you need me today," Rhodes would tell him.

CHAPTER XIII

AGAINST THE ODDS

THE GIANTS MIGHT have had that famed intertwined "🆖" on their cap, but there was something distinctly western about them during spring training in 1954. It took place in Phoenix, the hub of the so-called Cactus League, the counterpoint to Florida's Grapefruit League.

Not many major league teams opted for Arizona. But the Indians were one of them, and so that set up a natural, spring-long rivalry. There was another thing about Phoenix. It wasn't far from Hollywood.

Jim Ogle was a baseball writer for most of his life before retiring to become head of the Yankees' alumni association. "We'd always go to L.A. to play the Cubs, who owned a minor league team there," recalls Ogle. "That's where Leo would have his parties." And some parties they were too: "Gary Cooper, Bob Mitchum, Pat O'Brien, the director William Wellman. I'll always remember one night—there were several of us in one room, and Johnny Mercer was playing the piano and Doris Day was singing." It was a heady time for Hollywood and sportswriters, a kind of celebrity-jock merger that seemed to benefit everybody.

Leo's lifestyle never was appreciated by Alvin Dark, who quoted the Bible and whose Southern roots were intertwined with religion. But Dark, the team captain, did appreciate Leo's managing skills. One day that spring, Stoneham and Leo had a blowup over Leo's lifestyle, which was a world apart from Stoneham, a man who enjoyed getting quietly looped. Leo flared back and suddenly he was fired. Dark got wind of what was happening and made a proposition to Stoneham: "Let us keep him in line. We need Leo to win." And so Dark, and some of the senior players, would make sure that the Lip didn't get out of hand. There was too much at stake this season, with Willie coming back, with a new southpaw, Johnny Antonelli, acquired from the Braves (for Bobby Thomson!), and with Monte Irvin returning to full health. The Giants could win this thing, and didn't need to be disrupted with the season a month away.

Leo, meanwhile, promised to behave and to keep focused on what was going on. As Leonard Koppett, the baseball sage, points out in *The Man in the Dugout,* his seminal book on managers, the Giants of 1954 played "textbook 'counter-clockwise' baseball—hit to right, move the runners, manufacture one run at a time, get tight pitching and make the plays in the field. With Willie in center, of course, they not only made all the possible plays but a lot of impossible ones as well."

It was reminiscent of a time with the Dodgers, when Durocher disciple Gene Mauch gingerly asked Leo why he had gone against the percentages in making a certain move. "Kid," snapped Leo, "I make my own percentages."

There still was room for Leo's kind of managing, even though it was a different major league Willie Mays returned to. The Braves had escaped to Milwaukee, and in the American League, the St. Louis Browns had moved to Baltimore and called themselves the Orioles, trying to revive a grand old name while getting rid of their own sad monicker.

Coming into the 1954 season, Mays was twenty-three years old. On Opening Day, Willie's first game back from the Army, he faced a Dodger team that had a new manager named Walter "Smokey" Alston. (Alston, who eventually made the Hall of Fame, would ultimately be another reason for Leo to become grumpy and embittered at the end of his life.)

Before the opener, Leo beamed at the splendid weather. "I've been so amazed at everything I've seen during spring training that I keep warning myself that things can't be that good—our pitching, our hitting, our fielding, and now our weather," he said in good spirits from the dugout steps. But then he got annoyed before he could even bellow out his first "Stick it in his ear!" Frick came along to warn Leo and Alston about throwing beanballs—a curious welcome for Alston.

Mays broke a 3–3 tie by blasting a Carl Erskine pitch deep into the upper left field stands for the winning blow. The victory served as a symbol as well. The Dodgers had won two pennants while Willie was away. Now it was Willie's turn.

From the moment Willie joined the team in Phoenix, Leo harped on how it was going to be another championship season. It was on the players' minds all the time. By the end of June the Giants, confident, passed the Dodgers and moved into first place, just as Leo had been telling them they would. They had a 1-game lead when the teams opened a 3-game series at the Polo Grounds. Now was the chance to put them away. The Giants swept, with Willie belting a pair in the finale. He now had 30 homers.

While the Giants were producing an 11–2 rout over the Dodgers, and after Willie stroked one of his homers, Irvin was knocked down by Russ Meyer's first pitch. Then he was hit on the thigh by the next delivery. Of course, that meant a Dodger had to fall, and the player picked was Leo's old friend, Furillo. He hit the deck on a high, tight pitch thrown by Gomez. Furillo grabbed Westrum, but the umps separated them.

The papers proclaimed, as they did whenever a homer-hitter got off to a quick start, that Willie was ahead of Ruth's 60-homer pace, a barometer that measured every slugger's summer until Roger Maris finally broke the record. By the All-Star break the Giants had a 5½-game lead over the Dodgers.

In July, as the lead increased to 6½ games, Leo made one of his typical, cocksure remarks that made the Dodgers—and non-Giants fans—hate him so: "They're never going to catch us," he said.

With fresh inspiration, Brooklyn began to eat into the Giants' lead. By August the streaking Dodgers were only half a game out; the Giants had lost 7 of 8 games. Willie was still slugging homers, though, his count rising to 36.

One night before the Giants played Pittsburgh, Leo called Willie into his office and closed the door. "Willie," he said, "I want you to do something for me and the ball club."

"What's up, Mister Leo?" Willie asked.

"I want you to stop going for home runs."

Mays, whose slugging had landed him on the cover of *Time*, was shocked. Leo explained that Willie hit most of his home runs with nobody on base. But if he got more hits, and got on base more, the Giants would score more runs because then he'd be on when Irvin or Rhodes or Thompson came up. It would kick off rallies. He also told Willie, "You'll have a shot at the batting title." Mays was in the middle of the pack, at about .320, battling with Stan Musial, while Snider and Don Mueller were running away with the batting race.

Durocher was very convincing. Why, Willie even told him he liked the idea. And Leo asked Willie to change his stance, from batting in a slight crouch with his legs spread wide apart, to bringing his feet closer together and standing more erect.

Listening to Leo, Willie got only 5 more homers—and one of those was an inside-the-park job. But he also batted .379 over that stretch. He tore up the league.

With his new stance, he could rip outside pitches to right and right-center since the pitchers knew his power had been against high, inside deliveries and they had started to keep the ball away. That was fine against his old stance. Not for his new one, though. There was another thing Leo had predicted correctly. On the final day of the season, Willie had a chance to win the batting title.

Leo set the table for Willie when he moved him up in the batting order, from cleanup to third. It gave him more at-bats and more chances to catch Snider.

Joe Garagiola, who joined the Giants in 1954, remembers, "In my one month with Leo, he'd keep me on the bench and not in the bullpen because he wanted me to ride players. He'd say, 'Get on that guy!' His style that year was to pump you up. If you struck out but had one good swing, he'd concentrate on that one good swing. 'Oh, that was great,' he'd say.

"Before the game he'd meet with the pitcher and the catcher and give them a little pep talk. He knew the Dodgers were chasing us, along with the Braves, but he said, 'We're in first place, why worry? Let them worry. We pick up ground when we get rained out.' " That was the Giants' attitude, a winning attitude by their Peerless Leader.

In early September, with the Giants holding a 3-game lead, the Dodgers came into the Polo Grounds for 3 games. The Giants captured the first 2, and that essentially put the Dodgers in a hole too deep even for their Hall of Fame crew.

Leo reached back to memories of Huggins for the pennant clincher. The little Yankee manager had liked to threaten players whom he knew would take the bait, and go on to try even harder.

The Giants were a game away from clinching the pennant on the last Monday of the season, at Ebbets Field to boot. Maglie, whom Leo loved to save for these hated Dodgers, started for New York (he brought in a career record of 21–8 against Brooklyn). Maglie was getting hit in the third inning, holding a 2–0 lead, and Leo was pacing in the dugout. He was never shy about lifting a pitcher, not even Maglie. And this year, Leo had masterfully juggled two outstanding relievers, Hoyt Wilhelm and thirty-six-year-old Marv Grissom.

The Dodgers got Maglie shaky when he walked Reese and Snider and Hodges, then gave up a pop fly single into short center, in front of the sprawling Mays who tore a huge divot going for the ball. Reese scored. Runners were on first and third, with only one out, and Durocher already had someone warming up.

Leo didn't plan to take out Maglie, but he walked out to the mound to talk to him. As soon as Leo got to the foul lines, Maglie walked off the mound toward him and shouted, "What are you doing here? Get back in the dugout where you belong."

That frosted Leo, who screamed back, "I got nine other pitchers out there who want to win this game. I don't need you. Either you get the next hitter out, or you're out of the game."

Leo never intended at that moment to yank Maglie. But maybe, just maybe, it would stir him. It did.

Maglie got the next batter on a double play, then he stormed into the dugout. Leo was sitting next to the water cooler. Maglie took a swig of water and spit it all over Leo's pants. "How do you like that?" he asked. Then he took a seat at the other end of the bench and went on to win the game. Mays outhit Mueller and Snider to win the batting title—just as Leo had figured.

For the victory parade, Leo insisted that Dark, the team captain, and Mays, share the front car. Fifteen brightly colored open cars rode up Broadway—the traditional route for heroes—from the Battery to City Hall. This time, the Giants had New York to themselves. The Yankees were out of it, the only time in a ten-year stretch they did not win a pennant. A million people turned out for the Giants' ticker tape parade. Then, down at City Hall, Leo introduced each player, who wore a bright white uniform, while cheers rang through the crowd.

In any other city, every politician would be behind the team that won. But there were three teams in New York then. Abe Stark, a politician from Brooklyn who also owned the clothing store that gave a player a free suit if he hit Stark's billboard in Ebbets Field, started to speak to the crowd. "Wait till next year," he said. It was the famous echo. Even the Giants behind him booed.

The Cleveland Indians were awesome. The Yankees had won 103 games—and still trailed them by 8.

The Giants had won the pennant by 5 games over the Dodgers, amassing 97 victories. But Cleveland was the heavy favorite. The Indians beat out the Yankee team that had won more games for Stengel than any he managed. And besides, the Giants had a history of failure in the Series. For that matter, so did Durocher. The Giants had been in the Series thirteen times and won only four.

The Indians had pitching and hitting. Their starters were all-star-quality righties—Bob Lemon, Early Wynn, Mike Garcia, Bob Feller, and Art Houtteman. They had the American League's top home run hitter in Larry Doby. They had Al Rosen and Vic Wertz and Bobby Avila, who led the American League in batting average. Lemon, Wynn, and Garcia all led the league in some pitching category.

Despite Cleveland's roster of stars, the Giants weren't in awe of them. They had handled them routinely in Arizona, and had played them exclusively for two weeks during spring training.

Can you lose an entire World Series based on one play in the opening game? Maybe not. But perhaps Willie Mays's catch in the first game caused the Indians to think, What do we have to do to beat these bastards?

Bob Lemon (23–7) started against Maglie, who was 14–6, even though Durocher had Antonelli, a 21-game winner. Thus Maglie was a surprise starter, but when the eighth inning began, he and Lemon, the old pros, were locked in a 2–2 tie.

Doby led off with a walk, and Rosen beat out an infield hit. First and second, none out, and Vic Wertz was up. He was 3 for 3 against Maglie—a triple in the first, a single in the fourth, another single in the sixth. He was a left-handed power-hitter. Durocher had seen enough Maglie against Wertz this day, though, and he called for Don Liddle, a left-hander, to face Wertz.

Most hitters like to swing at a relief pitcher's first pitch. Willie, in center field, was thinking that with his hot bat Wertz wouldn't waste any time if he liked the pitch. And that's what happened.

"I saw it cleanly," Willie remembered. "As soon as I picked it out of the sky, I knew I had to get toward center field. I turned and ran at full speed toward center with my back to the plate. But even as I was running, I realized I had to be in stride if I was going to catch it, so about 450 feet away from the plate I looked up over my left shoulder and could see the ball. I timed it perfectly and it dropped into my glove maybe 10 or 15 feet from the bleacher wall. At that same moment, I wheeled and threw in one motion and fell to the ground. I must have looked like a corkscrew. I could feel my hat flying off, but I saw the ball heading straight to Davey Williams on second. Davey grabbed the relay and threw home. Doby had tagged up at second after the catch. That held Doby to third base, while Rosen had to get back to first very quickly."

The Giants escaped the inning. The game went into extra innings.

Willie made another stab of a Wertz drive that game, but few remember it. It wasn't for an out, but it might have saved the game. It was the tenth inning, Grissom was pitching, and Wertz came up again. He hit a screwball, Grissom's best pitch, to left-center. Mays had been playing Wertz to pull and was in right-center. Willie chased the ball and caught it bare-handed after it bounced. He held an inside-the-park homer to a double.

Then, in the bottom of the tenth, with Lemon still pitching, Mays stepped up. Leo told him to steal if he got on. The Indians had put in a new catcher, Mickey Grasso, and Leo noticed that during his practice throws, his arm wasn't as strong as Jim Hegan's. Willie drew a walk. As Leo figured, Willie had no trouble stealing second. Then, with first base open, the managing game began. Al Lopez decided to walk Hank Thompson. This would set up a double-play possibility with Irvin coming up against Lemon. Monte had been 0 for 3 against Lemon.

But Leo didn't let Monte get to bat again. All season long Leo had been juggling his pair of supersubs—the left-handed-hitting Dusty Rhodes, the right-handed Bobby Hofman. It seemed that whenever Rhodes connected, the ball was going places. Dusty had 56 hits that year, but 15 were homers. Leo's pinch-hitting calls that season were touched by genius, abetted by an improbable pinch hitter who could get the job done. Leo knew Dusty played for him.

Leo was risking a tricky situation this time though: putting up a pinch hitter for one of your leading batters with a World Series game on the line. Stars don't like being shown up. But Leo knew Monte's disposition—he was a good-natured guy—and made the move.

Lemon's first pitch was the only one he threw. Dusty jumped

on it and pulled it down the right field line—a shot maybe 270 feet away—but the ball sailed into the stands. A 3-run home run and the Giants (with Leo's managing) won the opening game of the Series.

The next day the Indians came back with their other 23-game winner, Early Wynn. Leo responded, again, with his super pinch hitter. He had discovered an unusual weapon, a pinch hitter you could use at any time in the game, ahead or behind or tied. It was not the traditional role, but Leo was not a traditional manager, if anyone noticed.

This time Rhodes came up to pinch-hit for Irvin in the fifth inning, with the Indians leading, 1–0. Wynn had been pitching a perfect game till then. Mays led off with a walk and dashed to third when Thompson singled for the first Giants hit. Irvin, on deck, stepped toward the batter's box. Leo called him back. Again, a bold move, embarrassing him in front of the crowd.

But Leo wanted Rhodes, even though it was early in the game and there wasn't even anybody out. He had seen Wynn strike out Irvin earlier.

Rhodes hit a high fly to short center. Doby was playing way back, which was a mistake since Cleveland manager Al Lopez should have had him in, trying to stop Mays from scoring on a fly ball. And there was another problem. Doby and his slugging co-star, Al Rosen, were both injured and could not play effectively. Doby had knee problems, probably the reason he was playing back so he wouldn't have to chase a long drive. For this dinker, he ran and ran, but it fell in front of him and Mays came home. The Giants scored another to take the lead. Then, in the seventh, Dusty came up with no one on base because Leo had left him in to play left field. This time he belted the ball for a long homer. He didn't need the friendly foul pole.

In the ninth inning that 3–1 lead looked shaky. Antonelli had been getting in and out of trouble all day. This time the Indians had two on, two out—and Wertz up. He belted a pair of balls foul. Then he swung again and hit a long shot to left-center. This was the weak spot in the field that had bothered Leo when he left Rhodes in the game. He had warned Willie: get anything hit to left-center. So Willie ran back and positioned himself for the difficult catch. Suddenly, Rhodes loomed in front of him, waved him off, and made the catch to end the game. And kept running—all the way to the clubhouse steps.

When Leo showed up after his five-hundred-foot walk from the dugout, Dusty already had a cigar in one hand and a beer in the other. "What were you worried about, Skip?" said Dusty. "I had it all the way. And how about that homer? I guess that was a cheap one, too."

In 2 games at the Polo Grounds Leo had been forced to use only three players who weren't in the starting line up—Rhodes and Liddle and Grissom.

Leo was wondering about his star center fielder even with the 2-game lead. Willie had gone 0 for 5, and the Series was shifting to Cleveland. In Game 3, the Giants were facing the Big Bear, Mike Garcia, a 19-game winner and the American League leader in earned run averages and shutouts. Yet, Leo had reminded his players from the moment they had clinched: We know these guys.

Before the Giants left for Game 3 and Cleveland, Leo was handed a fistful of telegrams. He glanced at them quickly, then read one carefully. He handed it over to a group of writers. It was from Rickey: "YOU DID A GREAT JOB YESTERDAY," wrote Rickey. "JUST AS YOU HAVE DONE ALL YEAR. IN MY BOOK YOU RANK AMONG THE GREAT MANAGERS OF ALL TIME. I JUST WANTED YOU TO KNOW I AM THINK-ING ABOUT YOU."

In the big Cleveland ballpark, the Giants took a first-inning lead and nursed that 1–0 edge going into the third. This time, Leo did it again—Leo and Dusty, that is.

The Giants loaded the bases, and Irvin was next. Baseball has a long list of relievers who became celebrities mopping up for famous starters. But Leo had come up with something new: the designated pinch hitter. Leo made the move again: Rhodes for Irvin. He sent up the sub even though his club was leading; it was early in the game, and it meant he would lose his regular left fielder. And Rhodes ripped Garcia's first pitch into right, sending in Mueller and Mays. The Giants went on to win, 6–2.

In Game 4, what would be the championship game, one of Leo's best friends, Jeff Chandler, the actor, sang the National Anthem before the game. Leo's pals, Danny Kaye and Toots Shor, sat in box seats provided by Durocher.

This time, Leo let Irvin bat—and he produced a big game. The Lip bought a managerial break because the Indians were forced to go to a left-handed reliever, Hal Newhouser, and that permitted the right-handed Monte to remain beyond the early innings.

In the second inning, Irvin, who had been hitless the first three games, doubled Thompson to third. A couple of errors by the Indians, now jittery, led to a pair of Giants runs. Then in the fifth, the Giants, enjoying a 4–0 lead, filled the bases. Leo figured Monte would have a better shot against the southpaw than Dusty. But this was the type of situation in which Leo had made a move in the earlier games. Monte even looked at Leo to see if he was going to bring in Dusty. Not this time. Leo just clapped his hands and yelled, "Let's go." Monte stayed in and slammed a single to score 2 runs. It was the only game Leo stuck with Irvin, and these were the only 2 runs Irvin batted in.

The 4-game sweep rocked not only Cleveland, but Las Vegas gamblers and New York wise guys as well. It ended the American League's dominance over the National League which would soon carry over to the All-Star Game also. It was the first time in forty years a National League team swept the series in 4 games.

The Giants arrived at 8:29 that night at the Marine Air Terminal at La Guardia, where almost three thousand fans had to be restrained from running onto the tarmac. They cheered Leo, they cheered Willie, they cheered Monte, they cheered Liddle.

At the victory party back in New York that night, with Stoneham cutting a giant cake with Giants cap made of icing atop it, Leo cried continuously, hugging Willie between sobs. Genius manager he might have been all these years, but world champion he had never been until this moment. In a quiet aside, he told Willie, "I've never won the big one until now. I wondered whether there was something in me that prevented it." Now, he joined Mr. McGraw as a champion Giants manager.

Others agreed. He was the manager of the year, the Giants sweep was voted the sports upset of the year, Willie was the player of the year.

Before the World Series checks were distributed, there was little time to savor the honors. Rumors from both coasts said the Giants were considering leaving New York for California. Their lease at the Polo Grounds was up in 1958.

"There is nothing, absolutely nothing to it," Stoneham said. "What makes anyone think the games will draw well in California?" he asked. There were too many old people on pensions there.

But Leo, more outspoken in late October, told the San Francisco press, "The Giants are in New York now, but things change."

"I can think of nothing more ridiculous," said Feeney.

* * *

Leo, in that self-destructive way of his, started to write his own departure ticket. If Leo was angling for a trip to California, he made one critically wrong move. At one of the many banquets where Durocher was feted after the championship season, Danny Kaye did an imitation of Stoneham. The impish Kaye slurred his words, hiccuped, and staggered around a little, bringing the dais—which included Jack Benny, Groucho Marx, and George Jessel—to tears of laughter. Stoneham, who wasn't there, read about it. In fact, all of baseball read about it. The scene became the most famous off-season incident. Stoneham seriously began to look around for someone to manage instead of Durocher.

Leo didn't know it, but his 1954 championship was to be his last and the 1955 season would end his connection with New York. Leo's hands were tied that year, or more precisely, the Dodgers' all-star lineup ran away with the pennant. The Giants, moreover, had done nothing to improve the club. Stoneham believed he could stand pat.

With player injuries, Leo juggled his lineup from top to bottom, losing his double-play combination, his first baseman, and his key pitchers. Antonelli, his 21-game winner of 1954, fell to a 14–16 record. Grissom and Wilhelm were to produce a total of only 8 saves between them. Only Willie prevailed, and mightily, with his 51 homers.

Before the Dodgers ran away, Leo tried one of his little tricks, the infuriating kind. In a game at Ebbets Field just two weeks into the season, Leo refused to disclose his lineup. Of course, he had to present it to the umpires, but until that moment no one in the park knew who was playing or pitching.

Giles, the National League president, admitted there were no rules violations. "However," he said, "the fans in the park are entitled to all information concerning line-ups . . . perhaps I will make some suggestions in the near future."

And Bavasi, the Dodgers' vice president, said, "We can't make Leo do something he doesn't want to do. We tried that for years when he was here."

Yet, Leo saved his most surprising reactions to defeat for the two ballplayers he had so much respect for: Maglie and Mays. Maglie had been the clutch guy for him over the years, but after a loss in late May to the Cardinals, Leo accused him of being "too lazy to cover first." He said of Maglie, "His spirit is gone." By then they were 14 games behind the Dodgers.

A few weeks later, Leo benched Willie. Mays had gone 3 for 26 when Durocher sat him down against the Braves in Milwaukee. "He hasn't been helping the club, he has been making bad throws and running bases the same way," explained Durocher. "He may need a rest."

Willie, publicly, never stewed. "He knows more about me than I know about myself," said Mays. "I don't feel tired, but that's the way it is."

Ironically, the high point of Leo's last season wasn't even with the Giants. It was managing the All-Star team.

The game brought together as rival managers the World Series opponents, Lopez and Durocher. Lopez's boys took an early lead, and so he rested Ted Williams, Harvey Kuenn, and Nellie Fox.

Leo had promised Giles he would try everything to win this game. (The league slowly was coming back to respectability after dropping 12 of the first 16 All-Star clashes to the American League.) So Leo kept Musial in the game. And in the bottom of the twelfth inning he crashed the winning homer. "He owed me that one," grumped Leo.

To one disgruntled American Leaguer, the way Leo had handled his team was the reason for the victory. "It was the 1954 World Series all over again," said the player. "Everything the guy did after that first inning broke just right."

By then, however, Leo was on the way out with the season half over. Everyone knew that Leo was finished in New York. Perhaps the greatest confirmation was offered by Leo himself, saying "No comment," when asked. Bill Rigney was ready to step into his shoes. It appeared, though everyone denied it, that Leo was headed for St. Louis. Stanky had just been dismissed, and Harry Walker had replaced him as interim manager.

Late in the campaign, Leo had a run-in with Antonelli. The left-hander stalked toward second base when he saw Fitzsimmons, on Durocher's orders, coming to relieve him in a game at Philadelphia. He refused to give up the ball. Finally, he dashed into the dugout and in the runway he came across Durocher. "I can't pitch for this club," shouted Antonelli. "I'm going back to New York."

"Twenty-five guys can't manage," Leo retorted. "Now get in the locker room and take off your uniform. You're suspended indefinitely."

That lasted one day, but what was the difference?

On the final day of the season, Willie hit his fifty-first home run, tying a Giants record set by Johnny Mize. Halfway through that final game, Leo called Willie over to his end of the dugout. The pair walked down the tunnel between the dugout and the stands and squeezed into a small bathroom used by the players. Leo placed both his hands on Willie's shoulders. "I want to tell you something," he began. "You're the best ballplayer I ever saw. Having you on my team made everything worthwhile. I'm telling you this now because I won't be back next season."

Willie was stunned, probably the only one in New York who hadn't realized what was going on. "How can you leave?" he asked him finally. "We're just getting started. I've only been back from the Army for two years."

Leo told him none of that mattered, that Stoneham already had decided on Rigney. Then he added, "I've already talked to Rigney about how to treat you. Besides, I'll always be looking out for you. All you have to do is call me."

Willie was standing on the toilet seat because there wasn't enough room for the two of them. He pleaded with Leo, "You won't be here to help me."

"Willie Mays don't need help from anybody," Leo told him, and kissed him on the cheek.

At game's end, Leo was photographed walking off toward the center field clubhouse, the defining "2" on his back, the big Chesterfield sign in front of him. Baseball as many of us knew it would never be the same. Leo was gone from New York.

CHAPTER
XIV

THE LAST
ROAR

NBC IMMEDIATELY GAVE Leo $52,000 a year to become a TV personality. The announcement was made by none other than RCA's founder, Robert W. Sarnoff. Leo's "in" at NBC, which was paying him $2,000 more than the Giants did, was Mannie Sachs, a top executive who functioned just under Sarnoff. Actually, he was hired as a sort of talent scout. But whether his front-office skills were negligible, or the network wanted to exploit his celebrity status and personality, he quickly was thrown to the cameras.

Leo was installed as the master of ceremonies for a new comedy hour. Then he starred on a segment of *Matinee Theater*, a weekday dramatic series aimed at America's housewives. He also appeared in a sketch with his friend George Gobel, did a report on Little League baseball on a new weekly show (where he predicted fame for a youngster named Norm Miller), and told jokes on the Ethel Merman special *Anything Goes*.

Durocher moved into a nineteen-room house in Beverly Hills, drove two Cadillacs, and contemplated the difference between show biz and baseball: "As the manager of a ball club, you make decisions *now*. In this business you can't operate that way. You can't do anything without coordinating with a half dozen other people."

He liked the idea of being a homebody, though, claiming he felt guilty that Laraine had given up her movie career to be with him, and that he had seen his children only during Easter and Christmas.

Leo's various debuts were more interesting than effective. After his second show he was out as the *Colgate Comedy Hour* emcee. Small wonder. The most influential TV critic in America, Jack Gould of the *Times*, wrote, "Leo Durocher's return to baseball should be arranged as soon as possible."

That gave him occasion to talk baseball. He criticized the Giants. They had only one pitcher, Antonelli, they had no second baseman, they could never catch the Dodgers. The Giants, and Rigney, fumed. Leo turned out to be right. The Giants finished sixth.

With Leo's career as an entertainer, TV style, stymied, NBC decided to put him behind the camera as a baseball broadcaster. The games were directed by a legend in the business, Harry Coyle, who brought a style and drama to televising baseball. It was a job he held more than thirty years. "When Leo came to us he was very independent," recalls Coyle. "You couldn't talk too much to him. But I'll tell you one thing, nobody knew baseball like Leo Durocher.

"At that time he was traveling with the Rat Pack—Frank Sinatra, Dean Martin, Joey Bishop, Sammy Davis, Jr., and Peter Lawford. And he was wearing these black Italian silk suits, going to their tailor, and the tailor was so insistent on the way the suits fit that Leo had the pockets sewn up so he couldn't put anything in the pockets to spoil the look. Leo couldn't even carry a wallet.

"He'd fly in from the West Coast to do the show. After he did a couple of shows, it was hard to tell him how I wanted him to improve himself, because when he flew back west, the Rat Pack would coach him. They'd critique him. So when he'd come back to the games, he had his own ideas.

"To show you how independent he was, one Saturday he got up in the sixth inning and left. He had to fly back home. And that's what he did. When Tom Gallery—he was a big executive—found out about it he was furious.

"As long as Leo was around, you always had to have a limousine. That was part of his deal. He was really a big shot. Real Hollywood.

"Did he do his homework? He really didn't have to. He knew baseball. He was good. We're in Pittsburgh, and we're doing a game and Kluszewski of Cincy gets a hit and he's on first base. And Leo says to Lindsey Nelson, the play-by-play announcer, 'Well, with Kluszewski on first base you know he's not gonna steal. Oh my God, there he goes!'

"Leo was a practical joker like you never saw. He played a lot of gin. In fact, one time on the plane he was wrestling in the aisle. The plane was half empty at the time, of course. But that's the way the baseball players of that time were, a kind of rowdy bunch. We rolled in the aisles. We were playing gin and I accused him of putting a card under the table. It wasn't bad, you understand."

People around Leo always remember him and money. "I don't know if Leo was cheap or what, but every time it came to pay a check for dinner or a cab, he never had a wallet. Because of his suit. He'd say, 'Hey, you got any change?, all I got is two thousand-dollar bills' And that's the way it would be every time he had to come up with money. So I went to a bank and got change for a thousand. The next time it happened he said, 'You got change for a thousand?' I pulled it out and gave him change."

Over the next few years, Leo was rumored repeatedly to be next in line for this or that managerial job. He almost latched on with the Continental League, devised by Rickey and Bill Shea—the powerful New York lawyer—to force baseball to return to the city. But Leo remained in radio and television.

By 1959, he was ready to return to managing. Almost five years out of the business had hardly brought him acclaim or critical success. But he announced that there was "a conspiracy" against hiring him. Who knows? Perhaps there was. Or perhaps the fact that he demanded a share of stock in any team he would join made the owners shy away more than his reputation warranted.

Leo also made copy for the gossip columnists. In 1959 the fifty-four-year-old Durocher dated a twenty-six-year-old blonde who was described as an actress, separated from her husband, the actor John Bromfield. Her name had a starlet's ring to it: Larri Thomas. Leo moved out of his Beverly Hills house, leaving Laraine with the two children.

Ms. Thomas's mother said she and her husband were "very fond" of Leo. "We were taken by him since our first meeting. He's a wonderful man."

Leo and Laraine divorced in 1960, and within a year she remarried. That was news, but not nearly as big as the news that Leo was coming back to baseball—and with the Dodgers, of all things.

The Dodgers now were in Los Angeles, with the colorless Walter Alston leading them. They had slumped in 1960 and management wanted a little life in that team. Not that they admitted it. "I'm very happy to have Leo with us," said Alston between smiles at a press conference.

Just a few weeks earlier, Leo had slogged into a funk. For Rigney had been hired to manage the brand-new American League team called the Angels. Rigney, his disciple! Over Leo!

Leo's salary was about $25,000, half of that of his last managerial deal six years earlier. But it didn't matter, he was back in baseball, coaching third, where the action was. And who knew? What if management got tired of Alston?

On his first afternoon back in uniform, Leo was kicked out—of an intrasquad game. He failed to stay in the coach's box.

In his first month he brought the rhubarb back to baseball. The Dodgers had barely started the season when Leo got into one of his defining moments—the famous sand-kicking antic with umpire Jocko Conlan.

The Dodgers' Norm Larker raised a high pop fly near the plate. Catcher Hal Smith of the Pirates staggered under the ball and missed it as it hit the turf, fair, down the first base line. But then the ball kicked across the line, making it merely a foul. So Conlan ruled. But the Dodgers claimed that Smith touched the ball with his mitt, making it fair.

Leo, in the dugout this game, flipped a towel. Conlan immediately thumbed him out. So Leo took out another towel, plus a batting helmet, and threw them out too. And then Leo came out himself, faster than the objects he had thrown. He did his old stuff, arms flapping, jaw moving, bellying up for position so that Conlan couldn't escape. And then Leo kicked sand on the umpire. But the follow-through landed Leo's shoe on Conlan's shin. Conlan kicked him right back. Bam, boom, kick, dirt flying. Leo was in pain. Conlan was wearing shin guards to protect him behind the plate; Leo merely had on team-issue socks.

Later, after composing himself (and presumably his story), Leo offered the fact that after he kicked dirt on Conlan, "he kicked me in the leg. I kicked an umpire once before, but it was accidental. This is the first time an umpire ever kicked me. Anyway, I never heard of anybody getting kicked out for tossing a towel inside the dugout."

If Leo hadn't heard of that, he certainly knew one didn't kick umpires in the shins. So Giles suspended him for three days.

Leo may have stopped moving his feet. But never his mouth. Later that season, he became annoyed when Willie Davis was slow in returning a hit by Roberto Clemente. Leo began jawing at Davis. That frosted Dodger second baseman Charlie Neal, who took Davis's side and began shouting at Durocher to mind his own business.

That was just for starters. Leo progressed in 1962 from arguing with his ballplayers to arguing with his manager. He second-guessed Alston so often he nearly lost his job. Leo was setting himself up for a fall once again.

The Dodgers were playing the Pirates, and Durocher sharply criticized Tommy Davis and Ron Fairly for making mental mistakes. Davis ran into his own bunt and Fairly blew a steal sign while on first. "Somebody," said Leo, storming in the dugout, "should take some money from those kids." In other words, Alston should fine them.

While the other players on the bench watched for Alston's reaction, the manager shouted, "You do the coaching, Durocher, and I'll do the chewing out and the fining." Then he booted Leo, figuratively, in the rear by adding, "Don't forget, we had to whistle three times to wake you up in the coaching box to take the signs."

This was hardly the first time Alston had to button the Lip. It was, actually, the third time that season alone. Buzzy Bavasi, the general manager, backed Alston, who was in his thirteenth year.

Leo had other problems that season, but those involved his health. He nearly died because of a reaction to a penicillin shot when the Dodgers returned to the Polo Grounds to play the Mets, the spiritual descendants of the transported New York teams. Jerry Izenberg, the columnist for the *Star-Ledger* of New Jersey, was on hand when it happened. "It was a twi-night at the Polo Grounds. The Dodgers were coming in to play the Mets. I was alone with Leo in the clubhouse, which is in center field, up the steps.

"I was talking to Leo when he suddenly grabs his chest. The only other person there is the trainer, I think. We lift him up onto a table. He's holding his chest and moaning 'I'm going, I'm going.' Just then, the traveling secretary, I think, walks by and Leo calls to him and the guy says, 'I gotta go.'

" 'Get Alston,' Leo says to me. So I run five hundred feet to the batting cage, all across the outfield and the infield. I get Alston. Then I've got to run back the other five hundred feet.

"By then, there's another writer or two hanging around and we go in to see Leo. And here's the scene I'm taking in. Leo whispers to Alston, 'Walter, come closer.'

" 'This is it,' says Leo. 'Tell them to win two for me.'

"So here I am looking at this shit and I'm thinking to myself, 'Is this great, or what?' Here Leo thinks he's dying and he knows the Mets have only won something like four games all year and he's putting a deathbed curse on them? He figures his final act, he'll make the headlines: Dodgers win 2 for Dying Leo, like they wouldn't kill the Mets anyway, right?"

So what happened? "Ah, it was no big deal. It wasn't his heart. He had taken a massive shot of penicillin. In those days the papers would say something like the guy had a hernia. But he had the clap or something like that, and he had a reaction to the penicillin."

Leo, and Alston, stood by as the Dodgers blew the pennant, failing to win down the stretch (Sandy Koufax was sidelined), and the Giants came along to tie them at the end of the regular season. That set up—was it possible, again?—a best-of-three playoff. As they did every eleven years, the Giants won this one in 3 games. In the ninth inning. Trailing by a few runs.

Eleven years after Thomson's blast, Leo was on the losing end and he didn't like it. It would have been different if he were the bench manager. Or so he said.

At a private party after the playoffs, he was quoted as saying, "We never would have lost the pennant if I had been managing." Leo always claimed he never quite said that, and anyway, it was said in private, wasn't it? What Leo insisted he said was, after someone asked him what he would have done, "I would have liked my chances with a 4–2 lead going into the ninth inning."

Bavasi chose not to believe him. The Dodger GM was so irate that he threatened to quit if O'Malley fired Alston. "Leo was disloyal to Alston," charged Bavasi.

Yet, Alston rehired Durocher the next year—or went along with the deal anyway.

Leo had no respect for the man he disdainfully referred to as "the farmer." Sitting on the bench, Durocher constantly was second-guessing Alston's moves. Many of the ballplayers agreed with their coach against the manager, often asking Durocher what he would do in particular situations.

Once, going into the bottom of the tenth inning in Cincinnati, nursing a 1-run lead, Alston asked Durocher what he'd do. Durocher told him to walk the potential winning run.

"How can you put the winning run on?" Alston asked him.

"If you're scared, go home," snorted Leo.

It worked—there was a game-ending grounder by the next batter. Later, Leo was changing into street clothes when a reporter asked Alston, in the adjacent locker, about putting the winning run on.

"Well, I thought about that," Alston said slowly. "It was a kinda tough decision, but I thought it was the right thing to do."

In disgust, Leo picked up his gear and moved to another part of the room. He never dressed next to Alston.

Leo stayed till 1964, along the way turning down Charlie Finley's offer to coach the A's, but accepting (he thought) the Cards' offer to take over the team from Johnny Keane.

This was a busy summer for Leo. For some time he had been dating a twenty-six-year-old woman from Middlebury, Vermont, named Carolyn Morin. In July, her French-born father, Rene, brought Leo to trial for alienation of affection—claiming that Leo had stolen his wife while dating his daughter.

During the course of the trial, Carolyn, more than thirty years younger than the fifty-eight-year-old baldish Leo, said she had turned down his invitation of marriage but was willing to reconsider. Leo hunched forward from his front-row seat.

Under oath, Leo said that, yes, he had given the mother gifts but they were meant for husband too. He also said he had given "very expensive" gifts to Carolyn, including a Thunderbird, a $1,700 diamond bracelet, a ring with a pearl setting, wristwatches, and cigarette boxes.

But the juicier stuff was told by her French-born father, a bricklayer, in broken English. Asked by his lawyer when Leo broke up their home, he replied, "My wife starts to get chilly, pretty soon she gets cold, then a deep freeze, like iceberg. My wife chilly in 1961, cold in 1962, and like Alaska in 1963." She would travel all the way to the Mets' games, he said, whenever the Dodgers came to New York, and Leo never invited him.

Leo won the case after a two-hour deliberation. Pretty soon he got involved in another suit brought by a man who claimed Leo had punched him in the Dodger Stadium parking lot after Leo refused to give his stepdaughter an autograph. That was settled privately.

Durocher lost the Cards job, though. They went ahead and won the pennant in 1964, after owner Gussie Busch had been ready to fire Keane. Keane quit to become the Yankee manager and preside over the demise of baseball's greatest franchise. And Leo . . . Leo never heard another word from the Beer Baron.

The Dodgers canned Durocher after a losing season, and they made sure he paid back all the money they had advanced him. He was out of a job again, but at least he didn't owe the Dodgers any money.

Phil Wrigley had plenty.

Wrigley owned two things people stepped on: chewing gum and the Cubs. By the time Wrigley tapped the sixty-year-old Durocher in 1966, the once beloved Cubs had finished in the second division for nineteen consecutive years. Since their 1945 pennant, every other team in the league from that era had won at least one title.

In desperation, Wrigley had even started a system unprecedented in professional sports history. He rotated a staff of coaches, bringing them up, then sending them to the minors after they got to know the big club. No one was running the show. The front office had coequals and they, too, had their own ideas of what should be done. It was presided over by a distracted owner who believed in a hands-off approach. Accordingly, there never was a strong man to make the thing run.

William Wrigley, Sr., now president and chief executive officer of Wrigley's, where he replaced his late father, recalls, "General Manager John Holland and I were talking and as I recall he said, 'Leo Durocher is the man to get it done.' We went to Dad and said, 'He's the best.' He was controversial and he talked a lot, but he was appropriate for the job that was ahead of him."

So after eleven years, Leo was back, in a situation that had daunted everyone who tried it.

"I am not the coach," he announced. "I am the manager. Only one man can run a ball club, and I'm it."

There was another thing he wanted everyone to get straight: "This is no eighth-place team," he said in the press guide.

And he was right. The Cubs finished tenth.

But Leo was enthusiastic. Players liked the idea of bringing in a veritable legend and having him run the show instead of the carousel of coaches.

(An interesting note to 1966: When Leo took over, ten of the other nineteen managers in the big leagues were his disciples. Stanky was on the other side of town with the White Sox; Dark was with the A's; Dressen with Detroit; Herman with Boston; Hodges with Washington; Rigney with the Angels; Bragan with Atlanta; Franks with the Giants; Mauch with the Phillies; and Westrum with the Mets. This might have been the finest testament to Leo's talents running a show.)

In spring training he peppered the infielders with hard-hit grounders, daring them to make the plays. Nearby, an eighteen-year-old blonde hovered, a Minneapolis girl who described herself as "a very good friend" of the Lip. From time to time, he'd put the bat down and wave to her.

Life wasn't easy for Leo that first year. The Cubs opened in San Francisco, then moved to Los Angeles. The Giants and Dodgers off the bat, back to back. The symbols of his past, and the two best clubs in the league to boot. Then these same clubs immediately came back to Chicago to help Leo open his tenure at Wrigley Field.

Leo began the season in last place and stayed there. He screamed at press interviewers. He was suspicious. After all, when he returned to Los Angeles, it was to face a Dodger club still run in the front office by Bavasi—who had said only weeks before that baseball had passed Leo by.

It was important for him to look spiffy when he took the field in his new uniform. On his desk in the manager's office, he took his cap with the "C" off a hat blocker, and he traveled with a wooden block to keep his caps firm. "Got to look professional," he explained.

By the time the amateurish Cubs returned to Chicago, they were 1–5. They won some more games before the season ended, but not many.

Despite Leo's early-season prediction (actually written for him by Cubs vice president Blake Cullen), this descent into the poorest record of his managerial career shouldn't have been surprising. Chicago had some wonderful players in Ernie Banks and Billy Williams and Ron Santo and Don Kessinger, but the pitching staff was young, and Ferguson Jenkins started the season with the Phillies and wound up in a relief role.

Marvin Miller remembers how Leo wanted to appear in control. Leo especially liked to look good at someone else's expense. In the spring of 1967, Miller was flushed with his first major victory as head of the newly formed Major League Baseball Players Association. He had hammered out a remarkable new contract. As part of the agreement with management, he was entitled to speak to every club personally during spring training and update the players on union doings. Miller learned some things about Leo.

"Durocher's antiunion sentiments go fairly deep," says Miller in retirement, but with vivid memories. In fact, Leo might have been his greatest adversary except for the owners.

"As I've discovered in my fairly long life, when I find someone that virulent, an antiunion bastard, I also usually find other biases. I found that Durocher was basically anti-Semitic as well. For example, sometime later when Ken Holtzman was the player rep for the Cubs, I came for a meeting. I was out on the field and I didn't see Holtzman. Leo was on the field. I said, 'Hello, I don't see Ken Holtzman around and I'd like to talk to him for a minute. You know where I can find him?'

"Leo jerked his head around and said to one of his coaches, 'Tell the Super Jew that Miller wants to talk to him.'

"This was a thoroughly right-wing character in every way. Without trying to, I used to pile up anecdotes about Durocher. They don't point to anti-Semitism as such, but it was clear they were part of his animus toward me. He never said anything of that nature to me directly, but I got reports from players in which he told them, 'That goddamn Jew bastard.'

"I can pinpoint this one, and it's symptomatic, if not evidence, of his feelings toward unions. After negotiating the first collective-bargaining agreement for the pension plan in the winter and spring, we reported the results to the players in Phoenix. When I got to the Cubs, they had a very small clubhouse. Durocher sat in the back of the room. He wasn't supposed to be there, but I made it a practice all through the years never to ask anybody to leave unless we were discussing strategy or a strike vote. Especially when I was reporting on the pension plan because I was also negotiating not only for the players, but for the trainers, coaches, and managers as well. They're covered by the pension and insurance plans.

"Of course, the pension plan was of interest to managers and I was glad to see them attend. This was one of the most dramatic increases in pension that anybody had ever seen. Here was this great pension plan which the owners thought was the greatest thing since white bread, which had been in effect since 1947, and I came in and in our first negotiations we more than doubled all the benefits. We knocked out the contributions players had to make, had the owners pick up the gap in that. It happened that Durocher was probably the main beneficiary since the maximum benefit would go to someone with twenty years of service at age sixty-five. Durocher was both those, or close to sixty-five.

"He was already eligible for a pension. The maximum benefit before I came was $723 a month. Instead of $723 we came up with something like $1,800 a month. This wasn't the only benefit. We increased widow's benefits and life insurance and hospitalization.

"Durocher heard me out. When I got through reporting and paused for breath, a voice came from the back, in Durocher's unmistakable rasp: 'Let me get this straight. This top pension will go from $723 to $1,800 a month? Is that right?' And I said, 'Yeah.' And he said, 'Jesus. I spend more than that on the shithouse for tips.'

"That was his contribution for the day.

"I'll tell you something else about Leo. Once I came in, Durocher never paid one cent of union dues. Before I got there they had some illegal form of dues checkoff in which the club sent around a form that every player signed and fifty dollars was deducted from his salary. My understanding is that Durocher paid that. But after I got there, and we put in a perfectly legal dues checkoff, Durocher never signed."

In other words, Miller didn't think much of Leo. "He was a crude, crass individual. This was a character who used to attempt to bully people at all times. He beat up more people—older people and smaller people—in parking lots than you can count. A bum. He was an earlier version of Billy Martin. I'll tell you something, though. Billy Martin was a good union member. Even as a manager.

"I was always inclined to discount this business that he was unbiased or pro-black because of his relationship with Willie Mays. But I have no knowledge of any racial incidents.

"I didn't meet him in his prime. I've got to give him that. He was getting older. I don't think he was happy. He had been moved around. He had been suspended. He was having trouble with everybody. I don't think I ever saw him at his best."

But in 1967, Leo was named manager of the year and brought the Cubs, at long last, out of the hated second division. They finished third, posting a winning record and uncovering a minefield of pitching talent that included Holtzman's 9–0 record before going into military service.

The Cubs of 1968 again finished third.

And then there were the Cubs of 1969. In Leo's past there were years he never again could live up to. However, 1969 would be the year he couldn't live down. It was his last hurrah, but it stuck in his throat.

For the Dodgers, there had been the cry of "Wait till next year!" until Leo arrived. For the Giants there had been the post–Bill Terry blues. But both teams gained respectability under Leo. For Cubs fans, though, 1969 remains to this day the year that crystallized their frustrations, that made winning worse rather than better.

Leo turned sixty-four during the season. His boys won 9 of their first 10. They would stay in first for 155 consecutive days. Going into June, the Cubs had a 7½-game lead. Leo stirred things up in the coming weeks.

First, he married a well-known Chicago media personality and ex-wife of a department store mogul. Her name was Lynn Walker Goldblatt and she said she was forty years old. The wedding was a posh affair at the Ambassador West Hotel, attended by everyone from various Wrigleys to ballplayers.

Leo didn't keep the faith long. At least in a story recounted by Ken Holtzman to Rick Talley, the well-regarded Chicago newspaperman whose *The Cubs of '69* is the chronicle of that sad year. A few weeks after the marriage, Holtzman said, bridegroom Leo invited himself along on a date Holtzman had made with a Jarry Park usher in Montreal. Leo saw Holtzman talking to her before the game, asked if they had made a date, and told Holtzman to get her to bring a friend. She did and Leo and his pitcher double-dated. Leo stayed up late and didn't make the game the next day—he called in sick after throwing up when he awakened.

Until now, the Mets were the usual Mets, bringing up the rear. Suddenly, they started winning. As July drew to a close, the Mets were raging and the Cubs were faltering.

Meanwhile, Leo's bride asked him to visit one of his new stepsons, who was away at summer camp. Leo did. During the season, during a pennant race, visit a kid in camp? The facts were that Leo left in the middle of a game at Wrigley Field on a Saturday against the Dodgers. Well, it seemed like a good idea at the time, he said

later. The Cubs were winning. The official announcement was that
Leo had left the game because he didn't feel well. He had planned
to go to the camp in Eagle River, Wisconsin, Saturday night anyway
and be back Sunday. This is what he announced after the fact, after
he didn't show up Sunday. But part of the story was exposed when
a reporter was tipped off that Leo was visiting his twelve-year-old
stepson, Joel Goldblatt, Jr. The camp even had a sign posted, "WEL-
COME LEO DUROCHER."

Leo's longtime friend, accountant, and executor of his will,
Harvey Wineberg, accompanied Leo to that camp—which was owned
by Wineberg's father-in law. "You had to understand Leo's frame of
mind. The week before, there was a dinner in Washington, D.C.
Walter Alston, Casey Stengel, and Leo were nominated as managers
of the century. I happened to be there. Tony Kubek was the master
of ceremonies. Casey Stengel won, which everybody knew he would.
Afterward I was talking to Leo when Tony Kubek came up to him
and said, 'Leo I can't tell you how sorry I am. I had everybody's name
on a card, and I dropped your card. It fell out by mistake.' And Leo's
name, despite being one of the three people, was never mentioned
all evening."

Kubek, asked to recall the incident, says he cannot. But Wineberg is quite clear on it. "Now, if you knew Leo, you knew it didn't
set too well with him. So next week was the weekend he was supposed
to go see his stepson at my father-in-law's camp. He had a flight I
arranged for him, he was supposed to leave after the game. A one-
thirty game, it would be over at four, he could get a five o'clock flight
and be there at six-thirty. I tried to talk him out of going because I
didn't think it would be a good idea for him to leave town. I was
going up with Leo because my wife and kids were at the camp.

"Anyway, I get a call from Leo *in the middle of the game.* He
says, 'Tell the plane to be ready, we're leaving.' I tell him, 'Leo, you
can't do it.' He says, 'It's my plane, I can do anything I want.'

"So he goes up there, we spend the night, and the next day
we're ready to go back—in plenty of time to make the game. Probably
nothing would have happened if he made it. But as the plane's landing
he says to me, 'Call Amalfitano at the field and tell him to run the
team today.' I asked, 'Why?' He said, 'I don't feel well.' I said, 'You
seem okay to me.' And then he says, 'If baseball doesn't need me, I
don't need them.'

"I knew he was still stewing from the week before. In no way was it justified, but that's how he was. I think just leaving in the middle of the game, nobody would have known. But then when he doesn't show up for the next day—and someone put up a sign at Eagle River 'WELCOME LEO DUROCHER,' and someone called the paper. Nobody bought the story he was sick. But I'm telling you, he was just angry."

So was old man Wrigley. For the papers, Wrigley said merely, "We got our signals crossed." But he threatened Leo with dismissal and scolded him for ten minutes. Leo told the press he had had a hernia flare-up.

The Cubs still had their nice lead, but things weren't happening the same way. It was a long, hot summer, and the boys were getting tired. As they began to founder, Leo became the target for the reasons: He played them too often, he yelled too much, he was . . . he was being Leo.

So the chiding he would give Holtzman, seemingly good-natured when calling him a "kike," took on a different edge when he also blasted him for being "gutless." And the times he called Santo "dago" then seemed more ominous with Leo pouting. The racial names didn't seem as charming anymore.

Leo was unhappy with Banks—or, more precisely, with Banks's presence. The great player was thirty-eight years old, a Chicago legacy, but not the kind of player Leo was looking for. Who knew what he was looking for? Some players to this day claim he went nuts when they lost. Others say he remained calm, which reinforces the common wisdom that Leo was tougher on the guys over the years when they won rather than when they lost.

After June, the Cubs were 43–43, while the Mets were 60–30. From September 4 to September 23, they went from 5 games ahead to 6 games behind, producing the worst record in the major leagues. The Cubs lost the pennant by 8 games. Put another way, the Mets won the pennant by 8 games. At least, that is the way most of the Cubs prefer to look at it. Leo conceded in later years that the Mets pitching had done in his boys. Maybe he was right. Maybe, too, he shouldn't have flogged Jenkins as a "quitter" in September (Jenkins completed 23 of 42 starts). Or maybe he shouldn't have permitted Dick Selma to go a week without starting, then start him twice in two days. Also questionable was his berating of his rookie center fielder, Don Young, after he blew two fly balls against the Mets ("Two little fly balls—he just gave up on one and stood there under the other").

Jerome Holtzman, the Chicago newspaperman, remembers, "Durocher never told the players it was okay if they lost a game, so there was a lot of pressure. If he had told them that, it might have gotten better."

Holtzman, like so many other sportswriters around Leo, had a roller coaster relationship with him. There was a stretch when Leo was angry at Holtzman and lied to him about who his pitcher would be. "He was a pathological liar," says Holtzman. "This was in 1969, and Leo never came out of his hotel room on the road. I asked him if Holtzman was going to pitch and he said, 'No, Hands is pitching.' I was ready to write that but the other writers tipped me off that it would be Holtzman. I waited till we got to the ballpark and I watched Holtzman warming up. I said, 'Leo'—and I said this in front of the players—'you told me Hands,' and he said no, he told me Holtzman.

"We started going at it. Someone was yelling, 'Hit him, Jerry, hit him.' Santo pulled us apart. Well, Holtzman pitched a 6-hitter, and one of the Cubs said to me, 'It was a great night for the Holtzmans.' "

Holtzman also remembers a distracted Durocher that season, someone who kept his distance from the players but who also played cards until ten minutes before game time. And there was the time Durocher allowed Jenkins to bat in the ninth inning. "It was an irrational thing to do," says Holtzman. "I asked him about it and he said one of his pet phrases, 'We went down with our best.' But to me, I thought he was afraid of making a move. I think he also was afraid of Jenkins."

Perhaps all these incidents conspired to send the Cubs into despair. It was a team without a core, which allowed the Mets' Jerry Koosman to hit Santo without retaliation in what became a symbol of the leaderless team. In fact, even when things were going well, Talley recounts, Banks collared Ken Holtzman and said, "We've got a nine-game lead but we're going to get beat."

When a stunned Holtzman asked him why, Banks replied, "Because we've got a manager and three or four players who are waiting to get beat."

As the collapse was complete, Leo said on his radio show the players had "quit." Players don't forget a word like that.

With the collapse, the rumors began. That toddling town has always had its share of criminals and wise guys. Couple that with Leo's well-known gambling proclivities, and some people who couldn't accept what happened to the Cubs in 1969 jumped to the conclusion Leo was throwing the games.

Former Commissioner Bowie Kuhn remembers an investigation of sorts and recalls telling Durocher not to accept drinks at restaurants from people he didn't know. But nothing more.

Still, an intriguing insight into Leo's gambling habits emerged from that investigation which involved Sinatra, Las Vegas, and a barrel of money. On his ESPN television show in 1992, Dick Schaap told of how Leo had "stolen" $25,000 worth of Sinatra's chips at a Vegas casino, then was discovered by Sinatra, who got his good friend Jilly Rizzo to confront Leo and tell him never to darken Leo's door again.

The "real" story? Harvey Wineberg recalls this happening: "I had heard about Leo stealing the money, too. But I must tell you I don't believe that. There was a time Leo called me in the middle of the night. He was kind of down and out mentally. He had just lost his job in Houston, or maybe it was after Chicago, and he says, 'Come on out here with a suitcase.' And I said, 'Who is this?' It's three in the morning, which is one in the morning in Las Vegas. And he said, 'It's Leo.' I said, 'Why should I come out there?' And he says, 'I just won a lot of money.'

"And he said, 'Sinatra bankrolled me, but I paid it back and I won a lot of money, and come out and get it.' I told him I wasn't going to come out and get it. Just give it to the cashier and get a receipt. I asked, 'Are you going to pick this up on your tax return?' and he starts screaming at me, 'Nobody does that.' And I said, 'Well, you're not a nobody.' And then I said, 'Who were you with?' And he tells me Sinatra, and I asked, 'How many people saw you win that?' and he says, 'I don't know. Thousands.' Anyway, I ended up putting it on his return.

"The point is, Sinatra gave him some money to gamble with, and he paid him back. My guess is that Leo never would have done something like that, stolen from Sinatra."

LeRoy Neiman, the artist, recalls the magnanimous nature of the Sinatra-Durocher relationship. Neiman's works hang in the great galleries of the world, as well as in many clubhouses. He has an artist's eye and a sympathetic ear, and players feel warmly toward him.

"Frank called me and commissioned me to do a painting of Leo," says Neiman.

" 'How should I do it?' I asked Frank.

" 'You know him,' Frank told me, 'do it any way you want.'

"This must have been in the early seventies. Leo was buying a house in Palm Springs near Frank, and Sinatra was giving it to him as a housewarming present.

"So I tried to get photographs of Leo and I finally saw one that I think captured him and what he was about. I sent it out to him."

Neiman was busy with other things one day when he got a conference call. Sinatra and Durocher were on the phone.

"They were crying. They thought it was great. Leo told me, 'You captured me.' We were close friends for life after that."

Perhaps, as Jerome Holtzman suggests, "if the Cubs had won in 1969, they would have won two, three in a row." Instead, they finished second in 1970 and tied for third in 1971.

With 37 games remaining in 1971, the Cubs trailed the Pirates by only 4½ games. Milt Pappas, who would pitch 5 shutouts and win 17 games, had just lost to the Astros, giving up a checked-swing double on an 0–2 count. That was intolerable to Leo. He called for a clubhouse meeting before their next game. The team-wide blowup that followed was due in part to a generation gap. No longer were the ballplayers of the 1970s—products of the antiestablishment 1960s—going to sheepishly take a scolding from an old man. Only Leo never figured this out. He reamed everyone, again mentioning the 0–2 count to Pappas.

"Why," piped up Joe Pepitone, "are you always blaming people? Pappas didn't mean to throw that pitch. Santo didn't want to be in a slump." Pepitone went on to say that when he played under Ralph Houk on the Yankees, Houk stuck up for his players. "That's why we won pennants."

That did not set well with Durocher.

"What are you, a fucking clubhouse lawyer?" said Leo. Then he named two of his favorites, Billy Williams and Glenn Beckert, as guys who showed up every day and took batting practice.

That last statement made an impression on Santo. He had

skipped batting practice in order to get out of a slump. He thought a day away from the cage might help. "What are you trying to say, Leo? That I don't practice hitting?" said Santo.

"Well, did you today?" shot back Durocher. More words flew, and then Durocher said, "I didn't want to bring this up, but the only reason the Cubs are giving you a Ron Santo Day is that you asked Holland for one because Banks and Williams had one."

"Bring Holland down here! Ask him!" shouted Santo, out of control. Players held Santo, who was screaming. Calmed down, he sat for a few minutes and looked around. No Leo. To him, that meant Durocher was talking to Holland, trying to get their stories to agree.

Santo ran into Durocher's office. Leo and Holland were talking. Santo lunged for Durocher. "I wasn't going to hit him," Santo recalls. "No way. But he thought he could handle himself, that's how dumb he was. He wasn't afraid to get hit. That wrinkled bastard wanted to prove he was still playing with the Gashouse Gang or something."

Later, when Santo confronted Holland in front of his teammates, the player cried out of frustration. Pepitone and Jenkins yelled at Durocher, who wheeled and said, "I quit." He went to the shower.

It was twenty minutes to game time. Someone started to talk and soon Durocher put his uniform back on and walked onto the field.

The club had been broken apart at that moment, but no one announced it. Leo's days were dwindling. It took a full-page ad in the Chicago papers by Phil Wrigley to try to stem the blood. In the ad, he said that Leo had brought the team back as a contender, and that "the Dump Durocher Clique might as well give up. He is running the team, and if some of the players do not like it and lie down on the job, during the off-season we will see what we can do to find them happier homes." There was a P.S.: "If only we could find more team players like Ernie Banks."

The season had a month to go, but Holtzman insisted on a trade. How dare Wrigley suggest that Banks was virtually the only team guy? And the old man's letter didn't endear Leo to his players at all.

But it meant Leo would be back in 1972. And there was going to be one big difference. Wrigley had heard the complaints from players, so had Holland. So these two who had created the college of coaches came up with another innovation: a coach to act as liaison between the manager and his players. It was Hank Aguirre, the former pitcher, and his title, incredibly, was "information and services coach." His job was essentially to explain Leo's moves to the players and the press. Leo, remember, never explained to his players—why should he? Huggins never had—and Leo by now was at war with the press.

There was almost an apologetic air about Leo being rehired. In the press release, it was pointed out that, except for the Cubs' "rebuilding year of 1966," Leo's teams had played 51 games over .500.

Leo predicted his 1972 team—with Holtzman and Banks gone—would win the pennant. But in July, the club went into a tailspin. One day Wrigley called Holland and told him to stay next to the phone. Wrigley was about to fire Leo. Leo was dismissed after 90 games, on the eve of the All-Star Game with the Cubs at 46–44. Another one of his disciples, Whitey Lockman, replaced him.

Durocher wasn't out of baseball long. One month, in fact. For with 31 games remaining, he was named manager of the Astros to replace the fired Harry Walker.

The Astros? Didn't they play in the Astrodome, the place he once described as "a million-dollar ballpark with a nickel infield and a ten-cent scoreboard?" Wasn't the Astrodome the place with the exploding scoreboard? The place where, in 1968 after a ninth-inning homer defeated his Cubs, the scoreboard read "Sorry About That, Leo." The place where, upon reading that message, he tore a telephone out of its socket in the dugout and hurled it onto the field.

To Leo, the fast infield took away baseball as he knew it—the bunt, for example. He threatened to wear spikes on the slippery AstroTurf. He once dressed a player in galoshes and a rain hat after the roof leaked.

This was the place he hated, the symbol of what baseball had become. This was the place he was coming to at the age of sixty-seven. Did anyone really think this would work?

Not Norm Miller, at any rate. Miller, destined for problems with Leo (he was the player rep, after all), is now the Astros' director of advertising sales. Ask Miller, a former outfielder, about Leo and you get this response: "Leo? He traded me.

"I remember him coming in, how he tried to blend in with the guys, how he played poker with the guys every day. The Astros of that time were the best bunch of guys I ever was with. We were glad to get rid of Harry Walker. We didn't want any more crap."

It had gotten so bad under the tyrannical Walker that he was dismissed with the club playing .557 ball, in contention for division honors. Leo immediately set a place for himself in the card game.

"And someone asks Leo, 'Where'd you get those boots?' Miller recalls. "And he says, 'My buddy Frank's bootmaker.' And someone said, 'Hey, Leo, we don't give a fuck about Frank.' "

Only 31 games remained when Leo took over, and the club barely made it to .500, finishing 16–15, 10½ back of the Reds, about to launch their Big Red Machine the first time.

No matter to Leo. No matter about the Astrodome. No matter about this new type of ballplayer, the one who disdained Leo's "Whatever happened to sit down, shut up, and listen?" Leo had Cesar Cedeno, whom he kept touting as "the next Willie Mays."

Everything was so different now. Leo couldn't get away with being Leo anymore. One of his newspaper buddies from New York, the columnist Jimmy Cannon, had uttered some words that symbolized the new journalism. During the National Anthem, the young writers were chatting and kidding, and Cannon said with a scowl, "Would you shut up? You sound like a bunch of chipmunks."

And so the word spread from New York—the young sportswriters gave themselves the nickname "chipmunks" as a title of honor. The greatest chipmunk question of them all was uttered by the irrepressible Stan Isaacs of *Newsday*. A pitcher being interviewed spoke of his baby and mentioned that his wife was feeding the infant. "Breast or bottle?" asked Isaacs.

Despite the newly irreverent press, Leo was going to enjoy Houston, going to enjoy their rinky-dink spring training set-up in Cocoa, Florida, where even the manager slept in a single bed in a dormitory room in the middle of nowhere. The veterans lived two to a room for seven weeks, the minor leaguers eight to a suite. No movie theaters, no stores, no restaurants.

Leo was gracious that spring, which would be his last. Harry Shattuck, now assistant sports editor of the *Houston Chronicle*, remembers: "Leo stayed in the dorm, in a twin bed just like everyone else. At 5 P.M. each evening, after practice, when the media would gather for cocktail hour, Leo usually would join in.

"Leo was a charmer that spring. And keep in mind he was coming to Houston from an experience in Chicago where reporters and Leo almost never got along, where players were constantly at odds with him.

"I remember being entertained the first time he told the story about Frank Sinatra calling him at his Palm Springs hotel during the night and saying, 'Leo, get dressed, we're taking a trip.' Sinatra, according to Leo, would board Leo and himself and others on a private jet and travel all over the nation and world.

"He told stories of Hollywood, of Willie Mays, of great Giants and Dodgers games. And the spring was great fun. For a while. What I know I remember was Leo telling the Sinatra story. Again and again. And other stories again and again. He loved to boast about his famous friends. It got old. And older."

The most famous incident of Leo's last year in baseball has to do with his antiunion activities. Marvin Miller nearly went to court over it. Miller was touring the teams in his annual spring-training updates, just as he had done six years earlier with the Cubs. This one was supposed to be with the Astros before their game with the Rangers in Pompano Park. "The Astros were coming up from Cocoa. What I learned later was that Durocher and Spec Richardson—he was the general manager—had gotten together and decided how best they could sabotage this meeting.

"Unlike any other kind of situation I had ever heard of before, they asked players, Who would rather not make the bus trip? Early in the morning. And of course [and here, Miller chuckles] a lot of people opted for that before realizing this was the date of the meeting of the Players Association.

"So what you had were the rookies and other players who might not make the team, and the player rep. Durocher and Richardson set the bus trip for some ungodly hour, 5:30 A.M. He was really trying to discourage them from coming.

"The meeting was called for in the contract. You really didn't need anybody's permission to schedule a meeting. The meeting was called for either in the clubhouse or on the field.

"It was a nice day and so we held the meeting out in center field. Our usual practice was for the players to sit around in a semicircle and I'd stand up and give them various reports. My back was to home plate. I noticed a ball bouncing. Then I'd hear a thud on the grass. I didn't pay much attention to it. Finally I saw some players muttering to each other and they got their gloves. Then they got up and they stood between me and the infield. I turned around and I saw why. Durocher was standing there with a couple of his coaches and he was pointing—and he's hitting fungoes right at me. It looked to me like they were having a contest, who could come closest to hitting me.

"I didn't pay much attention because the players who had gotten their gloves were insurance that the balls wouldn't hit me. After about an hour of the meeting, he sent a coach out and said, 'Come on, we've got to get going.' I told the players I didn't want trouble with the manager, but I wanted them to know that we had a contractual right, that it was a violation of the contract, and I would take appropriate steps later."

Indeed, Miller immediately contacted Feeney and threatened to file a charge of unfair labor practices for attempting to coerce the players into not attending a meeting. Miller also told John Gaherin, baseball's director of player relations, what had happened.

"Eventually, Feeney announced a fine. I forget how big it was, but Durocher made a big thing about never paying it. He paid it."

Norm Miller also has amusing memories of that morning. "I was the player rep. The morning of the meeting with Marvin Miller, they didn't take the regular players down there. They had a game plan. Now the inmates run the asylum. If that happened today, they'd be hitting balls at Leo."

But then Norm Miller was asked what he thought of the incident and he told a reporter, "I think Leo was totally wrong." The next day, Leo scratched the player's name off the work schedules. And then Miller got hurt getting out of a cab, popping his knee.

"I was in the training room, being wheeled in," says Miller.

" 'What the fuck's wrong with him?' asked Leo and walked out."

The injury set back the Astros' plan to trade Miller. That happened eventually.

Now, twenty years later, Miller can see humor in his time with Leo. "He came in the last few weeks of 1972 and he didn't manage. All he wanted to do was make a name for himself in the media. We didn't need another old manager.

"Let me tell you another ironic story. I was growing up in Sherman Oaks, California, and playing Little League, and a TV network in 1956 did a piece about it. He was the reporter. I stood next to Leo and he said, 'Some day this kid will be in the big leagues.'

"I was, and he fired me."

Leo fired himself in 1973. Some players remember him falling asleep in the dugout. Or his constant paeans to Cedeno, who finally confided, "I don't want to be the next Willie Mays. I want to be the first Cesar Cedeno." Preston Gomez, his number one coach, made many of the decisions. So did Richardson, who often called to the dugout phone in the middle of a game.

This was so unusual that pitcher Jerry Reuss, who had his own radio show, even mentioned this on the air. Within a few days, Reuss was off the air.

The front office was frozen. The famed Judge Roy Hofheinz, who created the Astrodome, which he dubbed "the eighth wonder of the world," had suffered a stroke. He was wheelchair-bound and knew little of what was going on. He'd sleep in the wheelchair. There would be periods of alertness, when he made decisions, but they were based on only brief stretches of lucidity. Within two years, credit companies would be running the Astrodome empire.

More and more, as the season wound down and it was apparent they were no better than a .500 club, Leo berated his players after losses. On the bus rides to and from the airports and stadiums and hotels, there was a nasty air. Players would mock the sixty-eight-year-old, who chose not to hear them. But once, Leo picked up a "motherfucker" uttered by pitcher Don Wilson. Durocher got up in the bus and demanded, "What did you say?"

"Motherfucker," repeated Wilson.

CHAPTER XV

THE LION IN WINTER

L EO LEFT BASEBALL with a winning percentage of .540. There are now ten managers in the Hall of Fame (since he retired, Walter Alston and Al Lopez got in). But only five have a better winning percentage. Only five have more victories than the 2,010 his clubs produced. Two thousand and ten victories are a lot of happiness, controversy, screaming.

He almost got back into baseball again—in Japan, of all places. And at the age of seventy. But a bout of hepatitis on the virtual eve of his departure in 1976 ended that scheme. One can barely imagine Leo and Japanese umpires.

He stayed married, officially, to Lynn until 1981, when they divorced. She said she couldn't take his gambling, which had gotten so bad that he tried, unsuccessfully, to get some of her money. But they really broke up a few years after the Cubs relieved him of his uniform. He developed heart problems, was operated on by the re-nowned surgeon Michael DeBakey of Houston, and briefly got back with Lynn. DeBakey himself telephoned her to make the reconcili-ation. She wasn't happy about that ploy.

Leo continued to keep up his associations with his old baseball buddies and young women.

In 1977 he entered a hospital in Brooklyn to have a penile implant.

"He wanted to come in when no one knew," recalls Annie Perasa, who became his nurse. "When he came in he was the talk of the hospital because on the form where you list next of kin he wrote 'Frank Sinatra.' When they brought him in, she came in with him, a very attractive, tall young woman, much taller than he was. Her name was Jeannie." Perasa remembers Leo's friend as a woman in her late twenties, perhaps early thirties. "She was very caring toward him. She'd come in and stay with him twelve hours a day. The first time he was in for a week." Leo actually came in three times for the procedure, which wasn't working. Perasa adds, "For a man his age I couldn't get over what good physical condition he was in."

The penile implant is for men who can't have ejaculations. Leo was almost seventy-two years old.

"You had to test it with a wraparound cuff. It was like a blood pressure machine. Put it on his penis. We used to kid with him and say, 'Okay, let's see if this thing is working.' "

Understandably, Leo didn't want other patients to know he was there. "I said to him, 'You know, Leo, none of these kids know who you are.' And at the end of that stay, I had him out of the room delivering the mail because he had to get up and walk. I had him walk over to pediatrics and see the kids. Of course, only a couple of people knew who he was. He'd deliver the mail to them and talk with them."

The story at the hospital—which also treated prominent mob figures named Gambino and Columbo—was that Sinatra paid for Leo's surgery in cash. There were rumors too that Frank once visited Leo, but after the normal hours, when few people were around.

"You know about the famous Sinatra phone call? I think it was Memorial Day weekend. I was giving out enemas because the next day was our surgery day. So I'm running down the hall and Leo called me in and said, 'Get in here. I got somebody on the phone I want you to talk to.' I said, 'I can't talk on the phone, I'm too busy. I've got to give out these enemas.' So he got hysterical laughing. And he gets on the phone and says, 'Well, Sinatra, this is the first time you've been turned down for a bucket of shit.' And he hung up.

"His language? It was fine. He would curse a little bit. I asked him about the nickname. He said, 'That's what I got for answering back everybody. But I don't curse around ladies.'"

Leo had a generous nature. He asked Annie to keep his 1954 World Series ring until he was released.

"I'll tell you how nice he was. For my fortieth birthday, my husband, Danny, called him in Palm Springs. He said, 'Oh, how could I forget Annie?' Typical ballplayer fashion, he sent me a picture and autographed it, 'To Number 40—Good Luck, Leo.'

"He was a very pleasant man. He was also a very clean man—clean-smelling. It was unusual for a patient in the hospital to have all the things he had: after-shave lotion, snappy bedclothes.

"He'd walk with his friend Jeannie. I remember he had such a beautiful bathrobe, a Pierre Cardin robe. And for a man his age, as I said to my husband, 'What a body.' No fat. All lean. He was just some piece of work.

"He idolized this girl. She was young enough to be his grand-daughter. I know they lived together for three or four years on the Sinatra estate in Palm Springs. He was very proud of that."

Leo had another passion in his later years. The Hall of Fame. Each year, the vote would go on and Leo's name would come up. And he'd lose. He never complained publicly about it.

Monte Irvin is one of the voting members on the veterans committee, the one that, year in and year out, declines to nominate Leo for the Hall of Fame. Some old-timers simply don't get enough votes. In Leo's case, it's as if some of the voters are actually voting against him, rather than not voting for him.

"In 1991 we thought we could get him in—the vote was close but he just missed," says Irvin. "It was a shame because shortly afterward he passed away. We wanted him to smell the roses. After that vote was when he said that if he ever got in, he would reject it, and that's when he told his friends that if he was voted in after his death, to reject it in his memory. But I discounted that, figuring it was just said in anger. We're still trying to get him in.

"What do they say against him? Either you liked Leo or you didn't. I guess maybe some guys there just didn't like him. We point to his record. He did it in 1951. He did it in 1954. And in those days if you asked anyone who was the best manager in baseball, they'd say Leo Durocher. So since he was the best manager, let's put him in the Hall of Fame. It's that simple."

There have been repeated reports that Stan Musial has a vendetta against Leo, that Stan continually declines to vote for him. "Why Stan was against Leo, I don't know," says Irvin.

"What a perfect manager he was in 1951 and 1954. And I think he was the only manager that could have made us catch the Dodgers and then win it on the last day. The way he did it was, he never put any pressure on us, he never said, 'Come on, let's catch them.' He always said, 'Come on, let's see how close we can get.' If he had put pressure on us, then we would have thought we'd have to win."

There was a moment in that 1951 season, Irvin recalls, that defined how Leo could rally the troops at the moment all seemed lost.

"When things were darkest, he had compassion. He'd try to figure out why. For instance, in 1951, we won the first game and lost the next eleven, he called us together and said we've got a much better club than this. That eleventh game we lost, it was at Brooklyn.

"We could hear Furillo and Robinson and a few of those other guys hollering, 'Eat your heart out, Leo. You'll never win this year. You son of a bitch.'

"And Leo said to us, 'Well, fellows, if that's not enough to make you go out and win, nothing will.' We went out on a tear and won sixteen in a row."

And if Leo's adopted son Chris is sad about anything regarding his father, it is the way baseball finally treated him. "There's still a collusion in the commissioner's office about him getting into the Hall of Fame, because of what went on in his prior life. It made him bitter at the end. It tore him apart. He had done so much for baseball. It would have meant so much to him to be voted into the Hall."

And what would the Hall of Fame have meant?

"I think he would have lived to be over a hundred."

Early in 1989, shortly after he had written out of his will a friend named Jean Alexander, Leo got into a terrible car accident while driving his beloved Cadillac. The eighty-three-year-old Durocher suffered serious head injuries after a car made a sudden turn into his right-of-way in Palm Springs.

"He was never the same," contends Wineberg. "They thought he was going to die right there. He recovered but he had a big scar on his forehead. He was never the same, and his body was never the same.

"He was becoming somewhat reclusive anyway. His friends had all left him—I mean, they all died. He didn't feel he had anybody. He was always angry at baseball. He would do some things for Peter O'Malley, because Peter was the one owner he respected. He would show up once in a while, and he would do some old-timers' games in Texas for a few years for Equitable because he thought he owed them that. But he wouldn't go anywhere.

"He felt that baseball snubbed him in later years. When the Cubs got in the playoffs in 1984, they never even asked him to come, or suggested it would be nice if he were there. He was invited to a lot of things but he turned them all down. And the truth is that he was driven a lot by money and if you gave him enough he'd make an appearance, but if you didn't, he wouldn't. That's not his fault. That's not hard to blame in today's world. That's what athletes do. If you don't ask for enough money, you can be out every night killing yourself.

"After the accident, not getting in the Hall of Fame just absolutely wiped him out. That's all he had been living for for two, three years. And in 1991, when it was so close, I think he lost by one vote. If Campanella had attended along with Red Barber, he would have made it. I guess they both weren't feeling well. I understand a few years ago, Ted Williams walked out saying, 'If Leo doesn't get in, nobody gets in.' "

Chris Durocher also remembers what effect the accident had on his adoptive father. "Along with his not getting into the Hall of Fame, it was his downfall. The doctor said to him, 'Get off your butt. Get out.' But he missed his car. It was an '88 Seville with only a few thousand miles on it. He would only get out if he could get a new car. He really was inactive for almost two years. He had been so conscientious about his health, but he let it go. We could see him and tell him but it was hard to talk to him."

Leo had a young woman friend named Florence. He let her use his car. Then she used to drive him everywhere. He had also returned to the church some years earlier. Leo became an usher at Our Lady of Solitude in Palm Springs, faithfully attending every Saturday night.

One day Bavasi attended the church. The basket was passed in front of him. He put a dollar in it. The basket didn't move. Bavasi put another dollar in it. Still, the basket remained in front of him. He looked to the end of the aisle, and there was a smiling Leo, holding the basket, putting the arm on him for a bigger contribution.

Father Arnold Fox, who was three years older than Leo and an octagenarian himself, recalled that Leo still thought about the Hall of Fame voting. "At the end, he told me didn't care. But I remember he even went in a wheelchair to the meetings by plane. He thought he'd be elected."

314 ◊   GERALD ESKENAZI

Leo moved into a modest condo about five years before his death. He was eighty-one years old. A remarkable thing happened.

"After I met him, he told me he was bothered a lot by his foul language," recalls Father Fox. "He said, 'Would you help me lose it?' He said as a coach how he'd fly off the handle. I guess he got to the stage where he wanted to be reconciled with God."

So Father Fox worked with Leo on his cursing. "I counseled him. And I think it worked. He stopped cursing."

"I liked him very much," said the eighty-nine-year-old priest. "I played a lot of baseball myself. He used to say, 'I don't let anything bother me,' but one thing that bothered him—he was a very neat man—was getting packages every day. People would send him equipment, balls, gloves, and he'd have to box them and ship them back.

"When he moved here he said he wanted to get away from Hollywood and that crowd. He was very devout the last years.

"If you hear why he hasn't been accepted to the Hall of Fame, let me know. I don't know what the reason can be."

So Leo, near the end of his life, had gone back, in a manner of speaking, to his West Springfield roots, to the church, to watching his mouth. "I think that as Leo got older he really mellowed," says Wineberg. "He wasn't drinking, he wasn't doing a lot of things. He really became a much softer, warmer person. He loved my kids. We were in Mexico with him, my wife and I and my youngest daughter. We made him her godfather because we thought he'd like it, even though we don't have godfathers for girls in the Jewish religion.

"He told me—after the Hall voting in 1991—he said, 'I want you to turn it down for me posthumously.' First of all, it's not up to me, I told him. And he put something in writing, and I told him I didn't think it was a good thing. I called the librarian at Cooperstown and they told me no one had ever done that, and I remember kidding Leo. He said, 'Well, that's what I want you to do,' and I said, 'The trouble is, you'll never know.' "

Leo had one last farewell to baseball. He visited New York and the annual Baseball Writers show, the one that Tallulah Bankhead had once starred in, the one that used to roast Leo when he was with the Dodgers and the Giants. It was early 1991. He was rheumy-eyed and walked slowly, but he brought along a beautiful tuxedo. He was the center of the private cocktail party that preceded the dinner. Jim Leyland of the Pirates spoke of how proud he was to sit next to him on the dais.

Leo told Willie stories, and Dusty Rhodes tales, and Giants stories and Dodger stories. He got the biggest hand at the dinner.

"The award we gave him was the Casey Stengel 'You Could Look It Up' Award," recalls Jack Lang, the writers' executive secretary. "It was for winning the pennant in 1951 and 1954. He had never been recognized here before. He never had won any honors here.

"His face was like dried parchment, but he still had that deep resonant voice, and the moment he walked into a room, you knew he was there. Dressed like a million dollars. He had on a black tuxedo that was so sharp.

"He was delighted to see a lot of the old people—Chub Feeney and Lee MacPhail, people he hadn't seen in a lot of years. It was like his last hurrah. I think the main reason he came back—I kind of coerced him into believing it would help—was that this would help get him over the hump for the Hall of Fame. That he was getting recognition at last and the Hall of Fame Veterans Committee would put him in. That's what he was hoping for when he came back here."

Six months later, Leo entered the hospital on the fortieth anniversary of Bobby Thomson's historic homer. When he died of natural causes a few days later on October 7, 1991, he was eighty-six years old.

Laraine Day and Chris handled many of the arrangements. There was some surprise by those attending that so few people from baseball's front offices, the commissioner's office in particular, had attended.

"More surprising was how few people from the entertainment world were there," says Ms. Day, who has been married for many years to a retired CBS executive, Mike Grilikhes. "Once Leo couldn't provide enough tickets for them or entrée into the entertainment world. I was surprised at how few came. He had entertained them. That was more shocking to me than the fact baseball didn't send anyone official."

Willie, of course, spoke, allowing that many people disliked Leo Durocher but how "he never treated me anything but perfect," and how "I have lost a dear father."

Behind the casket hung the painting of Durocher by LeRoy Neiman. In the painting, frozen forever, Leo Durocher is being ejected from a game by an umpire.

Appendices

How Leo Durocher stacks up against managers in the Hall of Fame
(listed in order of victories)

	GP	W	L	PCT
Connie Mack, Pirates, A's	7,878	3,776	4,025	.484
John McGraw, Baltimore (A & N), Giants	4,879	2,840	1,984	.589
Bucky Harris, Senators, Tigers Red Sox, Phillies, Yankees	4,410	2,159	2,219	.493
Joe McCarthy, Cubs, Yankees, Red Sox	3,489	2,126	1,335	.614
Walter Alston, Dodgers	3,657	2,040	1,613	.558
Leo Durocher, Dodgers, Giants, Cubs, Astros	3,740	2,010	1,710	540
Casey Stengel, Dodgers, Braves, Yankees, Mets	3,812	1,926	1,867	.508
Bill McKechnie, Pirates, Cards, Braves, Reds	3,650	1,898	1,724	.524
Al Lopez, Indians, White Sox	2,459	1,422	1,026	.581
Miller Huggins, Cards, Yankees	2,569	1,413	1,134	.555
Wilbert Robinson, Baltimore (A), Dodgers	2,813	1,397	1,395	.501

LEO DUROCHER'S PLAYING RECORD

Year	Club	League	POS	G	AB
1925	Hartford	Eastern	SS	151	536
1925	New York	American	PH	2	1
1926	Atlanta	Southern	SS	130	408
1927	St. Paul	A. A.	SS	171*	594
1928	New York	American	2B-SS	102	296
1929	New York	American	SS	106	341
1930	Cincinnati	National	2B-SS	119	354
1931	Cincinnati	National	SS	121	361
1932	Cincinnati	National	SS	143	457
1933	Cincinnati–St. Louis	National	SS	139	446
1934	St. Louis	National	SS	146	500
1935	St. Louis	National	SS	143	513
1936	St. Louis	National	SS	136	510
1937	St. Louis	National	SS	135	477
1938	Brooklyn	National	SS	141	479
1939	Brooklyn	National	SS	116	390
1940	Brooklyn	National	SS	62	160
1941	Brooklyn	National	SS-2B	18	42
1942	Brooklyn	National			
1943	Brooklyn	National	SS	6	18
1944	Brooklyn	National			
1945	Brooklyn	National	2B	2	5
American League Totals				210	638
National League Totals				1,427	4,712
Major League Totals				1,637	5,350

World Series Record

Year	Club	League	POS	G	AB
1928	New York	American	2B	4	2
1934	St. Louis	National	SS	7	27
World Series Totals				11	29

All-Star Game Record

Year	League	POS	AB
1936	National	SS	3
1938	National	SS	3
All-Star Game Totals			6

Member of National League All-Star team in 1940; did not play.

SOURCE: *The Sporting News.*
*Led the league.

R	H	2B	3B	HR	RBI	BA	PO	A	E	FA
60	118	13	4	1	—	.220	317	502	59*	.933
1	0	0	0	0	0	.000	0	0	0	.000
62	97	9	5	2	33	.238	245	393	43	.937
60	150	27	10	7	78	.253	420*	559*	56*	.946
46	80	8	6	0	31	.270	158	274	25	.945
53	84	4	5	0	32	.246	197	299	22	.958
31	86	15	3	3	32	.243	240	380	24	.963
26	82	11	5	1	29	.227	212	344	20	.965
43	99	22	5	1	33	.217	283	429	30	.960
51	113	19	4	3	44	.253	275	422	29	.960*
62	130	26	5	3	70	.260	320	407	33	.957
62	136	23	5	8	78	.265	313	420	28	.963
57	146	22	3	1	58	.286	300	392	21	.971*
46	97	11	3	1	47	.203	279	381	28	.959
41	105	18	5	1	56	.219	287	399	24	.966*
42	108	21	6	1	34	.277	228	322	25	.957
10	37	9	1	1	14	.231	102	131	10	.959
2	12	1	0	0	6	.286	17	28	4	.918
		(Did not play)								
1	4	0	0	0	1	.222	23	11	0	1.000
		(Did not play)								
1	1	0	0	0	2	.200	3	4	0	1.000
100	164	12	11	0	63	.257	355	573	47	.952
475	1,156	198	45	24	504	.245	2,882	4,070	276	.962
575	1,320	210	56	24	567	.247	3,237	4,643	323	.961

R	H	2B	3B	HR	RBI	BA	PO	A	E	FA
0	0	0	0	0	0	.000	1	1	0	1.000
4	7	1	1	0	0	.259	13	17	0	1.000
4	7	1	1	0	0	.241	14	18	0	1.000

R	H	2B	3B	HR	RBI	BA	PO	A	E	FA
0	1	0	0	0	0	.333	4	0	0	1.000
1	1	0	0	0	0	.333	0	3	0	1.000
1	2	0	0	0	0	.333	4	3	0	1.000

LEO DUROCHER'S
MANAGERIAL RECORD

	G	W	L	PCT	Standing	
1939 BKN N	157	84	69	.549	3	
1940	156	88	65	.575	2	
1941	157	100	54	.649	1	
1942	155	104	50	.675	2	
1943	153	81	72	.529	3	
1944	155	63	91	.409	7	
1945	155	87	67	.565	3	
1946	157	96	60	.615	2	
1948	75	37	38	.493	5	3
1948 NY/ N	79	41	38	.519	4	5
1949	156	73	81	.474	5	
1950	154	86	68	.558	3	
1951	157	98	59	.624	1	
1952	154	92	62	.597	2	
1953	155	70	84	.455	5	
1954	154	97	57	.630	1	
1955	154	80	74	.519	3	
1966 CHI N	162	59	103	.364	10	
1967	162	87	74	.540	3	
1968	163	84	78	.519	3	
1969	163	92	70	.568	2	
1970	162	84	78	.519	2	
1971	162	83	79	.512	3	
1972	90	46	44	.511	4	2
1972 HOU/N	31	16	15	.516	2	2
1973	162	82	80	.506	4	
24 yrs.	3,740	2,010	1,710	.540		

World Series
1941 BKN N	5	1	4	.200		
1951 NY N	6	2	4	.333		
1954	4	4	0	1.000		
3 yrs.	15	7	8	.467		

SOURCE: *The Sporting News.*
NOTE: Durocher was Sporting News Manager of the Year in 1939, 1951, and 1954.

Bibliography

Barber, Red. *1947—When All Hell Broke Loose in Baseball.* Garden City, N.Y.: Doubleday, 1982.

Campanella, Roy. *It's Good to Be Alive.* Boston: Little, Brown and Company, 1959.

Cohen, Stanley. *Dodgers! The First 100 Years.* New York: Carol Publishing Group, 1990.

Creamer, Robert. *Baseball in '41.* New York: Penguin Books, 1991.

Durocher, Leo, and Ed Linn. *Nice Guys Finish Last.* New York: Simon & Schuster, 1975.

Fleming, G. H. *The Dizziest Season.* New York: William Morrow and Company, 1984.

Frommer, Harvey. *New York City Baseball.* New York: Macmillan, 1980.

Goldstein, Richard. *Superstars and Screwballs: 100 Years of Brooklyn Baseball.* New York: Dutton, 1991.

Golenbock, Peter. *Bums.* New York: Putnam, 1984.

Gregory, Robert. *Diz.* New York: Viking, 1992.

Holmes, Tommy. *Dodger Daze and Knights.* New York: David McKay Company, Inc., 1953.

Hood, Robert E. *The Gashouse Gang.* New York: William Morrow and Company, 1976.

Hynd, Noel. *The Giants of the Polo Grounds.* Garden City, N.Y.: Doubleday, 1988.

Kahn, Roger. *The Boys of Summer.* New York: Harper & Row, 1972.

Parrott, Harold. *The Lords of Baseball.* New York: Praeger Publishers, 1976.

Polner, Murray. *Branch Rickey: A Biography.* New York: Atheneum, 1982.

Reichler, Joseph L., ed. *The Baseball Encyclopedia.* 4th ed. New York: Macmillan, 1983.

Rosenfeld, Harvey. *The Great Chase: The Dodgers-Giants Pennant Race of 1951.* Jefferson, N.C.: McFarland & Company, Inc., 1992.

Seidel, Michael. *Streak: Joe DiMaggio and the Summer of '41.* New York: McGraw-Hill, 1988.

Shatzkin, Mike, ed. *The Ballplayers.* New York: William Morrow and Company, 1990.

Smith, Robert. *Baseball.* 2d ed. New York: Simon & Schuster, 1970.

Sneft, David, and Richard M. Cohen. *The Sports Encyclopedia: Baseball.* 7th ed. New York: St. Martin's Press, 1987.

Sullivan, Neil. *The Dodgers Move West.* New York: Oxford University Press, 1987.

Talley, Rick. *The Cubs of '69.* Chicago: Contemporary Books, 1989.

Thomson, Bobby et al. *The Giants Win the Pennant! The Giants Win the Pennant.* New York: Kensington, 1991.

Magazines and Journals

American League Red Book. St. Louis: The Sporting News, 1992.

Carter, Craig, ed. *The Complete Baseball Record Book.* St. Louis: The Sporting News, 1991.

Mann, Arthur. "Baseball's Ugly Duckling—Durable Durocher." *Saturday Evening Post,* August 19, 1939.

National League Red Book. St. Louis: The Sporting News, 1992.

Reynolds, Quentin. "Pop-Off Kid." *Collier's,* August 5, 1939.

Tracy, Dr. David. *Pageant,* 1953.

Woodward, Stanley. "That Guy Durocher!" *Saturday Evening Post,* June 3, 1950.

INDEX